Out in the Periphery

OUT IN THE PERIPHERY

Latin America's Gay Rights Revolution

Omar G. Encarnación

OXFORD
UNIVERSITY PRESS

Oxford University Press is a department of the University of Oxford. It furthers
the University's objective of excellence in research, scholarship, and education
by publishing worldwide. Oxford is a registered trade mark of Oxford University
Press in the UK and certain other countries.

Published in the United States of America by Oxford University Press
198 Madison Avenue, New York, NY 10016, United States of America.

Library of Congress Cataloging-in-Publication Data
Names: Encarnación, Omar Guillermo, 1962–
Title: Out in the periphery : Latin America's gay rights revolution / Omar G.
Encarnación.
Description: New York : Oxford University Press, 2016.
Identifiers: LCCN 2015026332| ISBN 978–0–19–935664–5 (hardback : alk. paper) |
ISBN 978–0–19–935665–2 (paperback : alk. paper)
Subjects: LCSH: Gay rights—Latin America. | Gay liberation movement—Latin
America. | BISAC: SOCIAL SCIENCE / Gay Studies.
Classification: LCC HQ76.8.L38 E53 2016 | DDC 323.3/264098—dc23 LC record available at
http://lccn.loc.gov/2015026332

CONTENTS

ACKNOWLEDGEMENTS

In thinking about the ideas for this book and putting the book together, I have accumulated numerous debts that I am happy to record here. My greatest debt is to the activists who shared their struggles with me, whether in person, via research emissaries to Argentina and Brazil, by phone, or via the wonderful technology of electronic mail. In Argentina, I am grateful to Héctor Anabitarte, Gabriela Adelstein, César Cigliutti, Marcello Suntheim, Pedro Paradiso Sottile, Rafael Freda, Irene Ocampo, María Rachid, and Mónica Santino. Among these individuals, I am especially grateful to César, for his willingness to respond to my many inquiries, for facilitating many contacts in Argentina, and for granting access to the archives of the organization that he presides over, the Comunidad Homosexual Argentina, and to Rafael for his encyclopedic knowledge of Argentina's gay rights politics. In Brazil, I am thankful to Luiz Mott, Marcelo Cerqueira, Toni Reis, and, especially, Paulo Iotti. Without the contributions of these individuals this project would have been considerably poorer, perhaps not even possible. I am also indebted to the many Latin American scholars and observers of Latin American gay politics who were willing to share their insights with me, especially Osvaldo Bazán, Santiago Joaquín Insausti, Analia del Franco, Mabel Bellucci, Pablo Ben, Edward MacRae, Jorge Schwartz, and Peter Fry.

In the United States, three scholars deserve special recognition, and for very specific reasons. At the start of the project, Javier Corrales ably helped me in developing the theoretical scaffolding of the study. In particular, he pushed me to find a way to account for external influence in a manner that did not overwhelm the domestic environment. Toward the end of the project, James N. Green stepped in and was uncompromisingly rigorous in his review of my interpretation of Latin American gay history, especially with regards to the case of Brazil. Thanks to him, this study, which started as an ordinary political science project, gained a broader inter-disciplinary dimension. My dear friend and Bard colleague Karen Sullivan, a medievalist, was always available for that most useful of purposes: an outsider's perspective on things.

A number of articles that preceded the book provided useful venues for getting feedback from colleagues, anonymous reviewers, and ordinary readers, for which I am very grateful. The book's core argument first appeared in "Latin America's Gay Rights Revolution," *Journal of Democracy* (April 2011, Vol. 22, No. 2). Portions of chapters 3 and 4 provided the empirical foundation for "International Influence, Domestic Activism, and Gay Rights in Argentina," *Political Science Quarterly* (Winter 2013-14, Vol. 128, No. 4). Some of the ideas found in the conclusion were first discussed in "Human Rights and Gay Rights," *Current History* (January 2014, Vol. 113); "Why is Latin America so Progressive on Gay Rights?," *The New York Times* (online), January 28, 2014; "Gay Rights: Why Democracy Matters," *Journal of Democracy* (July 2014, Vol. 25, No. 3); and "The Ghost of Roe: How the United States Fell Behind on Same-Sex Marriage," *Foreign Affairs* (online), July 2, 2015.

I am also indebted to several research assistants who over several years helped me to complete the study, including Alex Elson, Gabriel Sub, Naomi LaChance, and Rachel Thompson. At Oxford University Press I am most grateful to my editor, Angela Chnapko, who expressed enthusiasm about this project from the very first email I sent to her suggesting the book, and to the anonymous reviewers recruited by Oxford for their thoughtful comments and suggestions for improving the analysis. Fieldwork in South America during the Spring of 2013 was made possible by a grant from Bard College.

As always, John and Amos were a source of love, support, and encouragement.

Out in the Periphery

Introduction

As fate would have it, I completed this book on the rise of "gay rights" in Latin America in June 2015, the very month that the United States Supreme Court ruled in *Obergefell v. Hodges* that same-sex couples are entitled to all the benefits and responsibilities of marriage under the American Constitution's Fourteenth Amendment clause of equal protection under the law.[1] Although the decision was widely expected—after all, some 70 percent of Americans were already living in a jurisdiction allowing same-sex marriage—its arrival was nonetheless stunning. Indeed, the decision was quickly proclaimed a "landmark," one of those rare cases that legal scholars and schoolchildren alike will study for years to come because of its profound effect on American society.

For those of us who study international gay politics, however, the *Obergefell* decision felt differently. Above all, the decision underscored the irony of how the country that birthed the contemporary gay rights movement fell behind nineteen other countries in introducing the right to same-sex marriage at the federal level. These countries include not only European liberal stalwarts, like the Netherlands and Sweden, but also several countries in Latin America, a region where the social and political climate for gay rights has historically been among the most inauspicious in the Western world. Yet today, in a remarkable turn of events, Latin America basks in the glow of a cascade of international media stories proclaiming the region "out of the closet,"[2] "surprisingly progressive on gay rights,"[3] a "gay heaven,"[4] and, most tellingly yet, the site of a "gay rights revolution that stretches from the Rio Grande to the Tierra del Fuego."[5]

Latin America's gay rights revolution was launched without much fanfare in 1996, when the Buenos Aires City Council enacted a ban on antigay discrimination. This was the first policy of its kind for any jurisdiction in Latin America. A civil unions law followed in 2002 that granted same-sex couples residing in the Argentine capital some of the benefits of marriage like pension and property inheritance rights and hospital visitation privileges, provided that the couple had proof of cohabitation for at least two years. These gay rights advances paved the way for the legalization of same-sex marriage and adoption in Argentina in 2010, the second nation in the Americas to do so (after Canada), and, at the same time, only the tenth one in the entire world. Soon to come were laws allowing for a change of gender without approval from a doctor or a judge, banning "ex-gay therapy" to overcome same-sex attraction, and providing reproductive assistance to homosexual couples under the national healthcare system. Understandably, today Argentina sits atop international rankings of countries most open to gay, lesbian, bisexual, and transgender (LGBT) issues, such as the recently developed Gay Friendliness Index (GFI).[6]

Roughly contemporaneously with developments in Argentina, same-sex marriage was introduced in Brazil, Uruguay, Mexico City, and several Mexican states; and four other nations, Colombia, Ecuador, Bolivia, and Chile, permitted same-sex couples to enter into civil unions, an option also made available to heterosexual couples. Less known, but no less important, is that since Panama removed sodomy as a crime from its penal code in 2008, homosexuality has been completely decriminalized in Latin America, and that virtually every country in the region bans discrimination on the basis of sexual orientation. These advancements make Latin America among the most advanced regions with respect to gay rights, comparable, in fact, to most parts of the developed West. It is telling that same-sex marriage was introduced at the federal level in Argentina not only ahead of the United States but also of France and the United Kingdom.

The comparison with other parts of the world is even more flattering to Latin America. Gay rights are contracting across the post-Communist world, especially in Russia, which in 2013 enacted an antigay propaganda law that for all intents and purposes criminalizes homosexuality. In parts of Africa, Asia, and virtually the entire Middle East, homosexuality remains a crime punishable by death. Not surprisingly, in recent years Latin America has begun to exert considerable global leadership on the issue of gay rights. The origins of the 2011 United Nations Resolution on Human Rights, Sexual Orientation, and Gender Identity, a landmark agreement that recognizes for the first time gay rights as human rights and that calls for ending discriminatory laws against LGBT people in all corners of the world, are found in the "Brazilian

Resolution." First introduced in 2004, the Brazilian Resolution was the first international effort focused on extending human rights protections to the LGBT community.[7]

Certainly, enacting gay rights into law has not been a panacea for the ills of Latin America's LGBT population. Homophobia, for one, is very much alive in the region. Consequently, the majority of LGBT people in Latin America remains vulnerable to discrimination and even deadly violence, including, paradoxically enough, in those countries where gay rights advances have been most pronounced.[8] Brazil is routinely cited by local and international human rights activists as one of the most dangerous places in the planet for homosexuals. But the change in the law and the social context in which this change is taking place is striking. Latin American culture is steeped in machismo, and the region is home to almost half of the world's Catholic population, including the two largest Catholic countries (Brazil and Mexico). For centuries, the Catholic Church in Latin America has promoted the view of homosexuality as a sin, if not as an outright abomination, a point stressed in family life and echoed by the legal establishment, the education system, and government policies.

So how to explain Latin America's surprisingly robust embrace of gay rights? What social and political forces have made the region the undisputed gay rights leader in the global South and countries such as Argentina an example to the world's leading democracies on how to advance equality for the LGBT community? And why are Latin American countries, despite a common heritage, moving at different speeds in recognizing gay rights, especially same-sex marriage? These are the questions animating this research.

A COMPELLING BUT FLAWED CONVENTIONAL WISDOM

If there is a conventional wisdom about the rise of gay rights in Latin America, that wisdom points in the direction of developments outside the region, and more specifically to a global spread of gay rights engendered by the maturity of the gay liberation movement in the developed West, especially the United States. *Newsweek International* nicely summed up this view in a 2007 cover story about the state of gay rights outside of the United States and Western Europe titled "Legal in Unlikely Places." The article asserted that "now matured in the West, gay power is growing worldwide, even in the original land of Machismo," a not-too-thinly-veiled reference to Latin America. It further noted that "the major developing countries in Asia, Latin America and Africa are following the liberal road—sometimes imitating Western models, sometimes not—but in all cases setting precedents that could spread to the remaining outposts of official homophobia."[9] Implicit in this accounting of gay rights developments across Latin America and the developing world is a "centering" of gay rights politics in the Western experience, and a corresponding "center-periphery" dynamic about the global spread of gay rights—as something that originated and matured in the developed West and that was emulated by or exported to the developing South.

The conventional wisdom, this study argues, provides a compelling but flawed explanation of Latin America's gay rights advances. On the compelling side, no fewer than three hypotheses that draw from a large body of social science scholarship suggest how developments flowing from the developed West have shaped the rise and evolution of gay rights in Latin America. First, and foremost, is the idea that Latin America has been engulfed by a tidal wave of "global queering." This is the process by which Western, especially American, homosexual cultures, practices, and identities have become internationalized since New York's 1969 Stonewall Rebellion, widely regarded as the seminal event in the founding of the contemporary gay rights movement.[10] Post-Stonewall, gay liberation fronts that formed across the United States and abroad (fueled by tourism, the HIV/AIDS epidemic, and the advent of the information age, among other forces) have led to the emergence of the "Global Gay," an individual whose taste in food, clothing, and entertainment is essentially the same whether he or she resides in New York, Mexico City, or Moscow.[11]

Second in line is the notion that Latin America has embraced gay rights as a consequence of having internalized the norms of the "international human rights regime." For any civilized country, this regime presently includes the extension of civil rights to the LGBT population. How Latin America came to internalize human rights is explained by the political science framework of "international socialization," which deconstructs the process by which developing nations are induced into accepting human rights norms and practices.[12] Key to this process are Western-based transnational activist networks, through their capacity to persuade, pressure, and even coerce recalcitrant nations into complying with human rights. Notable among these networks, at least in relation to gay rights, is the International Lesbian and Gay Association (ILGA). Since the early 1990s, ILGA has been busy naming and shaming Latin American governments for their mistreatment of the LGBT population.[13]

Third and last is the view of the emergence of gay rights in Latin America as an example of "policy diffusion." This conceptual framework explains how policy ideas, like same-sex marriage and civil unions, spread among countries.[14] Policy diffusion generally leads to a "bandwagon" effect as a result of countries influencing or mimicking each other. Support for the view of gay rights in Latin America as an example of policy diffusion comes from the influence that Spain, the first overwhelmingly Roman Catholic country to legalize same-sex marriage, in 2005, has exerted over Latin America. "Spain is the model for many Spanish speaking countries . . . because Spain has traditionally been a Catholic and conservative country," notes one study attempting to explain Spain's influence over Latin America in the area of gay rights.[15]

For all of its explanatory powers, the conventional wisdom leaves a lot to be desired. For starters, it has very little to say about why gay rights have progressed so unevenly across Latin America. While gay rights appear to have exploded in Argentina, Uruguay, Brazil, and Mexico, no meaningful progress can be detected in Cuba, Peru, Venezuela, and the Central American republics. In other countries, like Paraguay and the Dominican Republic, a gay rights backslash is underway with laws already in the books banning same-sex marriage and adoptions. In Chile, change has come, but very belatedly. Little can also be gained from the conventional wisdom about gay rights policy outcomes. Countries like Argentina and Uruguay have moved with relative ease to legislate same-sex marriage, while others, such as Bolivia, Ecuador, and Chile, have legislated same-sex civil unions that grant same-sex couples most, if not all, of the legal benefits of marriage, except for the name. Yet others, such as Mexico and Brazil, have struggled to legislate at the federal level either same-sex marriage or same-sex civil unions, leaving it to the courts to legislate gay rights from the bench.

Less apparent is that viewing gay rights politics in Latin America through the prism of external influence leads to serious distortions and misinterpretations about Latin American gay history—such as the view that gay rights activism in Latin America is a post-Stonewall phenomenon; or the impression that the strategies of Latin American gay rights activists to secure civil rights simply mimic those of their foreign counterparts. As will be seen in this study, Latin America's gay rights struggles are not a tropical or more sensual version of the American and European experiences. Argentina, Brazil, and Mexico, among other Latin American nations, decriminalized homosexuality in the nineteenth-century, more than a century before the United States and Britain got around to do it; and gay rights activism in Latin America developed independently of the Stonewall riots (which themselves were largely unknown in the United States until historians began to "rediscover" the riots in the mid-1990s, around the time of the riots' twenty-fifth anniversary, and the myth of the riots as the first instance of gay collective resistance began to build).

Moreover, the Latin Americans did not adopt international gay rights ideas wholesale or implement them with the same strategies employed by activists in the developed West. Instead, international gay rights ideas have been imbued with or wedded to local practices and implemented with the aid of local strategies and tactics. In so doing, the Latin Americans have often led rather than followed the developed West in devising ways to advance gay rights. Argentine gay activists were among the first to link sexuality to human rights, when they introduced the argument that "the free exercise of sexuality is a fundamental human right." They embraced this novel reading of the 1948 Universal Declaration of Human Rights, which is silent on the issue of sexual orientation, in the early 1980s. This was years before the rise in popularity in Europe and the United States of the argument that "gay rights are human rights." The Brazilian legal theory of "homo-affection," which argues that homosexual coupling is not just about sexual desire but also about the want to create loving and stable relationships, and that became the basis for the landmark legal case that ushered in same-sex marriage in Brazil in 2011, foreshadowed similar arguments in the United States by groups such as Freedom to Marry.[16]

Finally, the conventional wisdom fails to recognize that external influence is a double-edged sword, since it can both advance and hinder gay rights. Indeed, a compelling argument can be made that for the past two decades Western influence has worked mostly to undermine gay rights across the developing world. Having suffered important setbacks in their home turf, especially on the issue of same-sex marriage, foes of the gay community in the United States have turned to Latin America, Africa, and Asia in search of greener pastures and new audiences.[17] Underscoring this point, a report from the Human Rights Campaign, the United States' largest gay rights organization, notes: "When you scratch the surface on a lot of the backsliding that's going on in a lot of countries where it is getting harder to be LGBT, you find a lot of Americans."[18] Curiously, international anti-gay rights organizations and international pro-gay rights organizations function in strikingly similar ways. In both cases, external groups provide local groups with training, political expertise, and financial resources.

DECENTERING GAY RIGHTS

Seeking to remedy the many challenges and shortcomings posed by externally based explanations of Latin America's gay rights revolution, this study proposes the notion of "decentering gay rights." My intention behind this idea is not to deny the importance of international influence by proving how the "local" has trumped the "global" in Latin America—far from it. Rather, my goal is to focus on the interaction of global influence and domestic factors in determining the shape of national gay rights policy in Latin America; and more specifically, to demonstrate how the domestic environment has mediated external influence with respect to gay rights across Latin America. This kind of analysis has been lacking so far, at least with respect to gay rights.

Owing to an analytical bias for wanting to showcase the decisive manner in which external factors shape domestic conditions, usually through persuasion and pressure, much of the scholarship on transnational politics, especially the scholarship on international socialization, ignores or undervalues how the domestic context interacts with external influence. Even when the importance of the domestic context is acknowledged, it is left for the most part unsaid how precisely this context matters.[19] Little, if anything, is said about the cultural, legal, and political conditions in which actors operate outside of the developed West and how these conditions might affect the reception of outside influence.

Comparative work also commits the same sin of omission by being generally unconcerned with the role of external influence. The incipient literature on the spread of same-sex civil unions and marriage across Latin America broadly mirrors this point. This literature is primarily concerned with showcasing how internal domestic factors can best help us understand the wildly diverse landscape of same-sex marriage rights across the region, while ignoring or undervaluing the importance of the international environment. Thus far, analytical attention has focused on the internal composition of the gay rights movement, the movement's mobilizing capacities, resources, and connections to the political system and societal networks, and the configuration of the political system, especially the presence or absence of "veto players" such as Evangelical movements and "confessional" parties.[20]

At its most general level, this study contends that the domestic environment has worked to mediate international gay rights influence in Latin America by making the region internally receptive to international gay rights trends. A cocktail of cultural, legal, and political factors has contributed mightily to this internal receptivity. Modernization, for one, has had a doubly positive effect on gay rights. Rising incomes and educational levels have increased societal acceptance of homosexuality, while growing secularization has served to weaken the influence of the Catholic Church. Another reinforcing factor of internal receptivity for gay rights is a wave of constitutional reforms intended to extend civil rights protections to groups previously disenfranchised by the law, including sexual minorities.

These reforms have empowered the citizenry to approach the courts while at the same time strengthening the independence of the courts to rule in favor of gay rights. Yet another prominent factor is the advent of socially liberal left-wing governments in Latin America—part of the "pink tide" that has reshaped Latin American politics since early in this century. In many instances, these governments have partnered with gay activists to see gay rights enacted into law.

All of this said, my analysis privileges the activism by gay rights organizations. Of utmost concern to this study is highlighting the "crafting" of the gay rights campaign. By this I mean the arguments, messages, and strategies employed by gay activists to legitimize their demands, to motivate their followers, and to de-mobilize their opponents, as well as the arenas that gay activists chose in which to wage their struggles and the political alliances they make to assist them in those struggles. This crafting process underscores the dual role of Latin American gay activists as importers of international gay rights trends, such as same-sex marriage and civil unions, and adaptors of these trends to the local environment. It also explains why while the gay rights policies found across Latin America would be quite familiar to outside observers, the strategies by which these policies have become a reality across the region would be considerably less so.

Much of my thinking about the crafting of gay rights campaigns is inspired by the literature on "framing," which, as defined by social movement theorists, represents the "schemata of interpretation" that enable individuals "to locate, perceive, identify, and label occurrences within their life space and the world at large."[21] Framing helps social movements to "render events or occurrences meaningful and thereby function to organize experience and guide action." Framing performs this interpretive function by allowing social movements to simplify and condense aspects of the "world out there," in ways that are "intended to mobilize potential adherents and constituents, to garner bystander support, and to demobilize antagonists." Translated into layman's terms, framing gives meaning and purpose to the activism of social movements.

Effective framing involves the construction of a variety of "frames," including "motivational frames," which entail articulating a rationale "for engaging in ameliorative collective action; "prognostic frames," or "the articulation of a proposed solution to the problems, a plan of attack, and the strategies for carrying out this plan"; and "injustice frames," those arguments and actions that highlight and amplify grievance, suffering, and victimization.[22] Effective framing also hinges on the capacity of activists to evoke the local culture and political context, a point conveyed in the notion of "frame resonance."[23] As observed by a review of the literature on framing: "key to framing is finding evocative cultural symbols that resonate with potential constituents and are capable of motivating them to collective action."[24]

In highlighting these aspects of social movement politics, theorists of framing aim to draw a clear analytical distinction with "resource mobilization," the dominant theoretical paradigm for understanding the success and failure of social movements.[25] This paradigm, which has influenced the study of social movements since at least the 1970s, emphasizes organizational features, such as a large membership base, financial resources, extensive social networks, and access to the political system, as essential to the success of social movements, especially their capacity to exploit "political opportunity structures," those junctures provided by the political environment that allow social movements to bolster collective action and to press forward with their agenda.[26]

The Puzzle of Argentina

The primacy of crafting to advancing gay rights in Latin America is most compellingly suggested by the case of Argentina, whose gay rights struggles, alongside those of Brazil, comprise the empirical core of this study. For good reasons, Argentina is widely regarded as the paradigmatic example of gay rights success in Latin America and indeed the global South. As noted at the opening of this study, within a remarkably short period of time, the country has accumulated a stunning record of LGBT legislation, most notably a same-sex marriage law in 2010. None of this success could have easily been anticipated. On the one hand, other countries in the region were more likely contenders for the title of Latin American gay rights champion. These contenders would include Costa Rica, Latin America's most successful experiment with democracy; Mexico, which was spared military dictatorship for much of the twentieth century; Chile, the darling of the developmental set, for the remarkable social and economic progress attained in the last two decades; Uruguay, historically, Latin America's most socially progressive and secular nation; and, most of all, Brazil, a country famous around the world for celebrating sexual diversity and home to Latin America's largest and most politically connected LGBT community.

On the other hand, Argentina has traditionally been among the most challenging environments for gay rights in Latin America. Numerous social and political developments have contributed to the infamy that is much of Argentine homosexual history—indeed, only Communist Cuba comes close to matching Argentina's record of repression of homosexuality. Notable among these developments are the efforts by the medical community in the early part of the twentieth century to eradicate homo-sexual behavior, ensuing from a "homosexual panic" triggered by massive European immigration; the palpable hostility toward homosexuality that has traditionally run through the nation's two main political parties—the "Radicals" and the "Peronists"; and the crushing of gay rights organiza-tions by the military dictatorship in place between 1976 and 1983, which included targeting homosexuals during the country's "dirty war," a conflict infamous for its depravity and violence. By the time of democracy's return in 1983, what was once Latin America's most vibrant gay rights community had been completely eviscerated, and the homosexual population exhibited something akin to post-traumatic stress disorder.

Key to unlocking the "puzzle" of gay rights in Argentina, this study demonstrates, is the smart and sustained campaign for gay rights crafted by local activists. While in much of the world the campaign for gay rights took the form of a legal-political struggle to end discrimination against an historically oppressed minority, across Latin America and especially in Argentina the gay rights campaign was framed, more ambitiously and ideal-istically, as a human rights crusade. The crusade took international human rights principles and other ideas percolating in the international sphere to advance gay rights and wedded them to the local context, thereby generat-ing a gay rights campaign with considerable resonance in the national cul-ture. It succeeded in changing the law, but, more importantly, it succeeded in transforming society and the culture at large. By the time the Argentine Congress legalized gay marriage in 2010, there was a broadly based societal consensus in Argentina for eradicating all kinds of discrimination against the gay community, and supporting gay rights had become a very low-risk proposition for politicians from across the ideological spectrum.

THE PLAN OF THE BOOK

Chapter 1, "Latin America through Transnational Lenses," sketches the rise of the "international gay rights arc" in the post-Stonewall era, as suggested primarily by the US experience, and explains how this arc was transported to Latin America in the manner suggested by the literatures on global queering, international socialization, and policy diffusion. The analysis highlights that these approaches, although compelling, unintentionally distort Latin American gay history and politics. They also fail to explain the uneven embrace of gay rights throughout the region, and overlook the ambiguity of external influence when it comes to gay rights, given the rise in recent years of a powerful anti-gay rights international lobby. Chapter 2,

"Domestic Change, Foreign Influence, and Gay Rights," begins to demonstrate the analytical advantages of "decentering" gay politics by explaining how modernization, judicial and constitutional reforms, and socially liberal governance have dramatically improved the domestic environment for gay rights virtually everywhere in Latin America by making the region especially receptive to international gay rights trends.

Chapter 3, "Reinventing Latin America's Oldest Gay Rights Movement," moves the study beyond macro cultural, legal, and political factors conditioning the rise of gay rights and into the realm of gay rights activism and strategies by beginning to unpack the puzzle of how Argentina managed to best all other Latin American nations in advancing gay rights without having the largest or the most politically connected gay rights movement in the region. Opening the chapter is a review of Argentina's long history of state repression of homosexuality, especially the military's crushing of the Frente de Liberación Homosexual (FLH), an organization founded in 1971 that tied the Argentine gay rights movement to analogous gay liberation fronts in the United States and Europe and that worked to spread Stonewall's gay liberation politics across Latin America. After the advent of democracy, in 1983, the FLH's violent demise in 1976 would feature prominently in the folding of the campaign for gay rights into the national struggle for human rights. Closing the chapter is an analysis of the emergence in 1984 of the Comunidad Homosexual Argentina (CHA), the leading gay rights group in the posttransition era. A small but nimble organization, the CHA was hugely influenced by the activism to which Argentine gay leaders were exposed to while in exile during the military dictatorship, especially the shift in gay politics from "sexual liberation" to "social integration." This shift foreshadowed the marriage equality movement.

Chapter 4, "Human Rights and the Argentine Gay Rights Campaign," examines the strategizing behind the struggle for gay rights in Argentina. Premised on the idea that "the freedom of sexuality is a basic human right," the campaign had tremendous local resonance by capitalizing on the dark legacy of human rights abuses left behind by the military dictatorship and the animus toward homosexuality by the political class and the courts that prevailed in the new democracy inaugurated in 1983. Consequently, targeting society and the culture at large, rather than the legislature and the courts, became the early focus of gay activists. The campaign took as its model the activism of Argentina's large and influential human rights movement, from which gay activists borrowed a well-tested playbook for influencing hearts and minds. Repurposed by the CHA, this playbook included depictions of the Argentine state as "genocidal," a not-so-subtle inference to Nazi Germany, extensive use of *escraches*, a protest strategy entailing accosting and shaming public figures in order to trigger moral outrage and provoke debate about homosexuality, and media campaigns to influence public opinion that, aside from humanizing homosexuals, linked ending antigay discrimination to Argentina's human rights and democratic aspirations. By the time the campaign shifted focus to the courts and the legislature, in the early 2000s, the climate for legislating gay rights had vastly improved.

Chapter 5, "Gay Rights and the Paradox of Brazil," places the findings from Argentina in a broader comparative perspective by examining why Brazil, Latin America's most famously liberal nation when it comes to homosexuality, fell behind Argentina and other Latin American nations in legislating gay rights. The chapter discusses, first, three factors that have made gay rights an uphill struggle in Brazil: an entrenched homophobia in the culture that feeds from Brazil's infamous inequality, a large Evangelical movement with tremendous political sway, and an inauspicious legislative environment, especially a deeply fragmented party system that makes enacting any legislation regarding gender and sexuality quite difficult. The focus of our analysis, however, is on the differences between Brazil and Argentina with respect to how the campaign for gay rights was crafted and executed in the posttransition years.

In 1985, facing a political environment of democratization and civil society resurgence similar to that of Argentina, Brazilian gay activists crafted a very different gay rights campaign than Argentina's with respect to its themes, arenas, and alliances. Human rights pleas in Brazil, while prominent, lacked the resonance they had in Argentina. More importantly, lobbying the legislature and collaborating with state agencies to see gay rights enacted into law rather than transforming hearts and minds about homosexuality were the priority for gay activists. A close alliance with the Workers' Party (PT), the first party in Latin America to welcome gay activists into its ranks, aided in this effort. This alliance gave the Brazilian gay movement visibility and resources that were the envy of most gay rights movements in Latin America, but it had significant drawbacks as well. Aside from failing to achieve much in the way of legislative gains, the alliance with the PT made the political system rather than society and the culture at large the main arena in the struggle for gay rights. Consequently, the Brazilian campaign for gay rights would be less grounded in society than Argentina's as well as less focused on changing societal attitudes about homosexuality.

Chapter 6, "Insights from the Revolution," closes the study with a discussion of the implications of the Latin American experience for the comparative study of gay rights politics. The chapter begins with a broad discussion of how "decentering" gay politics, as understood in this study, contributes to our understanding of the global spread of gay rights. International influence is clearly important, but, in the end, the evidence from Latin America and beyond suggests that whether gay rights will emerge and be accepted by society at large hinges predominantly on the particulars of the domestic context, from broad social and political patterns, like democracy and development, to the types of activism waged by the local gay rights movement.

The activism of gay rights organizations brings to light a second insight: the need to go beyond the resource mobilization paradigm in order to better understand what makes for a successful gay rights movement. Tellingly, most of Latin America's gay rights movements, including the most successful one, Argentina's, do not fit the conventional image of a strong social movement—far from it, actually. Given an inauspicious social climate that has traditionally compelled homosexuals in Latin America to conceal their sexual orientation, until recently Latin American gay rights organizations have encountered significant obstacles in building up an organizational infrastructure. Gay rights organizations have also been shunned by the political system and even by other groups in civil society. For both political and civil organizations, an association with homosexuality has been viewed as detrimental to their own reputation.

Last but not least, the chapter concludes with a broad discussion of what the advent of gay rights means for Latin American democracy. The analysis recognizes the rise of gay rights as an important sign of the maturity of democracy and pluralism in Latin America, but also calls for sobriety when it comes to assessing what the advent of gay rights actually means to the region. Of utmost concern is increasing levels of violence, both symbolic and real, against LGBT people ensuing, ironically enough, from the dramatic gay rights advances made in recent times.

PART I

Decentering Gay Rights

CHAPTER 1
Latin America through Transnational Lenses

A lmost all accounts of the rise of the contemporary gay rights movement begin with the improbable tale of the 1969 Stonewall Rebellion;
a series of spontaneous riots by gays, lesbians, and transvestites at the
Stonewall Inn, a Mafia-owned bar on the west side of Manhattan. What
actually triggered the riots remains a point of contention among gay historians, with some pointing to the death of singer-actress Judy Garland,
a gay icon whose funeral was held just hours before the riots broke out,
and others inclined to see the riots as emanating from "all the previous
rebellions of the sixties—the civil rights revolution, the sexual revolution
and the psychedelic revolution."[1] There is little doubt, however, about what
transpired at the Stonewall Inn or about the riots' paramount importance
to the global rise of gay rights; and notwithstanding the fact that the riots
have been subjected to considerable mythmaking, such as the view that
Stonewall was the first instance of gay resistance in American history.[2]

On June 28, 1969, eight plainclothes police detectives entered the
Stonewall Inn, and began rounding up employees and patrons for serving
liquor without a license and for engaging in conduct that violated subsec-
tion 8 of the New York State Penal Code, which criminalized "solicitation
of men for the purpose of committing a crime against nature."[3] That sub-
section of the code, in essence, made homosexual activity, of almost any
kind, a criminal offense. As the police proceeded to force Stonewall employees, a few drag queens, and a lesbian into a paddy wagon, the patrons who
had gathered outside the bar began throwing bottles at the police officers, forcing the police to take refuge inside the bar and to call for outside

reinforcement. By then the melee had spilled into the neighborhood, which required deployment of New York's riot police to quiet down the unrest. Three days of demonstrations would follow, which provided the impetus for the rise of what is nowadays known as the gay liberation movement.

Stonewall's global importance to the rise of gay rights is most eloquently stated in the scholarship of its most prominent historian, Martin Duberman. "The 1969 riots are now generally taken to mark the birth of the modern gay and lesbian political movement—that moment in time when gays and lesbians recognized all at once their mistreatment and their solidarity. As such, Stonewall has become an empowering symbol of global proportions."[4] Curiously, this prominence accorded to Stonewall is a relatively recent occurrence. Indeed, Stonewall's prominence arose decades after the riots had taken place to compensate for the dearth of attention to the riots by mainstream historians. Even "liberal" accounts of the "radical" 1960s overlooked Stonewall, either by ending their analysis before 1969 or by failing to take note of the riots altogether.[5] Thus, accounts of the Stonewall riots and their aftermath that began appearing in the 1990s, around the time of the riots' twenty-fifth anniversary, like Duberman's, were trying to correct what was perceived by gay historians to be an egregious historical slight.

Among the most talked-about legacies of the Stonewall Rebellion is that it effected a radical change in the demands made by the gay community and the manner in which these demands were articulated by the then-dominant gay rights movement, the so-called homophiles.[6] Led by the Mattachine Society, founded in Los Angeles in 1950 by Harry Hay, a homosexual and a member of the Communist Party, and by the San Francisco–based Daughters of Bilitis, founded in 1955 as the first American lesbian organization, the homophiles "spoke in softer, gentler tones" and focused their activism on "education and information" in the hope of ending antigay discrimination and introducing a more enlightened view of homosexuality.[7] Key to their assimilationist agenda was the idea that "gay people are just the same as heterosexuals except for what they do in bed," hence the emphasis on "the common humanity between homosexuals and heterosexuals."[8] Accordingly, the homophiles called on homosexuals to "dial down the gay" (such as avoiding gender-bending clothing and effeminate mannerisms) in order to facilitate the integration of gays into the mainstream of society.

Stonewall simultaneously dealt a crushing blow to the homophile movement and its agenda and launched a new wave of gay rights activism. Front and center for this new wave of gay activism was "sexual liberation," or the affirmation of the diversity of the gay community. This began with the Stonewall riots themselves, which featured among their protagonists "the powerless and the disrespected," including "drag queens, dykes, street people and bar boys."[9] It is this legacy that separates Stonewall from other gay riots that preceded it and that are nowadays ignored save for the most judicious accounts of American gay rights history. As noted by journalist Linda Hirshman, author of *Victory: The Triumphant Gay Revolution*, what gave Stonewall its fame was not the rebellion itself but what happened a year later: the one year anniversary march that was initiated in 1970s, the world's first gay pride march. She notes that: "The march was a brilliant piece of political theater. The march had everything—pageantry, national ambition, outing, crowd psychology, simplicity, existence precedes essence."[10]

Another legacy of the Stonewall riots was to grant gays control of their own image, which prior to 1969 had been dictated by a hostile media, as suggested by the infamous *Time* 1967 cover story "The Homosexual in America," which used the terms "homosexuals" and "deviants" interchangeably, and the condescending 1967 *CBS News* documentary "The Homosexual," which depicted homosexuals as "pitiable creatures" incapable of sustaining romantic relationships. As remarked by historian Michael Bronski: "The Stonewall riots produced not only a movement which demanded complete civil rights for gay people, but also a social network which spread the once clandestine world of gay culture. No longer dependent upon a secretive underground or the assimilation of gay sensibility into mainstream culture, gay people built their own cultural resources, publishing houses, record companies, theatre groups, community-based newspapers, and magazines."[11]

THE INTERNATIONAL GAY RIGHTS ARC

Lastly, the Stonewall riots marked a significant reorientation in gay politics, by moving gay rights demands from "negative rights" toward "positive rights" and, eventually, "equal" rights.[12] While negative rights demand little of the state other than to let gay people be themselves, by respecting their dignity and desires, most notably by ending harassment of homosexuals and lifting blatantly discriminatory laws (such as sodomy laws), positive rights require the state to do things on behalf of the gay community, like enacting laws to prevent antigay discrimination in housing, government policy, and the workplace. Equal rights demand that the state laws treat heterosexual and homosexual individuals in the same way, including extending marriage rights to same-sex couples.

Prominent among the many gay organizations that helped push the gay movement away from negative rights and toward positive rights in the wake of the Stonewall riots was the Gay Liberation Front (GLF).[13] This organization has been described as "a militant coalition of radical and revolutionary homosexual men and women committed to fight the oppression of homosexuals as a minority group and to demand the right to the self-determination of our own bodies."[14] Its core premise was that "since every dimension of the existing system was bankrupt, a total transformation of society was desirable; and that to effect such a dramatic change, it was necessary to unite all oppressed minorities into a broad-based movement."[15] To those ends, the GLF promoted a "new-left" platform that "attacked ... consumer culture, militarism, racism, sexism and homophobia," advocating replacing the clinical term "homosexual" with "gay," embracing "coming out" as "a crucial element of the liberation experience," adopting "pride" as "an important feature of liberation consciousness," and calling for the end of discrimination on the basis on sexual orientation.[16]

Among the many advances of the gay liberation period was the 1973 decision by the American Psychiatric Association to remove homosexuality from its list of mental disorders. Around the same time, a number of American states began to rescind their sodomy laws, and several American cities and municipalities enacted ordinances protecting gays and lesbians from discrimination on the basis of sexual orientation in housing and employment, while some business corporations began to provide spousal benefits to same-sex couples. Stiff societal resistance met these early gay rights advances. Anita Bryant, a country-and-western singer, former beauty queen, and spokesperson for the Florida Citrus Association, led the biggest pushback against gay rights. Almost single-handedly, Bryant organized a successful campaign that overturned a 1977 Dade County, Florida, ordinance prohibiting discrimination on the basis of sexual orientation (the ordinance was reinstated twenty years later, in 1998).[17] Bryant's activism also launched the Christian Right movement as a formidable foe to the US gay community.[18]

Demands for positive rights, and eventually equal rights, intensified during the 1980s with the waning of the utopian phase of sexual liberation launched by the Stonewall riots.[19] This coincided with the advent of new generation of gay rights activists and organizations less concerned with issues of "sexual identity" than with the goal of promoting "social integration."[20] The integration or "mainstreaming" movement made a plea to society about the need to treat gay citizens as deserving of civil rights protections; encouraged gays and lesbians to "come out" of the closet, acting on the belief that self-disclosure of one's sexuality to family, friends, neighbors, and coworkers was the most powerful tool gay people had at their disposal for changing societal attitudes toward homosexuality; and encouraged gays to participate in society at large, including greater engagement with the political system.[21] Leading the campaign for mainstreaming was a new cadre of gay rights organizations noted for their media sophistication, political lobbying savvy, and fundraising prowess. The prototype of these organizations is the Human Rights Campaign (HRC), organized in the early 1980s to elect gay-friendly candidates to the U.S. Congress, and later transformed into an all-purpose gay rights organization working to advance gay civil rights and fight antigay discrimination. Today, the HRC stands as the world's largest gay rights organization.

As might be expected, by the late 1980s, the social integration movement was fueling demands for "marriage equality."[22] Demands for same-sex marriage first emerged in Northern Europe, and from there they spread to other parts of Europe, to North America, and to parts of the global South. A key argument in advancing marriage equality was that gay marriage is not a radical idea intended to destroy heterosexual society but rather a conservative idea that would work for the betterment of both gays and society at large. This argument signaled a milestone in gay history, if only because of the historic ambivalence (indeed, at times hostility) that homosexuals have harbored toward marriage, given its association with heterosexual society.[23] As noted by historian Josh Zeitz, "Practicalities aside, some early gay right leaders actively rejected marriage as a proscriptive and exclusionary heterosexual institution." Lesbian activists, in particular, deemed marriage "a patriarchal system that looks to ownership, property, and dominance of men over women as its basis." Zeitz adds that slogans such as "Smash the Nuclear Family" and "Smash Monogamy" pervaded the early liberationist days of the 1970s.[24]

TRANSNATIONAL PERSPECTIVES ON THE GLOBAL SPREAD OF GAY RIGHTS

Three distinct approaches explain how the international arc of gay rights shaped by the Stonewall Rebellion traveled from New York City to many other parts of the globe, including Latin America. Arguably, the most prominent is "global queering," a scholarship that marries assumptions about globalization and the popularity of "queer theory."[25] Behind global queering is the idea that "the gay and lesbian movements house identities, politics, cultures, markets, and intellectual programs which nowadays know no national boundaries."[26] More specifically, as contended by Dennis

Altman, global queering refers to the proliferation of gender and sexual identities (gay, queer, bisexual, transgender) as representing "the expansion of an existing Western category" and as "part of the rapid globalization of lifestyle and identity politics," in other words, "the internationalization of Western homosexuality" and the creation of the "Global Gay."[27] In making note of these phenomena, Arnaldo Cruz-Malavé and Marin Manalansan keenly observe that "queerness is now global. Whether in advertising, film, performance art, the Internet, or the political discourses of human rights in emerging democracies, images of queer sexualities and cultures now circulate around the globe."[28]

The internationalization of American homosexuality, as fueled by the culturally homogenizing effects of American capitalism, is generally believed to be the root cause of global queering. According to Peter Jackson, "Like McDonald's and Disney, global queering began in the United States and has transformed the planet's queer cultures by cultural borrowing or cultural imperialism as a result of American global hegemony."[29] The Americanization of global gay culture began, appropriately enough, with the emergence of multiple clones of New York's GLF in several places around the world, with the most notable ones being Great Britain's Gay Liberation Front, organized at the London School of Economics in 1970, France's Front homosexuel d'action révolutionnaire, formed in Paris in 1971, and Argentina's Frente de Liberación Homosexual, organized in Buenos Aires in 1971.

Gay liberation fronts around the world worked to spread the gospel of gay liberation championed by New York's GLF. In so doing, gay liberation fronts helped popularize Stonewall, which, by the time of its twenty-fifth anniversary, in 1994, was well on its way to becoming a global icon of gay resistance. According to one account, Stonewall's twenty-fifth anniversary marked a transition from "localized descriptions of a police raid in a Greenwich Village bar to globalized descriptions of a revolutionary movement for gays and lesbians everywhere."[30] Marking the anniversary was a massive parade departing from the headquarters of the United Nations in New York City, a site specifically chosen because of its global symbolism. The official guide to the celebration underscored the global significance attached to Stonewall. "People will celebrate the rebellion that transformed the existing Homophile Movement into our contemporary, global, Lesbian, Gay and Transgender Rights Movement."[31]

More recently, global queering has been fueled by the "LGBT Transnational Media," a vast network of Western-based information and entertainment entities invested in promoting gay identities and concerns.[32] Arguably, the most prominent component of this network is

Hollywood, whose influence over gay global popular culture can be seen in the popularity of television shows like *Will and Grace, Glee*, and *Modern Family*, movies like *Brokeback Mountain*, and the Broadway show *Rent*. This entertainment output is credited with promoting positive depictions of homosexuality in the United States and popularizing the white middle class and upper-middle class lifestyles of America's gay ghettos or "gayborhoods," such as New York's Greenwich Village and San Francisco's Castro District.[33] A related development is the foreign influence of American gay publications, especially glossy magazines such as *Out* and *Genre*. Supported by advertising from multinational corporations, these publications have contributed to the creation of a "transnational gay culture" defined by Western consumerism, together with the emergence of a "gay lingo," English words and phrases that have become part of the vocabulary of gay people the world over.[34]

In the end, however, it was the HIV/AIDS epidemic, the most calamitous event in contemporary gay history, that contributed the most to fueling global queering. The epidemic's legacy to the globalization of gay culture is complex, multifaceted, and far-reaching. Indeed, the epidemic is generally seen as the most consequential happening in shaping gay activism within the developed West, in helping export Western homosexual social and cultural norms across developing societies, and, more generally, in accelerating modernization in many parts of the developing world. Altman summarizes the point about AIDS and globalization by noting that "AIDS is both a product and a cause of globalization, linking the least developed and the most developed regions in the world. Despite attempts to close borders to its spread, as in the restrictions on entry of HIV-positive people applied to many countries, the spread of the virus made a mockery of national sovereignty."[35]

AIDS galvanized the US gay community like never before it; and this, in turn, had important reverberations for gay activism and policymaking around the world.[36] Across the United States and Western Europe, AIDS accelerated demands for legal protections against discrimination in housing, government, and the workplace, as well as for state recognition of same-sex unions, starting with domestic partnerships and ending with same-sex marriage.[37] Jonathan Rauch, an analyst at the Brookings Institution, observes that "in the 1980s, after the egalitarian onrush of the 1970s, came the plague of AIDS and the realization, first by homosexuals, then by their families and then by the society at large, that the absence of stable family structures was literally deadly. Gay partners discovered that without the protections of marriage they were often crippled in their ability to tend to one another; the straight world saw that a culture without marriage is one full of promiscuity, instability, vulnerability, and often tragedy."[38]

A related development triggered by the AIDS epidemic was the "NGO-ization" of gay activism, with the emergence of a myriad of gay organizations involved in lobbying the government to find a cure for the epidemic, providing legal services and healthcare and outpatient service to those afflicted with the HIV virus, and organizing AIDS-prevention education campaigns.[39] This phenomenon generated an unprecedented level of professionalization within gay activism. AIDS prevention campaigns, in particular, had a massive impact across the developing world. Originally conceived for American and European audiences, these campaigns were later exported to the developing world by regional multilateral organizations, such as the World Bank, the United Nations, the Pan American Health Organization (PAHO), and private charities such as the American Foundation for AIDS Research (AMFAR). Designed to curb the spread of the epidemic, AIDS prevention campaigns featured intimate images of same-sex couples and frank sexual language, which were a novelty for many developing countries. Not surprisingly, international AIDS/HIV campaigns are often credited (both positively and negatively) with disseminating a "Western model" of homosexual sexuality and identity.[40]

Among the thousands of NGOs launched by the AIDS epidemic, none gained more renown and attracted more controversy than the AIDS Coalition to Unleash Power (ACT UP), the protest organization founded in New York in 1987 by activist-writer Larry Kramer. Its chief purpose was to expedite the approval process of medical treatments for the HIV virus, but its legacy would go well beyond that very specific objective. At the peak of its popularity and influence, in the mid-1990s, ACT UP had become "the most visible social movement in the U.S.," with chapters in some forty American cities and several European cities, including Paris, Berlin, and London.[41] The organization was noted for its provocative slogan, "Silence = Death," for its controversial symbol, a pink triangle (the marker for homosexual in Nazi Germany), and for staging acts of civil disobedience high on theatrics—such as blocking traffic in Manhattan's major avenues, disrupting trading at New York's Stock Exchange, staging funerals for AIDS victims in front of the White House, and interrupting Sunday mass at New York's St. Patrick's Cathedral.[42] Such tactics, as reported by the New York Times, gave ACT-UP a reputation for being "rude, rash and paranoid, and virtually impossible to please."[43]

A second approach to understanding the global spread of the international gay rights arc is "international socialization," a concept that is a staple of international relations theory especially popular for explaining the spread of human rights norms from the developed West to the rest of the world since the enactment of the 1948 Universal Declaration of Human Rights.[44] Although the Declaration itself is mum on the issue of sexual orientation, since at least the 1980s, and in large measure due to the patient work of gay activists, gay rights have gradually made their way into what might be referred to as the "international human rights regime," or the cluster of social rights that all civilized societies are expected to adhere to.[45] In making the case that "gay rights are human rights," gay activists have taken refuge under several articles of the 1948 Declaration, including article 2, which affirms that every person is entitled to human rights "without distinction of any kind, including sex," and article 16, which proclaims the universal principle of "equality before the law."

"International socialization," as the term itself implies, is thought to represent the "induction of new members into the ways of behavior that are preferred in a society."[46] Behind this process of induction is a "spiral model" of change by which once recalcitrant states come to embrace human rights conventions. Western-based "transnational advocacy networks" are thought to be the engine behind this process.[47] These networks are described as "actors working internationally on an issue, who are bound together by shared values, a common discourse, and dense exchanges of information and services."[48] Because of their status as "nonstate" actors, transnational advocacy networks are able to act in ways not readily accessible to states and even international organizations. Margaret Keck and Kathryn Sikkink, two pioneers in the field of international socialization, note that transnational advocacy networks "are able to mobilize information strategically to help create new issues and categories, and to persuade, pressurize, and gain leverage over more powerful organizations and governments."[49] In so doing, transnational advocacy networks are able "to shape not only policy debates but also the nature of the debate."

Notable among the transnational advocacy networks active in the global promotion of LGBT rights is the International Lesbian and Gay Association (ILGA), an organization devoted to working "for the liberation of lesbian/gay women and gay men from legal, social cultural and economic discrimination."[50] Founded in 1978 in Coventry, England, as an umbrella organization for European gay rights groups for the purpose of lobbying intergovernmental organizations, by the mid-1990s ILGA had grown into a confederation representing some three hundred groups from over seventy countries, including members from Latin America, Africa, and Asia.[51] Among its many achievements are obtaining consultative status within the UN in 1993, a first for a gay and lesbian organization, getting the World Health Organization to drop homosexuality from its list of mental disorders, and lending critical support to fledging gay rights organizations across the developing world. More often than not, ILGA partners with local gay rights organizations to name and shame particular governments for their mistreatment of the LGBT population, hoping that this will lead to a change in policy and attitudes toward the LGBT population.

Following the lead of international gay NGOs such as ILGA, by the early 1990s major human rights organizations like Amnesty International began to name and shame countries for their failures to defend the human rights of the LGBT population. This was a huge victory for gay rights organizations. Like many other human rights organizations, Amnesty had for many years regarded gay rights as potentially detrimental to its worldwide mission of promoting human rights, defined largely as defending people subjected to political persecution.[52] In 1995, in collaboration with ILGA and other gay NGOs, Amnesty published *Breaking the Silence*, a wide-ranging report on human rights abuses perpetrated around the world on the basis of sexual orientation.[53] On May 7, 2006, International Day Against Homophobia (a day significant because it marks the occasion when the World Health Organization removed homosexuality from its roster of mental disorders, in 1990), Human Rights Watch introduced its "Hall of Shame." This report names five international public officials for their homophobic behavior and praises five countries for their LGBT rights advances.[54]

More recently, socialization into LGBT norms has been promoted by major Western powers. International support for gay rights by the American government commenced with the presidency of Barack Obama, whose administration is both credited with and blamed for pursing a "gay foreign policy."[55] Obama's most prominent statement on gay rights was made in an October 2011 speech to the United Nations General Assembly, in which he stated: "No country should deny people their rights to freedom of speech and freedom of religion, but also no country should deny people their rights of who they love, which is why we must stand up for the rights of gays and lesbians everywhere."[56] This speech was followed by an address by Secretary of State Hillary Rodham Clinton to United Nations Human Rights Commission's Geneva headquarters in December 2011 to mark the signing earlier that year of the UN Gay Rights Resolution. That resolution calls for the decriminalization of homosexuality in all corners of the globe. Borrowing from her famous 1994 Beijing speech in which Clinton argued that "women's rights are human rights and human rights are women's rights, she intoned: "Gay rights are human rights, and human rights are gay rights . . . no practice or tradition trumps the human rights that belong to all of us. And this holds true for inflicting violence against LGBT people, criminalizing their status or behavior, expelling them from their families and communities, or tacitly or explicitly accepting their killing."[57]

The third and last approach to understanding the global spread of gay rights is "policy diffusion." This concept refers to "the process in which an innovation is communicated through certain channels over time among the members of a social system. It is a special type of communication, in that the messages are concerned with new ideas."[58] Policy diffusion, more specifically, identifies junctures when a particular policy idea or innovation sparks a "wave" or a "cluster" of like-minded policies within a relatively short period of time by a great many different states. At work here is nothing short of a "contagion," meaning something that erupts in one or a handful of countries and rapidly spreads among many other countries. Recent instances of policy diffusion include democratization, privatization, healthcare reform, pension reform, gender quotas, the legalization of marijuana, and, of course, gay rights, same-sex marriage in particular.

Policy diffusion can happen through a variety of means, including the endeavors of influential opinion makers, such as celebrities, politicians, and business leaders; technocratic exchanges between and among governments; the foreign policies of major international players; multilateral collaboration; collective learning, international consultancy; and the socializing generated by transnational NGOs. But more often than not, policy diffusion happens autonomously as nations simply mimic each other's behavior, sensing that what works in one country might work in another one. Almost all of this is suggested by how same-sex marriage became all the rage in the developed West in such a short period of time. In 2001, the Netherlands made history by legalizing same-sex marriage, followed quickly by Belgium in 2003, and Spain in 2005, all of them by parliamentary action. Ten years later, some seventeen nations had extended marriage rights to same-sex couples, including several in the developing world.

Many factors and forces have aided in the diffusion of same-sex marriage, starting with several voices with great sway over elite opinion. Andrew Sullivan's landmark 1989 essay for the *New Republic*, "Here Comes the Groom," started the debate about gay marriage in earnest, at least in the United States, by making the case for the conservative nature of gay marriage. Sullivan argued that "it's one of the ironies of our society's blind spot toward gays that essentially conservative social goals should have the appearance of being radical. But gay marriage is not a radical step. . . . It avoids the mess of domestic partnership; it is humane; it is conservative in every sense of the word."[59]

Other calls for gay marriage were soon to come, such as a much-cited 1996 cover story in *The Economist*, which advocated societal acceptance of homosexuality, including extending marriage to same-sex couples. The magazine argued that now that homosexuals are less and less willing either to hide or to lead lives of celibacy, "the real choice for society is between homosexual marriage and homosexual alienation. No social interest is served by choosing the latter."[60] These views have been echoed by very prominent politicians, such as former New York City Mayor Mike Bloomberg; President Obama, the first sitting American president to endorse same-sex marriage; Spanish Prime Minister José Luis Rodríguez Zapatero; and British Prime Minister David Cameron. The last three politicians made gay rights a diplomatic priority.

THE QUEERING OF LATIN AMERICA

A visit to almost any Latin American country would provide ample evidence of the global queering of Latin America, even though Latin American homosexuality (especially male homosexuality) remains, in many regards, a world all of its own. Its peculiarities, as noted by anthropologist Richard Parker, writing in reference to Brazil, make it "a mistake" to view the Brazilian gay community as "as nothing more than an importation from abroad, a tropical version of the gay community as it exists in Europe or the United States."[61] Especially notable across Latin America is the so-called active/passive dichotomy among homosexual males, whereby a homosexual identity is adopted or attached only to those men who assume the passive role in homosexual relations but not those who assume the active role.[62] Even studies that try to highlight how the advent of the Western concept of "gay" in Latin America has since the 1970s helped erode the active/passive dichotomy acknowledge its surprising resilience.[63]

References to American gay culture, history, and politics transported by television, films, tourism, and the Internet, abound across Latin America, especially in business establishments that cater to the gay community, such as bars, bookstores, cinemas, restaurants, and gyms. The name "Stonewall," rainbow flags, and pink triangles are the most ubiquitous signs of global queering. But even somewhat obscure references to American gay history are not uncommon, such as Casa Brandon in Buenos Aires, a club, community center, art gallery, and performance space that honors the memory of Brandon Teena, the transgender teenager from Nebraska who was raped and murdered in 1993 and whose story was popularized in the film *Boys Don't Cry* (1999).

Images and stories about gay life in the United States are also prominently circulated in the Latin America media, especially in the larger and more globalized countries, like Mexico, Argentina, and Brazil. In some cases, the intention is to draw attention to controversial and/or exotic images of American lesbian and gay sexualities; in other cases the intention is to inform and even to laud gay rights progress. At times both purposes converge into a single mission, as was the case of the Brazilian media's coverage of the first Gay Games held in New York City in 1994, which were timed to coincide with Stonewall's twenty-fifth anniversary.

As analyzed by Charles Klein, the *Folha de São Paulo's* coverage of the opening ceremony of the games "does not contain any photos of this event but is surrounded by three photos from the San Francisco Lesbian/Gay Freedom Day Parade, which was held on the same day.[64] The largest photograph shows three women on a motorcycle—one is topless, the second wears a gas mask and the third has a shaved head." Klein adds that the point of the coverage is to show the "more scandalous (and non-Brazilian) aspects of US lesbian/gay/queer culture." In other instances, though, the coverage is deferential, as was the coverage of Stonewall's twenty-fifth anniversary. According to Klein, the *Folha* presents the Stonewall twenty-fifth anniversary march as an international political event worthy of two days of coverage in its "World Section," and "instead of images of scantily clothed leather people, we are shown masses of activists carrying picket signs, banners, and an enormous rainbow flag as they pass in front of the United Nations building."

Latin Americans have also eagerly adopted many of the political and philosophical arguments and cultural practices regarding homosexuality emanating from the United States and Europe. Beyond embracing the politics of gay liberation unleashed by the Stonewall riots, European and American debates about the nature of homosexuality have also been influential. Especially appealing to Latin American gay intellectuals has been the work of French philosopher Michael Foucault, who inspired an entire generation of Latin American and especially Argentine gay activists.[65] In *The History of Sexuality* (1978), Foucault argued that homosexuality was a relatively new social construction that the medical establishment had succeeded in turning into a pathological condition.

As for foreign cultural practices, none has been greeted more warmly than gay pride parades. Mexico City held Latin America's first gay pride parade in 1979, roughly a decade after this form of gay activism made its debut in New York City to mark the first anniversary of the Stonewall riots, and one of the first gay pride parades held outside of the US mainland. By the mid-1990s, gay pride marches had become commonplace in most major metropolitan areas of Latin America, including Guadalajara, Bogotá, Buenos Aires, Montevideo, Rio de Janeiro, and São Paulo. Among these cities, São Paulo's pride parade stands out. The city's first gay pride parade, held in 1997 down Paulista Avenue, the city's main thoroughfare, drew a paltry crowd of two thousand people. By 2005, however, attendance had soared to 2.5 million, and by 2009 São Paulo's pride parade was drawing crowds in excess of 3 million people, making that year's parade the largest public gathering in Brazilian history and, according to the Guinness World of Records, the largest of all gay pride parades held that or any other year.

As in the United States, gay pride parades have introduced a new means for mobilizing the masses, making demands against the state, and building collective identity, certainly quite distinct from strikes and public demonstrations, to say nothing of revolutionizing gay tourism.[66] While strikes and demonstrations seek to disrupt the normal course of things in an attempt to force public officials to respond (a strategy that more often than not results in annoying the public at large rather than forcing the government to act), the annual spectacle of pride marches, by contrast, aims to celebrate gayness and, notwithstanding their outlandishness, the ordinariness of gay people. As Javier Corrales has observed about Latin America's embrace of pride parades: "Like good old lefties, LGBT groups understand the power of a massive protest, especially in the streets. But their approach to taking the streets is not to go on strike, interrupt traffic during rush hour, shut down schools and hospitals, or vandalize private property, but rather, throw an annual gay pride march."[67]

Global efforts to curb HIV/AIDS have also contributed to the queering of Latin America. The virus first appeared in Latin America in the early 1980s, a few years after it was detected in the United States and Africa.[68] But this comparative advantage was wasted since Latin American politicians and health officials did not prepare for the eventual arrival of the virus, thinking that Latin American countries were different from the United States and Africa. Tim Frascas's chronicle of the rise of the AIDS epidemic in Latin America notes that public officials firmly believed that there was no decadent American-style gay culture or African-style poverty in Latin America to fuel an epidemic. "This is not Uganda," one smiling official told Frascas, implying that his citizens had nothing to fear due to their superior moral habits and modern health systems.[69] Aside from feeling morally superior to the Americans and institutionally better equipped than the Africans to handle AIDS, the Latin Americans were also quite naive about how AIDS would affect them. Mexicans were of the view that they "had stronger immune systems because they were frequently exposed to germs"; Chileans believed that "the Andes would shield Chile from this northern plague"; Brazilians felt that they were "sophisticated enough to have the disease."[70]

Once the epidemic began to spread like fire throughout Latin America, fueled by "sexual promiscuity, hypocrisy, and haphazard prevention," it was Latin America's small and poorly financed network of gay organizations that provided the first line of defense. This was a responsibility that these groups were simply not equipped to handle. Between 1986 and 1993, the number of people inflicted with full-blown AIDS in Latin America increased from fewer than 8,000 to 80,000; and the number of infected people was approaching 1,000,000 in Brazil, 500,000 in Mexico, 200,000 in Colombia, and 100,000 in Argentina.[71] Understandably, Latin American gay organizations looked to their counterparts in the United States for inspiration and assistance. This, in turn, strengthened activists' ties between the United States and Latin America.

ACT UP forged the most fruitful relationship between American and Latin American gay activists. The organization's Latino caucus, ACT UP Americas, a small cluster of activists of Latin American origin living in the United States, determined to bring ACT UP–style activism to the global South (a goal not always heartily supported by the mother organization, feeling itself already stretched battling for the rights of HIV patients in the United States), was the transnational nexus linking ACT UP and Latin American activists.[72] ACT UP Americas' role in the fight against HIV/AIDS in Latin America was multifold. The most urgent task was to assist local activists to confront the onset of the epidemic. To that end, ACT UP Americas published *Boletín de ACT-UP America*, a Spanish-language newspaper with articles on scientific findings about HIV/AIDS treatment, on drugs and therapies not yet available in Latin America, and on strategies for curbing infections. Another task was collecting and shipping medicines to Latin American countries, especially unused medicines, paraphernalia, and equipment made available to ACT UP activists as people in the United States began to develop resistance to the early AIDS medical treatment.

Last but not least, ACT UP America became heavily invested in educating Latin American activists about AIDS activism, a task that entailed nothing short of resocializing Latin American activists on how to promote their cause. M. Alfredo González, a founding member of ACT UP Americas notes that:

By the 1980s, the politics of social class was at the core of Latin American societal struggles, less so the politics of difference. The lexicon and methodologies that U.S. HIV/AIDS activists inherited from the civil rights, feminist, and gay rights movements were practically absent in Latin America. Southern activists knew about general strikes and popular revolts but not much about civil disobedience, creative non-violence, and of the "subordinate" expertise of lay-people who appropriate biomedical knowledge.[73]

International AIDS organizations also did their part to curb the AIDS epidemic in Latin America, while strengthening local gay rights activists, especially at the grassroots level. AMFAR financed some of the earliest AIDS prevention efforts in Latin America, including a grant in the early 1990s to the Sociedad de Integración Gay-Lésbica Argentina (SIGLA) to distribute free condoms in Argentina, against opposition from the Catholic Church, which believed that abstinence was the only effective deterrent to AIDS. Hoping to avert an epic disaster, international development organizations such as the World Bank assisted Latin American governments in designing a plan of action to combat HIV/AIDS, which in most cases included cleaning the blood supply, educational campaigns, and free and/or subsidized medical treatment. By 2003, the Bank had approved over $550 million in loans to help finance the implementation of HIV/AIDS prevention and control programs in seventeen Latin America and Caribbean nations.[74] The Bank's involvement in HIV/AIDS in Latin America has been most sustained in Brazil, where it cofinanced an HIV/AIDS prevention program that is widely praised as the most effective in the developing world.[75] The effectiveness of this intervention helps explain why Latin America is often viewed as less affected by the epidemic than other parts of the developing world.

Another early prominent actor in the fight against HIV/AIDS in Latin America was PAHO. Between 2002 and 2005, in conjunction with local gay NGOs, PAHO undertook what to date was the largest AIDS prevention campaign in Argentina, Colombia, Brazil, and Mexico. The campaign's main purpose was to develop an understanding of the causes of AIDS and ways to prevent it. But the campaign also created "a more tolerant environment for homosexuals in the four countries," by promoting more respect for diversity of sexual orientation.[76] This point was underscored by the publicity that accompanied the campaign, which featured a series of controversial posters and television ads showing males couples kissing and hugging and discussing in very frank language ways to prevent HIV infection. According to the organizers at PAHO, the advertisements of the campaign "presented homophobia as an interrelated problem of rights and health. They presented non-heterosexual people in a nondiscriminatory light, and took advantage of the controversy that the issue generated to promote a public dialogue among different sectors of civil society."[77]

International gatherings such as the International AIDS Conference, a conference that mixes politics, science, and activism, allowed Latin American activists to interact with their counterparts from Europe, the

United States, and other parts of the developing world. The conference was held for the first time in Latin America in 2006, in Mexico City, with some twenty-two thousand scientists, activists, and policymakers in attendance. Some six thousand of the participants came from Latin America. With the theme of "Universal Action Now," the conference featured a massive demonstration in the Mexican capital that highlighted issues of importance to the region, such as the increasing feminization of the epidemic, the risk of HIV infection among Mexican immigrants to the United States, and the epidemic's effects on indigenous communities. Among the conference's highlights was a presentation by Elena Reynaga, executive director of the Argentine Association of Female Sex Workers, a first for the conference. Reynaga called on international donors to allow funding intended to help sex workers to be administered by the women themselves, arguing "that many organizations do not actually understand women's complex needs with respect to HIV/AIDS prevention."[78]

SOCIALIZING BY NAMING AND SHAMING

A wealth of empirical evidence also supports the view that in the last decades Latin America has been successfully socialized into international gay rights norms. Some of the most compelling evidence comes from the pressure and shaming to which international NGOs have subjected Latin American governments for their horrid treatment of homosexuals. These endeavors began in earnest in the early 1990s, as international human rights activism in Latin America began to shift away from the abuses perpetrated against political prisoners by military governments and toward the oppression suffered by "women, street children, homosexuals, and indigenous peoples."[79] In the specific case of homosexuals, international human rights advocacy in Latin America has focused on documenting and exposing antigay discrimination and violence and in supporting the work of local gay rights groups.

A good example is the transnational advocacy of the International Gay and Lesbian Human Rights Commission (IGLHRC), founded in 1990 by American human rights activist Julie Dorf. Her activism was driven by the belief that "all people, regardless of their sexual orientation, gender identity, and HIV status are entitled to human rights."[80] By the early 1990s, the IGLHRC began issuing reports blasting certain countries in the region for their blatant discriminatory practices, including condoning the use of lethal violence against gay people. Among the first cases exposed was that of Colombia, where a self-styled moral campaign on behalf of "social cleansing" had degenerated into the killing of "disposable" people, including gays, lesbians, street children, and transvestites, by government-sponsored death squads.[81]

Another country targeted by the IGLHRC was Nicaragua, which in 1992, under the conservative government of President Violeta Chamorro, passed an antisodomy law that mandated prison sentences of up to three years for "anyone who induces, promotes, propagandizes or practices sexual intercourse between persons of the same sex."[82] This law served as a "constant threat" by allowing the police to intimidate, abuse, and extort lesbians, gays, and transvestites.[83] The IGLHRC also reported on the situation in Mexico, especially the morality campaign undertaken by the right-wing government of the National Action Party (or PAN) in the city of Guadalajara in the mid-1990s, which enhanced the power of the police to harass and arrest homosexuals, and in Brazil, with the release in 1997 of the report "Epidemic of Hate," which claimed that twelve hundred LGBT people had been killed in Brazil in the previous decade.

Through its Asylum Documentation Program, the IGLHRC was able to use high-profile immigration cases to highlight the dangers of being gay in Latin America and to embarrass major Latin American countries for their treatment of their LGBT population. In 1992, the IGLHRC was successful in getting Canada to grant refugee status to an Argentine homosexual for the first time. The case involved Jorge Alberto Inaudi, a twenty-eight-year-old former engineering student at the University of Córdoba who testified to the Immigration and Refugee Board, an independent agency within Canada's Ministry of Immigration, that while under arrest in 1989 and 1990 he had been raped and tortured by Argentina's federal police. He said that he had fled Argentina for Canada in 1990 because "he could not tolerate this police terror," noting that "the fact that they know me as a gay man and I am on file makes me vulnerable."[84]

In 1993, the IGLHRC accomplished a similar feat in the United States, which granted asylum to Marcelo Tenorio, a gay male from Brazil. This breakthrough in American immigration law was won on the grounds that Tenorio's sexual orientation put him in mortal danger in his home country. Threatened with deportation for having entered the United States illegally, Tenorio told an immigration judge that he fled Brazil in 1990 after he was stabbed outside of a gay bar in Rio de Janeiro in 1989 and that he feared for his life if forced to go home. To back this claim, the IGLHRC used data from Brazilian activists that claimed that a "homocaust" was occurring in Brazil, given the very high number of gay murders witnessed in the country since at least the early 1980s, most of them unsolved.[85]

By the mid-1990s, LGBT concerns were fully ensconced in the work of international human rights organizations, and this proved to be a very positive development for alerting the world to the plight of sexual minorities in Latin America. These organizations were especially attentive to instances of lethal violence against the LGBT population. In 1994, Amnesty International reported on one of the most horrific cases of sexual violence perpetrated upon a LGBT person in Latin America.[86] The report chronicled the killing in March 1993 of Renildo José dos Santos, age twenty-nine, a Brazilian councilman from the municipality of Coqueiro Seco, in the northeastern state of Alagoas, who, upon coming out as homosexual, was kidnapped from his home by four policemen and political enemies. He was subsequently tortured (his ears, nose, and tongue were severed and his legs broken), castrated, and sodomized before his body was set on fire and rendered unrecognizable and dumped into a river. This was one of the cases profiled in Amnesty International's 1995 book *Breaking the Silence*.

In the early 2000s, Amnesty International took Argentina to task for its treatment of the transgender community. In a report titled "Argentina: Death of a Transgender in Custody," the human rights organization investigated the killing of Vanessa Lorena Ledesma, a forty-seven-year-old transvestite active with the United Transvestites Association of Córdoba.[87] According to the report, Ledesma was detained during a bar fight and charged with damaging the bar. Five days after her arrest, on February 11, 2001, she died, and the police recorded her death as having been caused by "cardiac arrest." An autopsy revealed that she had been severely beaten while in police custody, as evidenced by severe bruising all over her body, and that there was a discrepancy between the date of her death recorded by the police and her actual time of death.

Over time, this kind of external reporting prompted action on the part of several Latin American governments. In 1996, in direct response to the toll that human rights violations (and reporting about these violations) were taking on Brazil's international reputation, the administration of Fernando Henrique Cardoso formulated the National Human Rights Program. This program identified the LGBT community as among the minorities most vulnerable to discrimination and violence in Brazil, but it failed to generate legislation banning discrimination on the basis of sexual orientation and identity. A better example is Chile's 2012 antidiscrimination law, which came on the heels of the vicious murder of Daniel Zamudio, on March 3, 2012, a twenty-four-year-old beaten so brutally by alleged neo-Nazis that he had to be put into an induced coma upon admission to the hospital. He died twenty-five days later of internal injuries.

Zamudio's death prompted the Chilean Congress to revive plans afoot since 2005 for an antidiscrimination law. Curiously enough, the law had been stalled over the issue of whether to include sexual orientation as a category of protection. But it was the global outcry that Zamudio's death generated that ensured passage of a law with protection for homosexuals. Mario Vargas Llosa, Peru's Novel prize-winning novelist, writing in the pages of the Spanish newspaper *El País*, best expressed the outrage triggered around the world by Zamudio's killing. "We can hope that the immolation of Daniel Zamudio should serve to shed light on the tragic condition of gays, lesbians, transgender in Latin American countries, where, without exception, sexual minorities are the object of scorn, marginality, persecution, and malicious campaigns that, by and large, have the overwhelming and enthusiastic support of public opinion."[88]

Western governments have also done their part to support the socialization of Latin Americans into international gay rights, especially since the advent of the Obama administration in 2008. Since announcing its support for LGBT rights abroad, under the leadership of Secretary Clinton, the US State Department has worked to promote LGBT rights across the region by, among other things, linking American and Latin American gay activists. In 2011, the Department of State's Bureau of Western Hemisphere Affairs (WHA) released a report titled "LGBT Rights in the Western Hemisphere and Opportunities for US Foreign Policy," the first of its kind for the department. It promoted "expanding public outreach and awareness of human rights for LGBT people, by creating and leveraging partnerships and utilizing multilateral venues like the United Nations and the Organization of American States."[89] Following the recommendation of the WHA report, in September 2012 the State Department sponsored a trip by prominent Latin American LGBT leaders to the United States.[90]

GAY RIGHTS POLICY DIFFUSION IN LATIN AMERICA

Some of the most compelling evidence of gay rights policy diffusion in Latin America concerns how policy developments from abroad have directly shaped gay rights legislation across Latin America. Mexico's federal antidiscrimination law, passed by the Vicente Fox administration in 2003, which covers discrimination on the basis on sexual orientation, pointedly drew upon foreign antidiscrimination laws. The final report that led to the drafting of the law noted that "the fight against discrimination in Mexico cannot ignore . . . vast discussions in what we might call 'the international public sphere,' which includes both agreements by government organizations and demands generated by non-governmental organizations."[91]

Civil union laws in Buenos Aires (2002), Uruguay (2007), and the Mexican state of Coahuila (2007) were inspired by France's 1999 Law of Civil Solidarity Pacts and the civil union laws introduced in several Spanish autonomous regions by the late 1990s that made such unions available to both homosexual and heterosexual couples. By being inclusive, gay activists and legislators were protecting themselves from the charge that they were pushing for "special rights" for gays. Same-sex marriage legislation in Latin America was also greatly influenced by developments abroad, especially in Spain. From Mexico to Argentina, the legalization of same-sex marriage in Spain in 2005 by Zapatero's left-wing administration spurred Latin American gay activists into action, prompted by the belief that if this was possible in Spain, it was also possible in their own countries.

Zapatero also influenced a new generation of left-wing leaders in Latin America, as suggested most vividly by the popularity of his speech to mark the enactment of same-sex marriage in Spain. That 2005 speech, which was broadcast live in television stations in countries like Argentina and that made headlines in all the major Latin American newspapers, has been widely quoted by several Latin American politicians and jurists to justify their support for gay rights. In the speech, Zapatero notes, "We are not legislating, honorable members, for people far away and not known by us. We are enlarging the opportunity for happiness to our neighbors, our co-workers, our friends and, our families. At the same time we are making a more decent society, because a decent society is one that does not humiliate its members."[92]

The Spaniards, however, did not just provide inspiration to Latin Americans. In what amounts to what has been described as "progressive colonialism," between 2000 and 2010 Spain spent some US$2 million promoting LGBT rights in Latin America, including $150,000 in Argentina alone around the time the same-sex marriage bill was being debated.[93] This spending reflected the efforts by the Zapatero administration to export to the world outside of Spain the same socially progressive policies for which Zapatero became known at home.[94] Zapatero's efforts to promote LGBT rights in Latin America were backed by Spanish NGOs, especially the Federación Estatal de Lesbianas, Gays, Transexuales y Bisexuales (FELGBT), Spain's leading gay rights organization.

According to lesbian and feminist activist Maria Rachid, who led the successful fight for same-sex marriage in Argentina: "We learned everything from the Spaniards."[95] Asked to mention one lesson her organization learned from the Spaniards, she said: "If you ask for civil unions you may fall short; if you ask for marriage equality your foes will offer you civil unions; so you might as well ask for what you really want." Unsurprisingly, the slogan employed in the campaign for same-sex marriage in Spain and Argentina was the same: "Los mismos derechos con los mismos nombres" (The same rights with the same names). And when Argentine legislators and gay activists sat down to write a same-sex marriage bill it was the Spanish 2005 same-sex marriage law that they used as their blueprint.[96]

Policy diffusion is also apparent in the increasing tendency of Latin American courts to engage in "transnational jurisprudence," the use of legal precedents from other countries' courts or international courts in their own deliberations, thereby facilitating the spread of ideas with respect to gay rights. Mexico's 2010 Supreme Court ruling that opened the way for the legalization of gay adoptions in Mexico City pointedly drew upon a 2008 landmark case from the European Court of Human Rights—*E.B. v. France*—which held that an unmarried woman could not be denied the right to adopt a child due to her sexual orientation and that same-sex couples should have the same rights to adopt as heterosexual couples and single parents to fully guarantee equality and freedom from discrimination.

More suggestive was the unanimous December 2012 ruling by the Mexican Supreme Court that declared it unconstitutional to deny the right to marry to three same-sex couples from Oaxaca. The ruling cited two famous cases from American jurisprudence: *Brown v. Board of Education*, which declared state laws establishing separate public schools for black and white students unconstitutional in 1954; and *Loving v. Virginia*, the 1967 landmark case that struck down laws banning interracial marriage. Citing the *Loving* decision, Justice Arturo Zaldívar Lelo de Larrea noted: "In comparative law it has been argued that discrimination that homosexual couples have suffered when they are denied access to marriage is analogous with the discrimination suffered by interracial couples from another era.[97]

Brazil's landmark 2011 decision by the Federal Supreme Court that put homosexual and heterosexual unions on the same legal footing, drew upon several international sources. Justice Celso de Mello cited the Yogyarkarta Principles, a 2006 agreement signed in Yogyarkarta, Indonesia, by a notable group of human rights experts to fight discrimination on the basis of sexual orientation and gender identity. Justice Ellen Gracie, the first female appointed to the court, cited Zapatero's speech at the time of the signing of Spain's same-sex marriage law, which, as noted previously, recognizes the "rights of our neighbors and family" in extending marriage rights to same-sex couples.

Although attractive and very compelling, externally based explanations for the rise of gay rights in Latin America leave a lot to be desired. Indeed, these explanations seem to obscure as much as they reveal. For a start, trying to understand the Latin American gay rights experience through the prism of international influence misrepresents and even distorts the history of homosexuality in Latin America by obscuring national developments and local histories. A case in point is the history of the decriminalization of homosexual behavior in Latin America.

Most Latin American countries began to decriminalize homosexual behavior more than a century before the United States and Great Britain undertook legal efforts to invalidate sodomy laws, as a consequence of the influence of the Napoleonic Civil Code of 1804 throughout the Iberian-Latin world.[98] With the monarchical order destroyed by the French Revolution, the Napoleonic Civil Code sought to rationalize French law by freeing it from its prerevolutionary legal order, especially Roman law and natural law. Brazil was the first Latin American country to copy France by eradicating all sodomy laws in 1830, following its independence from Portugal. Mexico and Argentina followed course in 1872 and 1887, respectively. By contrast, homosexuality was not completely decriminalized in the United Kingdom until 1981, after a decision by the European Court of Human Rights in *Dudgeon v. the United Kingdom*, which ruled that legislation that criminalized male homosexual acts was in violation of the European Convention of Human Rights; and in the United States until 2003, when the Supreme Court struck down all remaining sodomy laws in *Lawrence v. Texas*.

Also instructive is that the making of a modern gay identity in Latin America, especially male gay identity, owes more to national developments than to international influence. In the United States and Western Europe, modern homosexual identity, especially male homosexual identity, began to emerge in the late 1800s as a consequence of the advent of industrial capitalism and urbanization.[99] In some of the better-known accounts of the rise a male homosexual culture in cities like New York, London, and San Francisco, modern gay identity was propelled by the concentration of a large number of male homosexuals driven by a multiplicity of factors, including migration from the countryside to the city and the expansion of urban economies.[100] Being severed from their families and clustered with sexually like-minded people allowed gay urban immigrants to create a social milieu in which they could freely express their sexual orientation and begin to create the social infrastructure (cafes, bars, social clubs, drag balls, and charities) that in time would propel national movements of gay liberation.

The narrative highlighted above also holds true for Latin America's largest cities. Osvaldo Bazán's encyclopedic account of the history of homosexuality in Argentina—it begins with the European conquest and ends in the early years of the twenty-first century—describes a bourgeoning gay male culture in turn-of-the-century Buenos Aires fueled by capitalist expansion and massive European immigration.[101] Daniel Bao's account of the rise of contemporary homosexual culture in Argentina—which focuses on the years between 1900 and 1950, a period that witnessed the development of Argentina's industrial base and the rise of an affluent, consumerist society that brought alongside the formation of a strong middle class and the consolidation of bourgeois values—makes note of the development in Buenos Aires of a thriving homosexual subculture. In describing similarities between Buenos Aries and large European cities, Bao notes that "at the turn of the century a developed Argentine subculture of inverts had meeting places, their own argot, fashion, and sexual tastes and customs. They held balls and dances, got married to each other, and engaged in prostitution."[102]

Buenos Aires' experience is mirrored by other major Latin American cities like Rio de Janeiro and São Paulo, especially with respect to middle-class homosexual male culture.[103] James N. Green's landmark study of Brazilian male homosexual culture in the twentieth century notes that during the 1920s and 1930s, "literally hundreds of thousands of young men who became aware of their sexual desires and fantasies for other men moved to Rio de Janeiro and São Paulo, turning these cities into important centers for emerging homosexual subcultures."[104] By the 1960s, Green reports, a sexual identity in major Brazilian cities like Rio de Janeiro and São Paulo had developed that "was quite similar to the gay identity that developed in the United States in the 1930s and 1940s" and was aided by "urbanization, the expansion of the middle class, an endogenous counterculture, changes in gender relations, and international gay cultural influences."[105]

It is also misleading to employ the 1969 Stonewall Rebellion as some kind of marker for charting the birth of organized activism around the issue of homosexuality in Latin America. Instead, gay activism across Latin America has been triggered primarily by local developments generally linked to state repression of homosexuals. Nuestro Mundo (Our World), reputed to be Latin America's first gay rights organization, was organized in 1967, two years before the Stonewall riots, a point confirmed to this author by Héctor Anabitarte, one of its founders.[106] According to Anabitarte, the organization's founding "did not respond to anything happening outside of Argentina"; instead, the "fundamental" reason behind the creation of Nuestro Mundo by several workers affiliated with the national postal union was to fight "the anti-gay *edictos policiales*" (police regulations that regulated public morality). He notes that "the police detained people in the streets, in the parks, public bathrooms and sent you to the prison at Villa Devoto—for twenty-one days, and more if you were dressing in women's clothing. Moreover, the police were in the habit of informing the family of the reasons for the detention, leading many to lose their families and jobs."

Historians give credence to Anabitarte's claim that the birth of the Argentine gay rights movement is unrelated to Stonewall, by reporting that news of the Stonewall riots did not reach Argentine gay activists until the early 1970s, and that even then awareness of the riots was not widely disseminated. According to Bazán, Nuestro Mundo's creation was "an entirely indigenous event; the founders had no idea of any gay rights organizations existing outside of Argentina." Bazán adds that the organizers of Nuestro Mundo knew nothing about Stonewall, stating that "they received information very slowly, and most likely from tourists.[107] Moreover, Bazán notes that none of the publications produced by Nuestro Mundo make any reference to Stonewall.

Other Latin American nations echo the Argentine experience, insofar as they suggest that the rise of gay organizations responded more to local happenings than to foreign influence. Mexico's Frente de Liberación Homosexual was created in 1971 after "the firing of several gay employees at the Sears store in Mexico City"; the group later reorganized as the Frente Homosexual de Acción Revolucionaria in response to "numerous anti-gay assaults and murders and police harassment in the Federal District" and made its appearance at a march in 1978 in support of students arrested after the 1968 Olympics.[108] Gay groups began to organize in Brazil in the late 1970s, including SOMOS, created in 1978 by students and faculty at the University of São Paulo. The movement expanded after the military undertook a cleansing campaign in anticipation of the country's return to civilian rule, including a police sweep in 1980 that imprisoned fifteen hundred people in São Paulo on "public morals charges."[109]

Furthermore, to the extent to which international developments, especially the rise of the gay liberation movement in New York, helped fuel the activism of gay rights organizations in Latin America during the 1970s, this influence seems to have materialized in ways not reflected in the existing theoretical literature on how external influence is spread. On the one hand, the Latin American experience shows that when international influence has been the impetus for change, this impetus has not come from outside actors but rather from local actors acting as filters of external influence.

A case in point is the role of Latin American gay activists in importing gay rights trends. In the most suggestive experiences, this happened as a consequence of the creation of a large Latin American gay diaspora in the 1960s and 1970s.

In his amusing and very informative memoir *Perverts in Paradise*, João S. Trevisan, one of the founders of the Brazilian gay movement, writes that his involvement with the American gay rights movement in San Francisco propelled his activism in Brazil: "Paradoxically, by causing the exile of a large number of intellectuals and placing them in brutal contact with the outside world, the military caused a compulsory modernization, culturally speaking, in this period of Brazilian life. Years later, when the amnesty allowed them to return, they brought back experiences which they had absorbed in the time they had been forced to stay away from home." He adds that in addition to gay activism, exiled gays were exposed to "Eurocommunism, ecological concerns, feminism, and anti-racism."[110]

On the other hand, when international influence has been relevant, this influence has not always stemmed from the United States or Western Europe, but often from Latin America itself. A telling example is the influence on gay activism imparted by the Cuban Revolution. Green notes that "the political passions set loose by the 1959 Cuban Revolution had a contradictory effect on gay and lesbian activists. The fusing of Stalinist homophobia with Catholic morality reinforced traditional notions among leftists that homosexuality was counterrevolutionary. Yet at the same time, the impetus for social transformation inspired by Cuba fueled social contestation and offered a training ground for many who later formed the first generation of gay and lesbian activists."[111]

Cuban influence was especially felt around the time of the creation of the Argentina's Frente de Liberación Homosexual (FLH), the most influential gay rights organization outside of the developed West in the 1970s. Much the same way in which New York's GLF inspired the creation of Great Britain's Gay Liberation Front, organized at the London School of Economics in 1970, and France's Front homosexuel d'action révolutionnaire, formed in Paris in 1971, the GLF influenced the creation of the FLH in Buenos Aires in 1971—by inspiring the activism of already-existing local gay organizations. In the case of Argentina, the pre-Stonewall gay movement included the aforementioned Nuestro Mundo, which was one of several groups behind the formation of the FLH.

Directly inspired by the GLF, the FLH espoused an agenda of "sexual liberation" that aimed to destroy the heterosexual patriarchy for its oppression of women and sexual minorities, to shatter conventional norms about femininity and masculinity and sexual identity, and to encourage homosexuals to come out of the closet. But the FLH's ideological makeup extended far beyond that, and included a strong Marxist revolutionary rhetoric, a legacy of the Cuban Revolution, that was not a central component of the GLF. As noted by an FLH manifesto titled "Sex and Revolution": "The Homosexual Liberation Front considers that the historic moment has arrived for a revolution that simultaneously, along with the economic and political bases of the system, liquidates its sexist ideological bases, taking into account that the system of oppression would otherwise automatically reproduce itself after a revolutionary process that would only have altered the political and economic spheres."[112]

Understandably, when seeking models to emulate, Argentine activists were more inclined to look to Europe than to the United States. It was France's gay liberation front that most directly inspired the Argentines. This reflected not only the Marxist affinities between Buenos Aires and Paris, but also a rebuke of the American gay rights movement. As explained by Bazán, "The FLH was a left-wing organization, and as such it was very much anti-U.S. For that reason the organization shunned any formal affiliation with American groups." He notes, however, that the FLH leadership admired the black liberation movement, the Black Panthers in particular. "They (the FLH) could relate to being an oppressed minority fighting for their rights, although they did not share the Black Panther's advocacy of violence as a means for attaining their goals."[113]

Counterbalancing External Influences

Another powerful argument against viewing gay rights developments in Latin American through transnational lenses is that this perspective ignores the counterbalancing influence exerted by international groups working against gay rights in Latin America. In many regards, international influence when it comes to gay rights is a double-edged sword, since it can both advance and undermine the cause. It is arguably the case that during the last two decades, outside anti-gay rights groups have been more visible and influential in Latin America than those advocating for gay rights. For years, the most prominent external opposition to gay rights in Latin America stemmed from the Holy See. In both discreet and overt ways, the Vatican's concern over gay rights in Latin America has been building up for several decades. During the 1990s, when gay rights were in their infancy in Latin America, the Vatican Pontifical Family Council organized a series of meetings between "pious lawmakers" and "religious clerics," encouraging the former to defend the family and combat the so-called culture of death.

In some quarters, this push by the Vatican was viewed as an attack on abortion and homosexuality.[114]

The Vatican's campaign to undermine gay rights in Latin America, and elsewhere, gained steam with the creation of the World Congress of Families (WCF), a US-based organization formed in 1997 and supported by the Vatican and Evangelical conservative groups such as Focus on the Family and the Family Research Council. The American gay rights organization Human Rights Campaign has described the WCF as "the largest and most influential organization involved in anti-LGBT policies worldwide."[115] Among the organization's main "achievements" are Russia's infamous anti-gay propaganda law and the criminalization of homosexuality in several African nations, including Uganda. Its activities in Latin America began in earnest with the Third World Congress of Families, held in Mexico City in 2004, which condemned "homosexual unions" and instructed politicians of all political stripes "to take heed and block them."[116]

Spain's move in 2005 to legalize same-sex marriage, the first for an overwhelmingly Catholic nation, prompted the Vatican to intensify its antigay activism in Latin America. Opposition to the Spanish law from the Vatican was fierce, in no small part because Vatican officials feared that the legalization of same-sex marriage in Spain would open the way for the advent of same-sex marriage in Latin America. In a 2006 trip to Valencia to address the Fifth World Congress of Families, Benedict XVI, already famous for being one of the most homophobic popes in modern history (in 1987, as Cardinal Ratzinger, he authored the infamous "Rat Letter," which characterized homosexuality as "intrinsically evil"), called same-sex marriage "a threat to humanity" and urged Catholic notaries public to refuse to sign same-sex marriage licenses. In 2012, Benedict made worldwide headlines when he implied in a New Year's address that same-sex marriage was as serious a threat to humanity as climate change, by noting that laws undermining "the differences between the sexes were threats to creation."[117] Gay activists condemned the address as an act of "homophobic bullying" that could be used by opponents of gay rights around the world to legitimize antigay discrimination and even violence.

Benedict's successor, Buenos Aires Cardinal Jorge Mario Bergoglio (Pope Francis), is rightly credited with changing the Vatican's tone on homosexuality. He has famously called on Catholics to stop obsessing about social issues such as abortion, contraceptives, and homosexuality, and he is on the record as having said, "If someone is gay and seeks the Lord with good will, who am I to judge?"[118] Moreover, under his papacy, the Vatican has stopped denouncing the embrace of same-sex marriage by Catholic nations. There were no formal condemnations of same-sex marriage once it was legalized in Uruguay and Brazil in 2013 or in France that same year. This is all rather ironic considering that Bergoglio's ascent to the papacy, in March 2013, was viewed in some quarters as reflecting the Vatican's satisfaction with Bergoglio's vigorous opposition to Argentina's same-sex marriage law.

Arguably more consequential has been the arrival in Latin America of a large and diverse cast of American Evangelical organizations opposed to gay rights. Leading the way were proponents of "corrective therapy," otherwise known as "pray away the gay therapy," a practice generally associated with Evangelical churches that promise to "cure" homosexuality. This is part of the so-called ex-gay movement that began in the United States in 1976 with the creation of Exodus International.[119] Not surprisingly, perhaps, the arrival of the ex-gay movement in Latin America coincided with the surge in growth of American Protestant and Evangelical churches.[120] New York–based Colombian blogger Andrés Duque, who tracks the influence of the American Christian Right in Latin America, notes, "The rapidly rising neo-Pentecostal movements are supplanting their long-reigning precursor, the Roman Catholic Church. As they become more prevalent, they are playing more and more significant roles in any pushback against gay rights in Latin America; homophobia and aggressive campaigns against LGBT rights, plus ex-gay ministry approaches, are one of the signatures of the movement."[121]

More recently, Latin America has seen the arrival of policy-oriented antigay American Christian organizations, many of them defeated veterans of the American culture wars looking for greener pastures for spreading their antihomosexual agenda. Among the first groups to arrive in Latin America was the American Center for Law and Justice (ACLJ), the advocacy organization created by televangelist Pat Roberson in 1990 as a conservative alternative to the liberal American Civil Liberties Union. The ACLJ is responsible for drafting the infamous Defense of Marriage Act (DOMA). This act prevented the federal government from recognizing same-sex marriages from the time it was enacted into law by President Bill Clinton in 1996 until the Supreme Court invalidated it in 2013. An analysis of the activities of the ACLJ's Brazilian branch (the Brazilian Center for Law and Justice, BCLJ), part of ACLJ's global outreach to promote profamily policies, notes that "in its short existence, it is clear that the BCLJ is using some of the ACLJ's same tactics to try to win influence: wooing government officials and facilitating access to them, building alliances with key evangelical powerbrokers, and hiring local staff to serve as its face."[122]

A more recent arrival is the National Hispanic Evangelical Leadership Conference (NHELC), which through its subsidiary, Confraternidad Evangélica Latina, links Hispanic American Evangelical pastors with their counterparts in Latin America in the common effort to battle gay marriage, abortion, and pornography. Pastor Samuel Rodríguez, who describes his ministry as "mixing Martin Luther King Jr. with Billy Graham and then putting a little salsa on top," heads the NHELC; and its ministry against homosexuality in Latin America is advised by Matt Staver, a veteran of the American culture wars famous for accusing governments and department stores of waging a "war on Christmas," that is, the attempt to secularize Christmas.[123] According to Staver, the reason for his activism in Latin America is "that the U.S. government via the State Department is funding gay rights groups in other parts of the world, upsetting Latin American conservatives. They (the Latin Americans) are looking to us in America for help. Why? America through this current administration has been using a bully pulpit to try to tell them what to do on abortion and homosexuality and they don't like that."

Yet another sign of the counterbalancing effect of international influence in Latin America is the wave of antigay legislation introduced in the United States to thwart gay rights, especially the thirty state constitutional amendments defining marriage as the exclusive union of a man and a woman enacted across the United States since Alaska passed Ballot Measure 2 in 1998. The influence of such legislation suggests a compelling example of policy diffusion working to undermine rather than to advance gay rights. In 2005, inspired by the American experience, Honduras amended its constitution to define marriage as the union between a man and a woman, a move later emulated by Bolivia, Ecuador, and the Dominican Republic. Honduras's same-sex marriage ban was introduced against the backdrop of the 2004 American presidential campaign, in which President George W. Bush endorsed amending the US Constitution to ban same-sex marriage. "The same political campaign that Bush started is what Honduran conservatives are doing," according to Edgardo Javier Medina, a Honduran gay activist.[124]

The Puzzle of Uneven Development

A final argument against transnational explanations is how little currency they hold in explaining the adoption of gay rights across the developing world. Not only do these explanations fail to say much about why international influence appears to have had such an outsized impact on Latin America relative to Africa or the Middle East, but also why gay rights have been embraced by some Latin American countries and rejected by others. Presumably, all of Latin America has been subjected to the same external forces fanning global queering, international socialization, and policy diffusion. Yet there is considerable unevenness in how governments across the region have responded to these external influences.

As seen in table 1.1, despite sharing a similar culture and analogous levels of development, the nations of Latin America vary greatly in the speed and scope in which they have adopted gay rights. While some countries have made significant progress (such as Argentina, Brazil, Bolivia, Ecuador, Mexico, Colombia, Chile, and Uruguay), others lag far behind (Costa Rica, Cuba, and Venezuela), while still others have preempted the rise of gay rights by banning same-sex marriage via a constitutional amendment (Honduras and the Dominican Republic).

Table 1.1. GAY RIGHTS IN LATIN AMERICA (2015)

Same-sex marriage[a]	Same-sex civil unions	Same-sex adoptions[b]	Antidiscrimination law (sexual orientation)	Antidiscrimination law (gender identity)	Decriminalization of same-sex relations
Argentina	Bolivia	Argentina	Argentina	Argentina	Argentina
Brazil	Colombia	Brazil	Bolivia	Brazil	Bolivia
Uruguay	Ecuador	Colombia	Chile	Chile	Brazil
	Chile	Uruguay	Costa Rica	Colombia	Chile
			Colombia	Cuba	Colombia
			Cuba	Ecuador	Costa Rica
			Ecuador	Mexico	Cuba
			Mexico	Peru	Dominican Republic
			Uruguay	Uruguay	Ecuador
					El Salvador
					Guatemala
					Honduras
					Mexico
					Nicaragua
					Panama
					Paraguay
					Peru
					Uruguay
					Venezuela

Note: This information is limited to nationally recognized rights.
[a] Constitutional bans on gay marriage are in place in Bolivia, Ecuador, Dominican Republic, Paraguay, and Honduras.
[b] Constitutional bans on gay adoptions are in place in Bolivia, Ecuador, and Honduras.

Ironically, in the one place in Latin America where the United States has had the longest and most sustained cultural and political influence, Puerto Rico, an American possession since the 1898 Spanish-American War, the picture for gay rights remained unaltered until the US Supreme Court made same-sex marriage the law of the land in all fifty states and US territories in June 2015, with its historic ruling on *Obergefell v. Hodges*. In fact, whatever change there had been on LGBT matters in Puerto Rico prior to 2015, it was intended to curb rather advance gay rights. In 1999, the island enacted a law defining marriage as the union between a man and a woman and barring recognition of same-sex marriages conducted abroad. A decade later, in 2009, the island's Senate passed a proposed referendum that would have amended the Puerto Rican constitution by banning same-sex marriage, civil unions, and domestic partnerships. The bill died once it failed to get approval from the lower chamber. In February 2013, the Puerto Rican Supreme Court upheld a controversial ban on gay adoptions.

Furthermore, while some countries have welcomed American leadership on the issue of gay rights, others have deeply resented it. When in 2011 American ambassador Mari Carmen Aponte published a letter in a newspaper in El Salvador urging Salvadorans to become advocates for LGBT issues, local politicians complained to Washington that its representative in El Salvador was "disregarding our profound Christian values rooted in natural law, by trying to impose a new vision of foreign and bizarre values, completely alien to our moral fiber, intending to disguise this as human rights."[125] Religious leaders in the Dominican Republican threw a fit after the Obama administration appointed James Wally Brewster, an openly gay Obama fundraiser, as ambassador to the island. Vicar Pablo Cedano, Santo Domingo's archbishop, noted that "the nomination of Mr. Brewster shows a lack of respect, of consideration" and added, rather ominously, that "if he arrives, he'll suffer and will be forced to leave."[126]

Clearly, in order to fully understand Latin America's gay rights experience we have to unpack the domestic context. With that goal in mind, subsequent chapters attempt to "decenter" gay rights politics in Latin America. The point about decentering is not to deny the importance of external factors—far from it. Rather, the intention is to place the domestic context front and center as a means to suggest how this context has interacted with global influence. The next chapter examines several macro trends in the cultural, legal, and political environment in Latin America that in recent years have made the region one the most internally receptive for LGBT rights.

CHAPTER 2

Domestic Change, Foreign Influence, and Gay Rights

Among the many domestic factors favoring gay rights in Latin America over the last decades, one stands out as the most obvious: modernization. This is hardly surprising. A virtual truism among social scientists is that modernization, shorthand for social and economic development, leads to significant cultural change. As observed by one review of the modernization literature: "from Karl Marx to Daniel Bell, economic change brings pervasive cultural changes. . . . In particular, economic development is associated with shifts away from absolute norms and values toward values that are increasingly rational, tolerant, trusting and participatory."[1]

Data from the World Bank provide a snapshot of the sweeping wave of economic and social change afoot in Latin America in recent years. It is reported that "since 2003 there has been rapid economic growth in Latin America" and that "higher overall income plus some redistribution of it have led to higher percentages of the middle-income sector of most countries." It is further noted that between 2003 and 2012, the percentage of Latin Americans living in extreme poverty (US$4–US$10 per day) shrank to 38 percent, and that, as a consequence of this dramatic drop in poverty rates, "the extremely poor are no longer the majority in Latin America."[2] Contributing to this economic progress in Latin America are aggressive antipoverty programs targeting hunger and illiteracy, among other social ills, that have been introduced in recent years. Brazil's Bolsa Familia program, or Family Allowance, initiated in 2003 by the Lula administration, is credited with lifting tens of millions from extreme poverty in the last decade alone.[3]

At least two ways have been suggested about how the cultural changes flowing from modernization have aided in the development of gay rights. The most discussed among social scientists is the rise of so-called post-material values, such as feminism, environmentalism, and the extension of civil rights to minorities, including homosexuals.[4] According to post-materialism's leading theorist, Ronald Inglehart, rising prosperity leads to a transformation of individual values, away from "material values" that emphasize economic and physical security and toward "postmaterial values" that stress "autonomy" and "self-expression."[5] Inglehart finds this causal connection between modernization and postmaterialism in advanced industrial societies, especially Western Europe, but, as suggested by the Latin American experience, postmaterialism is also very much a reality among developing countries.

There are no multiyear data suggesting a direct cause and effect between social and economic development and support for gay rights in Latin America, since public polling on the subject of gay rights in the region is a very recent phenomenon. But recent surveys show impressive rates of approval and/or acceptance of homosexuality in the Latin American countries with the highest levels of social and economic development, especially education, such as Argentina, Uruguay, and Chile. By contrast, gay rights appear to be struggling in the less developed parts of Latin America, such as the Andean region, the Caribbean, and Central America.

A broad view of public opinion on homosexuality in Latin America can be seen in table 2.1, which draws from a survey conducted by Vanderbilt University's Latin American Public Opinion Project (LAPOP).[6] The LAPOP survey shows national levels of tolerance for homosexuality based on the question, "How strongly do you approve or disapprove of homosexuals being permitted to run for public office?" This question is analyzed using a 1–10 response scale, with responses 7 and higher deemed "high tolerance," responses ranging from 4 through 6 deemed "medium tolerance," and responses 3 and lower deemed "low tolerance." Two Latin American nations, Argentina and Uruguay, join the United States and regional leader Canada in earning the rating of "highly tolerant." In all of these countries, acceptance of homosexuality stands at above 50 percent. In Brazil, acceptance exceeds 40 percent. In the rest of the countries, however, acceptance of homosexuality does not exceed 30 percent.

Unsurprisingly, the level of tolerance toward homosexuality mirrors public attitudes toward same-sex marriage. Another LAPOP survey, summarized in table 2.2, finds that support for same-sex marriages in the Americas is highest in Canada, where 63.9 percent of the public support

Table 2.1. TOLERANCE TOWARD HOMOSEXUALITY IN THE AMERICAS

Above 50%	50%–40%	40%–30%	30%–20%	20%–10%	10%–0%
Canada (75.3)	Brazil (44.4)	Costa Rica (39.4)	Panama (28.6)	Guatemala (19.9)	Jamaica (5.3)
Argentina (66.5)		Mexico (37.8)	Bolivia (26.7)	El Salvador (19.3)	Haiti (4.7)
Uruguay (62.1)		Colombia (36.7)	Peru (25.3)	Honduras (17.7)	
United States (62.1)		Chile (36.0)	Ecuador (24.0)	Guyana (15.4)	
		Nicaragua (33.8)	Paraguay (23.7)		
		Venezuela (30.8)	Dominican Republic (20.1)		

Note: See text for discussion of the research method.
Source: "Gay in the Americas," *Americas Quarterly*, Winter 2010.

it; followed by Argentina (57. 7 percent); Uruguay (50.5 percent), the United States (47.7 percent), and Brazil, 39.8 percent. El Salvador, Guyana, and Jamaica are at the bottom, with 10 percent of the population or less endorsing same-sex marriages.

The second cultural phenomenon of significance to gay rights that is thought to occur as a consequence of modernization is a decline in religiosity. Indeed, after social and economic progress, religiosity is the most reliable predictor of whether or not gay rights will emerge in any country, with high levels of religiosity associated with low levels of societal acceptance of homosexuality and vice versa. All of this is also broadly reflected in the Latin America experience. Societal acceptance of homosexuality is highest in Uruguay, Argentina, and Chile, countries with Latin America's highest percentages of nonpracticing Catholics and secularists. By contrast, tolerance for homosexuality is lowest in Guatemala, which has one the region's highest percentages of practicing Catholics as well the highest percentage of Evangelicals.[7]

The connection between modernization and religiosity in Latin America, however, remains ambiguous, a point highlighted by Inglehart himself, drawing from his analysis of the World Values Survey, a cross-national database incorporating dozens of nations. According to these data, religion remains an important part of most Latin Americans' lives; in fact, only the Islamic world has a higher percentage of people attaching importance

Table 2.2. ACCEPTANCE OF SAME-SEX MARRIAGE
IN THE AMERICAS

Country	Popular approval of same-sex marriage (%)
Canada	63.9
Argentina	57.7
Uruguay	50.5
United States	47.4
Brazil	39.8
Chile	39.7
Mexico	37.8
Colombia	34.4
Peru	26.3
Bolivia	24.7
Panama	22.8
Honduras	22.6
Venezuela	22.5
Costa Rica	20.7
Surinam	20.3
Dominican Republic	18.3
Ecuador	18.4
Belize	17.5
Guatemala	16.5
Paraguay	16.1
Nicaragua	15.6
Trinidad &Tobago	15.4
El Salvador	10.3
Guyana	7.2
Jamaica	3.5

Source: "Support for Same-Sex Marriage in Latin America," AmericasBarometer Insight 2010 (No. 44), October 10, 2013. Published by the Latin American Public Opinion Poll (LAPOP).

to religion in their daily lives than has Latin America.[8] And yet Latin American social values and attitudes are more in line with those of Western Europe and the United States. Key to understanding this puzzle, as noted shortly, is the shifting nature of Latin America's religious landscape in recent decades. There has been a phenomenal growth of Protestantism that has offset an equally phenomenal decline in Catholicism, which means that while Latin America has become less Catholic, it has not necessarily become significantly less religious. Nonetheless, the decline of Catholicism has been dramatic in terms of both numbers and prestige, and this has had a huge impact on the development of gay rights.

Although Latin America remains overwhelmingly Catholic—the region is home to 41 percent of world's Catholic population and the world's two largest Catholic countries (Brazil and Mexico)—the Catholic Church no longer possesses a monopoly on religious belief and practice, as was once the case. Table 2.3 illustrates the current religious landscape in Latin America, according to data from the Pew Research Center.[9] It shows the overall percentage of Catholics in the region, as of 2014, at 69 percent. This represents a stunning reversal of fortunes for Catholicism in the region and explains a lot about a much-observed "crisis of Catholicism" in Latin America among scholars and political observers alike that goes well beyond empty church pews.[10] Addressing this subject, Frances Hagopian notes that "Catholic trade unions have vanished, Christian Democratic Parties are declining, and social movements are defined to a greater degree by issue area than by their religious identity."[11]

Table 2.3. LATIN AMERICA'S RELIGIOUS LANDSCAPE (PERCENTAGE)

Country	Catholic	Protestant	No affiliation	Other
Argentina	71	15	11	3
Bolivia	77	16	4	3
Brazil	61	26	8	5
Chile	64	17	16	3
Colombia	79	13	5	3
Costa Rica	62	25	9	4
Dominican Republic	57	23	18	2
Ecuador	79	13	5	3
El Salvador	50	36	12	3
Guatemala	50	41	6	3
Honduras	46	40	10	2
Mexico	81	9	7	4
Nicaragua	50	40	7	4
Panama	70	19	7	5
Paraguay	89	7	1	2
Peru	76	17	7	4
Puerto Rico	56	33	8	2
Uruguay	42	15	37	6
Venezuela	73	17	7	4
Regional average	69	19	8	4

Source: "Religion in Latin America," Pew Research Center, 2014.

As suggested in table 2.4, between 1910 and 1970, Catholicism's hegemonic presence in Latin America remained virtually unchallenged, with the percentage of Catholics in almost all Latin American countries exceeding 90 percent. Since 1970, however, a steep decline in Catholic affiliation has occurred across the region, in some cases a precipitous fall. If these trends persist, by 2025 the percentage of Catholics in Latin America will fall to 50 percent. This decline would offset any gains the Catholic Church might make in areas of the world, such as Africa, where it is actually gaining new converts.

More revealing are the fraying ties between self-identified Catholics and devotion to their faith. According to a 2012 survey by Latinobarómetro, a Santiago-based polling outfit, although nearly three-quarters of Latin Americans consider themselves Catholic, only 40 percent practice their faith, understood as attending church regularly and following Catholic teachings.[12] Central America has the highest rate of practicing Catholics, with a rate of about 48 percent, while the lowest rates are found in the Southern Cone (Argentina, Chile, Uruguay, and Paraguay), with an average

Table 2.4. CATHOLIC AFFILIATION IN LATIN AMERICA, 1910–2014

	1910	1950	1970	2014
Argentina	97	95	91	71
Bolivia	94	94	89	77
Brazil	96	93	92	61
Chile	96	89	76	64
Colombia	80	91	96	79
Costa Rica	99	96	94	57
Dominican Republic	96	96	94	57
Ecuador	88	98	96	79
El Salvador	98	99	93	50
Guatemala	99	99	91	50
Honduras	97	96	94	46
Mexico	99	96	96	81
Nicaragua	96	96	93	50
Panama	84	87	87	70
Paraguay				
Peru	95	96	87	56
Puerto Rico	100	94	87	56
Uruguay	61	62	63	42
Venezuela	93	91	93	73

Source: "Religion in Latin America," Pew Research Center, 2014.

of 37 percent. Among Southern Cone countries, the most extreme case is that of Uruguay, where only quarter of the public claims that religion is a very important part of their lives. The numbers are also revealing for countries for which information on long-term trends is available. The Latinobarómetro survey reports that there has been a significant drop in Catholic affiliation in Mexico over the last decade, where 31 percent of the country's Catholics said they currently practice their faith, compared to more than 60 percent in 1995. In Venezuela, the number of practicing Catholics has fallen by fourteen points over the last ten years, to 37 percent.

Among the factors impacting the decline of Catholicism in Latin America and fueling the rise of non-observant Catholics (so called cultural Catholics), is a rising tide of secularism, usually thought of as a direct byproduct of modernization. Roughly one in ten people in Latin America claims no religious affiliation of any kind. This group is the most likely to express tolerance for "Political Rights of Gays" (54.6 percent), followed by "Catholics" (42.3 percent), "other" (40.8 percent), "Protestant" (32.2 percent), and "Evangelical" (29.2 percent). As shown in table 2.5, these findings mirror the level of support for same-sex marriage across religious groups.

A more important factor driving the decline of Catholicism, however, is the explosive growth of Protestant and Evangelical churches. The Pentecostal-Evangelical population expanded from 12.6 million in 1970, to 118.6 million in 1990, and to 156.9 in 2005.[13] As of 2014, the percentage of Protestants in Latin America stood at almost 20 percent. Brazil is illustrative of this dramatic rise in the ranks of Protestants. According to a study from the Getúlio Vargas Foundation, while 83 percent of Brazilians called themselves Catholics in 1990, by 2009 that number had fallen to 68 percent. During the same time, Brazilians who identified themselves as Protestants or Pentecostals rose from 9 percent to 20 percent.[14]

Table 2.5. SUPPORT FOR SAME-SEX MARRIAGE AMONG RELIGIOUS GROUPS

1.	Catholic	30.8
2.	Protestant	20.1
3.	Evangelical	15.9
4.	No religion	43.7
5.	Other	30.9

Source: "Evangelism and Gay Rights in Latin America," AmericasBarometer Insight 2013 (No. 94), October 10, 2013. Published by the Latin American Public Opinion Poll (LAPOP).

Survey data on why people are defecting to Protestant churches point to reasons such as seeking "a more personal connection to God," a more "active worshiping experience," and a church "with a greater emphasis on morality."[15] These factors are echoed in the academic literature on contemporary religion in Latin America, which emphasizes the appeal of Evangelical churches, which are generally seen as more democratic in structure than the Catholic Church.[16] This, in turn, is seen as affording more opportunities for attaining positions of leadership within the church, especially for women and minorities. Evangelical sects are also seen as purveying a more positive message about self-improvement and ways to accrue material wealth, as suggested by the appeal of the so-called prosperity theology. Underscoring these points, Elio Masferrer, chairman of the Latin American Religious Studies Association, notes: "If the Catholic Church does not make changes to its centralized structures and authoritarian messages, it will suffer a genuine collapse within 15 years."[17]

But the Catholic Church's travails in Latin America also stem from several self-inflicted wounds, such as past support for political regimes notorious for their wanton disregard for human rights. Argentina's Catholic hierarchy was on the whole supportive of the "dirty war" waged against political dissidents and "social undesirables" by the military between 1976 and 1983, a support readily admitted by the church in a stunning public apology issued in 1996. Urged by Pope John Paul II to examine their consciences and their past political activities, Argentina's Roman Catholic bishops begged forgiveness for any crimes committed by Catholic Church members during the Dirty War: "We implore God's forgiveness for the crimes committed then by sons of the church, whether as members of the revolutionary guerrillas or as members of the state or the security forces," read the statement from Argentina's National Conference of Bishops.[18]

The apology did not spare the clergy from prosecution on charges of human rights abuses. In October 2007, former chaplain of Buenos Aires Christian von Wernich was sentenced to life in prison for conspiring with the military in murders and kidnappings. Witnesses in the trial spoke of von Wernich's duplicitous behavior in helping to extract confessions from those imprisoned, which aided the military in eradicating enemies of the dictatorial regime, even while offering spiritual comfort to family members looking for those who had disappeared while in the custody of the police. The apology has not done much to restore people's faith in the church either, given that the truth about the actions of the church during the dictatorship continues to emerge. Interestingly enough, the ascent of Buenos Aires Cardinal Jorge Mario Bergoglio to the papacy (as Pope Francis) has served to bring worldwide attention to the Argentine Catholic Church's dark history. In his position as head of the Argentine Jesuits under the military dictatorship, Bergoglio has been accused of failing to protect two young priests who were tortured by the military for their advocacy of liberation theology, and of condoning the theft of babies born to political dissidents.[19] The Vatican has vigorously denied these accusations.

A rash of sex and child abuse scandals have further tarnished the Catholic Church's reputation in Latin America, where, more so than in the United States and Europe, the Catholic Church has been very slow in addressing the accusations. The most egregious and damaging scandal across the Hispanic-Catholic world is that of Marcial Maciel, a Mexican church leader who rose to prominence within Catholic circles in Europe, Latin America, and the Vatican as the founder of the influential and wealthy Legionaries of Christ Order.[20] For decades, Maciel was plagued by a litany of scandals that went ignored by both Mexican church leaders and the Vatican; indeed, the Vatican fiercely defended Maciel against charges of impropriety. In 1993, during his third trip to Mexico, John Paul II offered a public tribute to Maciel as an "efficacious guide to youth," even after nine men, including two university professors and a lawyer, had already alleged that Maciel had sexually abused them.[21] It was not until 2006, after charges of a cover-up had erupted all over Mexico, that Benedict XVI removed Maciel from active pastoral duties and restricted him to a life of prayer and penance.

Two years after Maciel's death, in 2010, the Vatican released a report on Maciel that accused him of "leading a double life hidden from most Legionaries by creating a system of power that allowed him to silence his critics," as part of its efforts to signal a tougher stance toward sexual abuse.[22] The Vatican report also assailed "the most serious and objectively immoral behavior of Father Maciel, confirmed by incontrovertible witnesses, which amount to true crimes and show a life deprived of scruples and authentic religious feeling." The report does not include a detailed account of Maciel's crimes, but press reports from Mexico, Spain, and the United States allege that Maciel raped underage seminarians, telling his victims that he had instructions from the pope that they surrender themselves to him; maintained sexual relations with at least two women and fathered six children, two of whom he sexually molested; used millions of dollars from his charities to purchase several properties, including a luxury apartment in Madrid for one his mistresses; was a notorious drug abuser; and plagiarized some of the theological literature produced by his organization.[23]

Whatever its roots, the crisis of Catholicism in Latin America is having an undeniable effect on gay rights. For a start, many Latin American Catholics now find themselves at odds with the church on a wide range of social issues, including homosexuality. This is clearly suggested in the polling data that show high levels of support for homosexuality and same-sex marriage in countries where the percentages for nonreligious and nonpracticing Catholics are highest, but also polls that suggest that Latin American Catholics, much like Catholics in the United States and Europe, do not put homosexuality on the same plane as other "sins" dictated by their faith. Although 67 percent of Catholics in Argentina and 76 percent of Catholics in Brazil believe that abortion is never justifiable, only 39 and 55 percent, respectively, believe the same of homosexuality.[24]

A weakened church has also emboldened Latin American politicians to ignore the church's hyperbolic threats whenever gay rights are being legislated and to fight back in ways that would have been unthinkable in the not-so-distant past. Argentina's gay marriage legislation unleashed an epic battle of words between Cardinal Bergoglio and President Cristina Fernández de Kirchner, after Bergoglio called gay marriage "the destructive pretension of God's plan."[25] The president took this statement as a declaration of war and gave the cardinal a rhetorical smackdown by depicting the Catholic hierarchy as anachronistic, uncivil, and irrelevant, "a relic of the Inquisition," as she so famously put it.[26] In taking such a confrontational stance against the Catholic Church, Fernández de Kirchner was banking on the pent-up dislike among ordinary Argentines for the clergy. "The aggressive action of the Catholic Church during the current debate has only exacerbated a loathing that already exists within the population toward the Catholic hierarchy," said Marcelo Ferreyra, the Latin American coordinator for the International Gay and Lesbian Human Rights Commission.[27]

Following the legalization of same-sex marriage by the Mexico City assembly in 2009, the first Latin American locality to do so, church leaders threatened to excommunicate any member of the assembly who voted in favor of the law. Once that threat fell on deaf ears, Hugo Valdemar, spokesman for the Archdiocese of Mexico City, warned that the law would be "more damaging than narco-trafficking."[28] After the Mexican Supreme Court upheld the law, church officials sought to discredit the ruling. Cardinal Juan Sandoval Iñiguez, archbishop of Guadalajara, labeled the ruling "an aberration" and added, "Who would want to be adopted by a pair of faggots and lesbians?"[29] The cardinal also accused Mayor Marcelo Ebrard of bribing the justices: "I do not think the judges would arrive at such absurd conclusions, against the sentiment of the Mexican public, without there being very big motives, and the very big motive may be the money that they are given."[30] Ebrard responded by filing a defamation suit against the church and publicly chastised Cardinal Iñiguez for failing to grasp that "we live in a secular state, and in it, whether we like it or not, the rule of law prevails; the cardinal must obey the law like any other citizen of this country."[31] In a very unusual move, the Mexican Supreme Court censured the cardinal, in a unanimous decision supported even by the justices who had dissented on the gay marriage decision.

When Uruguay in 2007 became the first country in Latin America to legalize civil unions and gay adoptions, lawmakers broadly ignored a public document issued by Archbishop Nicolás Cotugno of Montevideo that warned about violating the human rights of children by using them as pawns to advance the wants of the gay community. "To accept adoption by homosexual couples would be to grant those who opted for the lifestyle of not being parents the right to be such, thus prioritizing their interests over those of the child," noted the prelate.[32] Once that document failed to persuade the lawmakers, Cotugno resorted to demeaning the capacity of gays to rear children: "A child is not something you make. I don't want to be too harsh in my comment, but with all due respect, a child is not a pet," he said.[33]

Lastly, having lost considerable moral capital and political authority because of sex and child abuse scandals and support for bloodthirsty dictatorships, Latin American church officials have found it very hard to demonize gay activists as criminals, deviants and predators. In Brazil, allegations of pedophilia against Monsignor Luiz Marques Barbosa of the diocese of São Paolo, which generated huge headlines and even prompted a congressional investigation in 2010 after a video showing the eighty-three-year-old priest in bed with an altar boy went viral over the Internet, undercut the church's efforts to denounce the gay community as a threat to the Brazilian family. When Mexico City officials legalized same-sex unions, the country's top cardinal, Norberto Rivera Carrera, remained strangely silent because at the time he was facing charges of sheltering a Mexican priest accused of sexually molesting children in California. "The Catholic Church was facing a credibility crisis," according to Mexican gay rights activist Alejandro Brito. Many church leaders in Mexico, including Rivera, "knew that if they fiercely opposed the gay-union law, the news media would eat them alive."[34] In Argentina, the church's somewhat muted reaction to same-sex marriage responded to an eight-year prison sentence given in 2009 to Eduardo Stroni, ex-archbishop of the province of Santa Fe, for having abused a seminarian.

A RADICALLY TRANSFORMED CONSTITUTIONAL LANDSCAPE

The fact that relatively poor countries in Latin America, such as Ecuador and Bolivia, have also embraced gay rights reveals the need to go beyond rising incomes and standards of living in understanding why the region has become so receptive to gay rights. Another critical factor is the transformation of the Latin American constitutional landscape triggered by the democratic transformation that occurred during the 1980s and 1990s.[35] Several factors spearheaded these constitutional reforms, including the need to undo the tampering with the constitutional order by authoritarian regimes in order to justify or facilitate their dictatorial power grab; the desire to modernize the judicial system by incorporating aspects of international jurisprudence, most notably international human rights law, especially international human rights accords much of Latin America is party to, such as the 1948 Universal Declaration of Human Rights and the American Convention on Human Rights, otherwise known as the Pact of San José de Costa Rica; and the hope to make democracy itself and democratic institutions, including the courts, more responsive to groups and citizens demanding equality.[36] By the time the constitutional reform process was concluded in the mid-2000s, Brazil, Colombia, Ecuador, and Bolivia had enacted brand-new constitutions, and Argentina, Chile, and Mexico had dramatically revamped their old constitutions.

First and foremost, constitutional reforms in Latin America have worked to support gay rights by incorporating into the framework of the national constitution new stipulations that favor the extension of civil rights and human rights protections to sexual minorities and other oppressed groups. These stipulations have made accessing the courts and demanding rights easier for advocacy groups and ordinary citizens. It is telling that the newest Latin American constitutions explicitly incorporate gay rights. Ecuador's 2008 constitution limits marriage to heterosexual couples while creating civil unions with all the obligations of marriage for same-sex couples. Bolivia's 2009 constitution defines marriage as the union of a man and a woman but bans discrimination on the basis of sexual orientation and gender identity.

Almost all of the rest of Latin America's constitutions speak to the desire for equality under the law in lofty and ambitious terms and, more importantly, provide the means by which ordinary citizens can address their claims of injustice and discrimination. Some of the earliest and boldest steps took place in Colombia, which in 1991 enacted what is widely regarded as one of the world's most progressive constitutions because it affirms the country's ethnic and cultural diversity. Article 13 of the constitution notes that the state will provide conditions for "real equality" and undertake measures "in favor of marginalized or discriminated groups." The constitution also provides access to the courts through *tutela* suits, which entitle any Colombia citizen "to challenge violations of constitutional rights" and which make Colombia "perhaps the most open system of judicial review."[37] As noted shortly, gay activists have used this constitutional provision to petition rights from the state, with considerable success.

Developments in other Latin American nations mirror Colombia's experience. Argentina's *amparo* (or protection of individual guarantees) was introduced in 1994, as part of a sweeping revamping of the national constitution launched by the Carlos Menem administration that also granted constitutional status to all human rights treaties signed by Argentina, with the hope of preventing the human rights atrocities of the past from recurring. The Argentine *amparo* allows suits against government officials for violations of statutorily or constitutionally defined rights, which means "that judges are now arguably less constrained by traditional civil law approaches (especially the rule that decisions only apply to the direct parties and do not create a precedent) and are increasingly attempting to set broad policy grounded in rights-based jurisprudence."[38] The *amparo* provision in Argentina was key to activists' plan to legalize same-sex marriage, as court rulings in favor of same-sex marriage by several lower courts served to pressure the legislature into legislating same-sex marriage.

Mexico's *amparo* grew out of the judicial reforms undertaken by the Ernesto Zedillo administration in 1994, one of Latin America's most ambitious processes of judicial reform of recent times (which is ironic given that, at the time, Mexico was still regarded as "a semi-authoritarian democracy").[39] It was intended to strengthen the capacity of the courts to advance and protect the human rights provisions.[40] As the only constitutional procedure available to citizens to defend human rights, Mexico's *amparo* protects citizens and their basic guarantees and protects the constitution itself by ensuring that "its principles are not violated by statues or actions of the state that undermine the basic rights enshrined within it."[41] In December 2012, the role of the *amparo* in facilitating gay rights was more than self-evident, when the Mexican Supreme Court, having heard an *amparo* complaint from three plaintiffs in the state of Oaxaca, ruled unanimously that the existing provision in the civil code that contended that "one of the purposes of marriage is the perpetuation of the species" violated the Mexican constitution's promise of equality under the law.

As part of the process of revamping national constitutions, Latin American nations have also expanded and strengthened the structures of federalism with the aim of bringing democracy closer to the people by granting autonomy to states, cities, and municipalities to manage their own administrative affairs, including passing their own laws as long as these laws can pass constitutional muster.[42] Brazil's federalism was significantly reinvented by the 1988 constitution, a key component in the process of returning the country to civilian government. The most notable feature of that reinvention was the fiscal decentralization of the state, a process that some studies have criticized for weakening or inhibiting the capacity of the new democracy to deal with perennial issues in Brazil such as poverty and inequality.[43] But fiscal decentralization was not without a silver lining, since it helped propel the much-observed policy of "participatory budgeting," which allows grassroots organizations, including gay groups, a say in spending priorities at the local level.[44]

Similar dynamics played out in Colombia, where as part of its constitutional reforms the country undertook a process of fiscal decentralization that put the country first after the two federal countries in South America (Brazil and Argentina) in the percentage of total spending by subnational governments.[45] Local governments in Colombia have used this new spending power to boost and expand the profile of the gay community. In 2006, Bogotá's mayor, Luis "Lucho" Garzón, who describes his politics as "Marxist-Lennonist—Marxist for the Marx Brothers and Lennonist for John Lennon,"[46] inaugurated South America's first gay and lesbian center, devoted to helping the local gay community navigate the city's complex social service bureaucracy, after activists convinced the mayor that overt discrimination kept many gay and lesbian citizens from availing themselves of city services.

Yet it was in the "city-states" of Buenos Aires and Mexico City that federalization had the most profound effect in advancing gay rights. In 1994, as part of the rewriting of the Argentine Constitution, the federal district of Buenos Aires was given extraordinary political autonomy (hence its current, formal name: The Autonomous City of Buenos Aires). Among the changes introduced by the constitutional reforms was the popular election of the city's mayor, with the first election going to future president Fernando de la Rúa, and the creation of a popularly elected city legislature, first elected into office in 1996. Prior to 1996, the president of the nation appointed the mayor of Buenos Aires, a major political perk. The advent of autonomy had an almost immediate effect in advancing gay rights. Among the first orders of business entertained by the new legislature was a provision in Buenos Aires' charter banning discrimination on the basis of sexual orientation. Enacted in 1996, this was Latin America's first gay rights legislation. It was followed, in 2002, with a domestic partnership law, a precursor to the national 2010 same-sex marriage law.

In 1997, Mexico City residents gained the right to elect their own mayor and legislature, a pivotal step in the city's emergence as a bastion of social liberalism in Mexico and the Americas as a whole. Under the Ebrard mayoralty of the Party of the Democratic Revolution (PRD), Mexico City's legislature liberalized divorce laws by allowing "express divorces" (which can be concluded in less than two hours provided that any children are of legal age, the wife is not pregnant, and neither of the spouses is receiving governmental assistance), legalized abortion in the first twelve weeks of pregnancy, introduced "passive" euthanasia by allowing terminally ill people to refuse medication or further medical attention to prolong life, banned smoking in bars and restaurants, and authorized same-sex marriage and adoptions. The last measure was legislated in 2009 and entailed redefining marriage as "the free uniting of two people."

Last but not least, the constitutional reforms of the posttransition period have aided gay rights in Latin America by strengthening the judiciary itself, historically "the weakest branch" of government in Latin America."[47] Judicial reform became "a buzzword in Latin America during the 1990's, and many nascent democracies in the region engaged in the dramatic revamping of their judiciaries with the stated intent of increasing judicial power."[48] Among the more notable reforms were those aimed at making the judiciary more independent by changing how judges are selected, introducing compulsory retirement for judges (especially members of the high courts), and creating "national judicial councils" designed to improve the quality of judicial deliberations. Traditionally found in civil law countries, such as France, where they were pioneered in the post-Revolution period, national judicial councils comprise leading legal scholars, prosecutors, and lawyers and act as overseers of the court system.[49]

A stronger judiciary has fueled what some have termed "the judicialization of politics of same-sex marriage policy in Latin America," understood as "when the courts begin to make decisions on policy traditionally made by the legislative and executive branches of the government."[50] This phenomenon has allowed the courts to extend marriage to same-sex couples in Latin American countries where the legislature is unwilling or unable to change laws limiting marriage to opposite-sex couples. The best examples so far are Colombia, Mexico, and Brazil, where same-sex marriage rights have emanated largely from the courts.

In 2007, Colombia's Constitutional Court ruled in favor of same-sex unions in a ruling authored by Rodrigo Escobar Gil, a justice noted for his socially conservative jurisprudence. Gil's opinion noted that "the absence of marriage protections for homosexual couples results in lessening the human dignity of homosexual couples," and that it "creates a form of discrimination precluded by the constitution."[51] In 2011, the Constitutional Court went further by mandating that the legislature allow same-sex marriage within a two-year time frame, noting that the civil unions law did not provide sufficient protections to same-sex couples, especially with respect to their right to form a family. The court granted the legislature two years to legislate same-sex marriage; otherwise same-sex couples would automatically be entitled to marriage rights.

In Mexico, same-sex marriage was put on a fast track after Mexico City's assembly legalized same-sex marriage in 2009. But it was a string of bold rulings from the Mexican Supreme Court that brought marriage to the rest of the country. After Mexico City's assembly voted to legalize same-sex marriage, by a vote of forty-three to seventeen, and Mayor Ebrard signed the legislation into law, the conservative administration of President Felipe Calderón took the city to court, arguing that the law was unconstitutional because it violated the article in the constitution "protecting the family." But in 2010, the Supreme Court, in a nine-to-two vote, upheld the law, arguing that barring same-sex couples from marrying was discriminatory, since it violated both the Mexican constitution's equal protection clause and international human rights treaties signed by Mexico. In subsequent rulings, the court upheld gay adoptions and forced other states to recognize same-sex marriages conducted in the federal capital. More recently, in June 2015, the court issued a decree that any state law restricting marriage to heterosexual couples was discriminatory and therefore unconstitutional. This is was, however, a "jurisprudential thesis," which means that it does not invalidate any state laws. It does, however, allow gay couples to seek injunctions from district judges in order to get a marriage certificate; these judges are now compelled to issue these injunctions.

In May 2011, Brazil's Federal Supreme Court, the country's highest court, ruled that the state had to guarantee equality in the way in which it treated homosexual and heterosexual unions, but it stopped short of mandating marriage for same-sex couples.[52] This ruling came after the court grew frustrated with the inability or incapacity of the national legislature to enact any gay rights legislation since the enactment of a new democratic constitution in 1988, which itself failed to ban discrimination on the basis of sexual orientation, alongside other categories such as gender, race, and age. The court's ruling led to divergent interpretations by the various Brazilian states, with some authorizing same-sex marriage and others choosing instead to allow same-sex civil unions. In May 2013, to clear up the national marriage picture, the National Council of Justice, a body that dates only to 2004 and comprises fifteen prominent judges, prosecutors, and lawyers, effectively federalized same-sex marriage. The council boldly determined that it was wrong of notary publics to have issued same-sex couples with civil union certificates in instances where the couple had specifically asked for a marriage certificate. The council also mandated notary publics change civil unions to marriage if that was the wish of the couple.

Yet another factor behind Latin America's internal receptivity toward gay rights is the ascent to power of left-wing governments in some of the region's leading nations—like Argentina, Brazil, and Chile, and in the mayoralty of Latin America's largest metropolis, Mexico City—and a robust embrace of social progressive causes such as homosexuality by these governments. Such developments are doubly significant, for they signal a dramatic reversal of fortunes for the Latin American Left and a radical reconsideration of the Left's stance on homosexuality. Around the time of the democratic transitions of the 1980s, the Latin American Left was close to extinction. Save for a few nations, such as Mexico, repression by right-wing military dictatorships had decapitated or crippled left-wing parties. Arguably more damaging was Communism's collapse in the former Soviet Union and Eastern and Central Europe after 1989, which dealt a double whammy to the Latin American Left by undercutting the appeal of Marxism and socialism while ending decades of Soviet support for revolutionary left-wing movements and causes.

But since the late 1990s, with the rise of the so-called pink tide, the Latin American Left has staged a much-discussed "resurgence."[53] By one account from 2005, "Three quarters of South America's 350 million people are now ruled by left-wing presidents, all of whom have been elected in the last six years."[54] Since then, the trend has continued apace, and shows no signs of slowing down, with the return to power of the Socialists in Chile in 2013 and the re-election of the Workers' Party in Brazil in 2014. To be sure, not every left-wing regime to have emerged from this tidal wave of leftism in Latin America is supportive, or even tolerant, of gay rights—far from it. After all, the Latin American Left has historically been quite conservative on matters regarding gender and sexuality. In fact, a strong case can be made that the Left in Latin America has been as conservative on the issue of homosexuality as the Right, if not more so,

Homosexuality, as Shawn Schulenberg observes, "is antithetical to the macho image of the left as portrayed by revolutionary leaders Che Guevara and Fidel Castro." For decades, these leaders "appropriated and deployed this imagery of the strong leader to appeal to wider societies used to following a caudillo (strongman)."[55] The Latin American Left has also been traditionally reluctant to confront the Catholic Church on the issue of homosexuality. Elisabeth Jay Friedman notes that Latin America's political Left "has an uneven record on women's rights and in fostering gender-based solidarity," a situation that is attributed to the unwillingness of left-wing presidents to confront the Catholic Church.[56] She writes: "Even the most left-wing presidents seem unwilling to frontally challenge gender and sexual hierarchies, in great part because the Catholic Church defends—and depends on these constructs."[57]

Notable, too, is the profound homophobia that permeates Marxism. The mere suspicion of being homosexual has historically been grounds for expulsion from left-wing organizations, ensuing from the Marxist perception of homosexuality as "alien" and "suspect."[58] Homosexuality was criminalized by the Soviet regime in 1934, under Joseph Stalin, and soon thereafter it became a key critique of capitalism, more specifically as the ultimate sign of "bourgeois decadence."[59] Accordingly, for much of the twentieth century, Latin American Communist parties have excluded gays and lesbians from their ranks on the grounds that homosexuality is incompatible with revolutionary goals. As seen later, some of the founders of the gay rights movement in Argentina and Brazil were expelled from Communist organizations. Indeed, some had to break rank from their left-wing parties and movements in order to form or join gay rights organizations.

Not surprisingly, a particularly virulent strand of homophobia has prevailed among the left-wing armed revolutionary movements that emerged across Latin America in opposition to right-wing military rule during the Cold War. Writing about the Brazilian experience of the 1960s and 1970s, James N. Green notes that one of the ironies of the Latin American revolutionary movement is that a movement "that proclaims a dedication to freedom, liberation, and a radical transformation of society" has "consistently marginalized men or women who did not conform to normative gender and sexual roles."[60] He reports of the "pain and trauma" endured by gay and lesbian revolutionaries at the hands of their left-wing comrades.[61] During the 1980s, Peru's Sendero Luminoso (Shining Path) and Túpac Amaru Revolutionary Movement, among the last radical left-wing movements to emerge in Latin America, "systematically executed homosexuals in the towns and cities that it captured."[62]

Nor it is surprising to learn that Latin America's best-known left-wing revolutionary governments are notorious for their hostility toward homosexuals. In Nicaragua's Sandinista Revolution, gays and lesbians, many of them among the most avid supporters of the revolution, were not allowed to "organize and march openly."[63] Under Hugo Chávez's "Bolivarian Revolution," Venezuela's constituent assembly, a body "dominated almost entirely by leftists," rejected a proposal to write into the constitution a ban on LGBT discrimination.[64] Thus, while the new Venezuelan constitution guarantees a wide range of rights—such as the right to employment, healthcare, and education—it does not protect against discrimination based on sexual orientation. This oversight signaled "a lost opportunity to integrate gay rights into the Bolivarian vision of social justice."[65]

And then, of course, there is the case of Cuba, Latin America's most orthodox left-wing regime, which provides the most compelling evidence that left-wing rule and pro-gay rights policies have not always gone hand in hand. Communist Cuba is usually cited as the most repressive country in Latin America when it comes to homosexuality, as well as the least evolved on gay rights.[66] From its onset in 1959, the Cuban Revolution stigmatized homosexuality and undertook the systemic repression of homosexuals—including the criminalization of homosexual behavior until 1979 and the enslavement of homosexuals in labor camps through the late 1980s.[67] There remains to this day a ban on independent gay groups and publications, and police brigades routinely raid bars patronized by gays and lesbians. One of the few independent gay groups to emerge in Cuba, the Cuban Association of Gays and Lesbians, was shut down by the government and its leaders arrested in 1997.[68] This repression is in keeping with the association of homosexuality with bourgeois decadence and moral decay that has marked Communist attitudes toward homosexuality since the 1917 Russian Revolution, a stance that, as noted previously, was embraced by most Latin American Communist parties, including Cuba's.

In the only known interview in which Fidel Castro was asked about homosexuality (an interview conducted in 1965 with the American journalist Lee Lockwood), Castro left very little doubt about the incompatibility of homosexuality and the goals of the Cuban Revolution:[69]

> Nothing prevents a homosexual from professing revolutionary ideology, and consequently, exhibiting a correct political position. In this case he should not be considered politically negative. And yet we would never come to believe that a homosexual could embody the conditions and requirements of conduct that would enable us to consider him a true Revolutionary, a true Communist militant. A deviation of that nature clashes with the concept we have of what a militant Communist should be.

Signs of progress in Cuba are evident, however. In 2010, in an interview with the Mexican newspaper *La Jornada*, Castro assumed direct responsibility for the abuses against homosexuals during the early years of the revolution. "Five decades ago, and because of homophobia, we sent gays to re-education camps and accused them of being counter-revolutionaries, ... If someone is responsible it is me," he said.[70] Since the creation of the National Center for Sex Education (CENESEX), directed by Mariela Castro, daughter of Cuban president Raúl Castro and Cuba's best-known gay rights activist, Cuba appears to be changing course with respect to homosexuality. Due to Mariela Castro's efforts, Cuba's state-run medical system has offered sex-change operations since 2012. But her calls for the kind of gay rights legislation that other Latin American countries have embraced—such as anti-gay discrimination legislation and same-sex civil unions and adoptions, have been summarily rejected by the top leadership of the Cuban Communist Party. In an interview with the author, while she was visiting New York City in 2012, Castro insisted that "there is nothing incompatible between the Cuban revolution and the advancement of gay rights," and that progress on LGBT rights in Cuba was not being hindered by ideological reasons, a statement that stands strikingly at odds with the historical record.[71]

In light of this dispiriting background, it is quite striking that so many left-wing governments in Latin America have in recent decades not only embraced gay rights, including same-sex marriage and civil unions, but also taken on the Catholic hierarchy for its conservative positions on homosexuality, as will be seen shortly. This embrace of gay rights by the Latin American Left has been most pronounced in what Kurt Weyland has characterized as the "moderate" Left.[72] This Left, according to Weyland, "tempers its pursuit of leftist goals prudently, respecting economic constraints, and political opposition"; and it stands in contrast to what Weyland has called the "contestatory" Left, which "challenges neo-liberalism, defies the structures of globalization, and attacks the political opposition."[73]

Brazil's Workers' Party (PT) paved the way for the Left's embrace of gay rights in Latin America. Unlike other political parties that formed or regrouped during the euphoric years of redemocratization of the 1980s, the PT stood out for its willingness to embrace the gay community.[74] Announced in time for the 1982 elections, the PT's first electoral platform made explicit reference to the need to respect homosexuals and to stop treating homosexuality as a medical problem or a matter for the police to deal with, as was customary at the time. Between 1985 and 1988, the party led the fight, ultimately unsuccessful, to write into the new constitution a ban on discrimination on the basis of sexual orientation. This was nothing short of radical for a left-wing party in Latin America. The PT was also the first political party in Latin America to run openly gay candidates for public office, to elect gay-friendly politicians at both the local and federal levels, and to advance legislation of concern to the LGBT community—from same-sex civil unions, to HIV/AIDS policy, to bans on antigay discrimination.

Under Socialist President Michele Bachelet (2006–2010), Chile, one of Latin America's most socially conservative countries, underwent some significant changes in its gender and sexuality policies. Bachelet made

Chile's National Women's Service "one of the biggest, best funded and highest ranked national women's agencies in Latin America," introduced gender parity in cabinet appointments, and took baby steps toward legislating LGBT rights; for example, directing the Labor Bureau to investigate charges of unjust firings on the basis of homophobia and transphobia.[75] In 2013, Bachelet returned to the presidency with 62 percent of the popular vote, the highest for any presidential candidate since the democratic transition, running on a platform that included legalizing same-sex marriage. These stances stood in sharp contrast to those adopted by her conservative rival, Evelyn Matthei, who famously remarked that as president "she would not do anything that is not indicated in the Bible."[76] In April 2015, Bachelet signed into law a same-sex civil unions law, which grants same-sex partners the right to inherit each other's property and pension benefits and join one another's health plans.

Another important development in the emergence of social progressivism within the Latin America Left, especially of the populist kind, is the reinvention of Peronism under the administrations of Néstor and Cristina Kirchner (2003 to 2015). As seen later, there is a long history of homophobic policies within the Peronist movement going back to General Juan Domingo Perón himself, for whom nationhood and masculinity were part and parcel of the same thing. Yet under the Kirchners social progressivism surged dramatically. The Kirchners supported a system of gender quotas that by the early 2000s had given Argentina the highest level of representation of females in all levels of government in Latin America.[77] They also pioneered LGBT rights, by ending discrimination against homosexuals in the Argentine armed forces, extending marriage to same-sex couples, and allowing anyone to change the gender he or she was born into, without authorization from a judge or a medical doctor.

Uruguay's Frente Amplio (Broad Front), however, best embodies left-wing social progressive policies in contemporary Latin America. *The Economist* has described José "Pepe" Mujica, Frente Amplio's leader and President of Uruguay from 2010 to 2015, as "a roly-poly former guerrilla who grows flowers on a small farm and swears by vegetarianism."[78] Since coming to power in 2004, the coalition of left-wing parties comprising Frente Amplio has positioned Uruguay at the vanguard of gay rights in Latin America. The legalization of civil unions in 2007, which granted same-sex couples rights similar to those of married couples on matters such as inheritance, pensions, and child custody, was followed by laws permitting gay adoptions, repealing a ban on gays serving in the military, and allowing transsexuals to change their names in all official documents, from birth certificates to passports, to reflect the gender of their choice. Those seeking to change their gender must be at least eighteen years old and must wait at least five years before requesting another gender change. In 2013 Uruguay legalized same-sex marriage.

What explains the Left's newfound support for gay rights remains an understudied question. Indeed, it is largely ignored by the growing literature on the surge in left-wing governance in Latin America.[79] But several factors immediately jump out, beginning with the example set by the European "New Left."[80] As it developed among Western European social democratic parties, "New Leftism" is concerned with expanding the Left's agenda beyond traditional issues such as wealth redistribution, by incorporating concerns like feminism, the environment, and gay rights.[81] Spain during the administration of Socialist Prime Minister José Luís Rodríguez Zapatero appears to be the model for Latin America's socially progressive left-wing governments. Under Zapatero's rule (2004–2011), Spain underwent a "Second Transition," a set of social policies designed to modernize Spain once and for all, including liberalizing abortion laws and stem-cell research, gender parity laws, a stricter divide in church-state relations, a pathway to citizenship for undocumented immigrants, and same-sex marriage.[82]

There is also a desire by the Latin American Left to reconnect with an anticlerical Republican history, a history that many decades ago had led many Latin American liberals to defy the Catholic Church on a wide range of social issues, from education, to divorce, to women's rights. As explained by historian Thomas Laqueur in his analysis of Argentina's 2010 same-sex marriage law, "This law fits exactly into a tradition of anti-clerical republicanism."[83] He adds that "Latin American countries grew out of a rebellion against conservative Spanish clerical governments. This keeps coming up again and again." These arguments are echoed in the tussle between church leaders and politicians that surrounded the legalization of same-sex marriage and adoptions in Mexico City in 2009. In the landmark ruling by the Mexican Supreme Court that validated the actions of Mexico City officials, the justices "hewed to Mexico's strict separation of church and state and said the constitution did not indicate that marriage had to be defined as the union of a man and a woman."[84] In citing the Mexican constitution, a document drafted in 1917 during the heydays of the leftist forces leading the Mexican Revolution that strictly prohibits participation from the church in politics, the justices were making the point that "while anti-clerical provisions are rarely enforced, they remain a potential weapon to be used by the government against prelates who challenge its actions."[85]

The Left's embrace of gay rights should also be seen as emanating from a desire to use social liberalism to restore the aura of radicalism lost with the embrace of bourgeois-capitalist democracy during the 1980s and 1990s. Coming out of the democratic transitions of the 1980s, Latin American left-wing parties by and large abandoned economic "statism" in favor of free markets, in keeping with the prevailing global trend dictated by the collapse of Communism in Eastern Europe and the former Soviet Union as well as the rise of neoliberalism in Britain, the United States, and leading international financial institutions such as the World Bank and the International Monetary Fund.[86] From this confluence of events emerged the so-called Washington Consensus, a set of economic prescriptions designed to reform the Latin American economies by mandating, among other things, privatization of state enterprises, liberalization of trade, and austerity in social spending. Thus, the adoption of the mantra that democracy and free markets go hand in hand forced the Latin American Left, not unlike social democratic parties in Western Europe, to find a way to differentiate itself from the Right, and the adoption of homosexual rights appears to fit well within that strategy.

The Latin American Left's acceptance of gay rights has also been encouraged by the changes afoot in gay activism across Latin America, especially the shift away from sexual liberation and toward discourses aimed at integrating gays into the mainstream of society. This shift has made gay rights more palatable to the Left. Diego Sempol, writing about the relationship between the Uruguayan gay rights group Collectivo Ovejas Negras (Black Sheep Collective) and the Frente Amplio, notes that beginning in the 1980s, with the transition to democracy, the emerging gay community began to abandon "the stress on identity aspects in order to advance an intersectional conceptualization of discriminations that enabled the construction of stronger alliances among LGBT organizations and student, feminist, afro-descendant and workers' movements. Primarily, the sexual diversity movement started using in its discourse, terms such as 'equality' and 'social justice,' which facilitated engagement with the Uruguayan left."[87]

THE RISE OF GAY RIGHTS ACTIVISM

Last but not least, when considering the internal receptivity of Latin America to international gay rights trends, we have to take into account the activism by Latin American gay rights movements. These organizations have been the engines powering Latin America's gay rights revolution. Curiously, the gay rights movement has been mostly invisible to Latin American scholars, even scholars of Latin American social movements. The leading text on Latin America social movements completely overlooks the LGBT movement.[88] The same thing can be said of the most popular textbook on Latin American politics at US colleges and universities—even the chapter devoted to Argentina makes no mention of LGBT rights.[89] This neglect is somewhat surprising not only because of the importance of the movement in lobbying legislatures and the courts and changing public attitudes toward homosexuality but also because it is not as if gay and lesbian groups in Latin America have been invisible—quite the contrary. They have, in fact, been as conspicuous as any other social movement in Latin America in the posttransition period, perhaps even more so than others when we consider the explosion in popularity of gay pride parades from Guadalajara to Buenos Aires since the late 1970s.

As shown in our analysis of the Argentine and Brazilian experiences, organizational capacities have mattered a great deal for the realization of gay rights goals—but not as much as one might think, coming from the perspective of dominant social movement theories. What has been most decisive in shaping successful gay rights activism in Latin America is not whether gay rights movements are strong in the conventional sense—membership rich, financially well endowed, and linked to the political system—but rather the skill of gay rights activists in transporting international gay rights ideas and adapting them to the domestic context, especially by framing their struggles in ways that evoke the local context. Moreover, our case studies suggest that Latin American gay rights activism is not the monolith that it is often presumed to be. There has been significant divergence in strategies and approaches for advancing gay rights across the region, and this divergence goes a long way toward explaining the different speed and scope at which gay rights have been adopted.

PART II
The Puzzle of Argentina

CHAPTER 3

Reinventing Latin America's Oldest Gay Rights Movement

Since becoming a full democracy in 1983, Argentina has accumulated an impressive gay rights record, one that has fully realized the international gay rights arc—from "negative" rights (or the wish to be left alone), to "positive" rights (or the desire for actual civil rights), to "equal" rights (or legal parity with heterosexual society). The last milestone came under the administration of Cristina Fernández de Kirchner, Argentina's first female elected (and re-elected) president, with the legalization of same-sex marriage in 2010.[1] Since then, Argentina has enacted laws allowing individuals to change their gender without permission from a judge or a medical doctor, banning "ex-gay therapy" intended to eradicate same-sex attraction, and providing reproductive assistance under the national healthcare system for same-sex couples and single women. These legal advances, which comprise as full a menu of LGBT rights as one could imagine, have earned Argentina the title of "global champion of LGBT rights."[2] More revealing is that Argentina is nowadays in a select group of nations regarded as being on the cutting edge of LGBT issues, such as Denmark, the Netherlands, and Spain, and ahead of more "developed" nations, such as the United States, Britain, and France.

Argentina's gay rights advances would be a momentous achievement for any country, but for Argentina they are quite remarkable. After all, the country is overwhelmingly Catholic (the world was reminded of this by the hysterical reception that greeted the election of Buenos Aires archbishop Jorge Mario Bergoglio as the New World's first pope); and Argentine culture, perhaps more than in any other in Latin America, celebrates machismo.[3]

Indeed, the country reeks of macho symbols—from the national dance of the tango, with its precisely choreographed movements by the dominant male and the compliant female, to the mythical figure of the gaucho, the rough and tough horseman of the pampas—to say nothing of the country's reputation as the land of "high testosterone generals, thick slices of red beef, and beautiful women."[4]

Unsurprisingly, homosexuality in Argentina has traditionally been viewed as alien or suspect and, generally, not only as a source of derision but also as a repudiation of the very essence of what it is to be Argentine. Writing about the development of homosexuality in Buenos Aires, the literary critic David William Foster notes that "thanks to the long conflict between the capital and the rest of the country, between *civilización* (civilization) and *barbarie* (barbarism), the culture of the former has been often associated with effeminate men." He adds that "Argentine machismo is typically associated with the mythical countryside: the Gaucho, the suburban *compadrino* (tough), and the Peronist unionized worker, many of whom are urban marginals or rural immigrants. For these groups, individuals who enjoy metropolitan privilege are viewed as dandies, a euphemism for effeminate."[5]

Nor is it surprising to learn that homosexuality in Argentina has traditionally been seen as taboo—something to be repressed rather than flaunted.[6] This is reflected in a dark history of state attempts to repress homosexuality, a history that, according to one account, "exhibits a viciousness hardly equaled anywhere else in Latin America"[7] and includes targeting gays during the country' infamous "dirty war" against political dissidents. As might be expected, then, for years after the democratic transition, the Argentine gay community exhibited a palpable case of post-traumatic stress disorder. During Buenos Aires' 1996 pride parade, which featured dark and defiant messages such as "Discrimination condemns us, the police kills us, and we are still standing,"[8] participants "fearful of the consequences of 'coming out' wore masks or partially covered their faces as they marched through the downtown streets of the capital city."[9]

Reflecting the social climate, official politics in Argentina have historically been hostile to homosexuality. Indeed, gay organizations have rarely found allies within the Argentine political system. Neither one of the two national political parties that have for decades dominated Argentine politics—the Radical Civic Union (a center-right party, and a traditional patron of the middle class); and the populist Justicialista Party, better known to the outside world as the Peronist Party (traditionally an advocate of the working class)—is known for its support of gay causes or tolerance of homosexuality. Quite the contrary, both have a history of homophobic policies, but especially the Peronists, who through their politics and policies have historically reinforced heteronormativity.

It is telling that Fernández de Kirchner, a Peronist, did not come into office in 2007 championing a gay rights agenda. She did not endorse the same-sex marriage bill until the bill was being debated in the Congress, after the courts were leaning heavily in the direction of ruling in favor of the constitutionality of same-sex marriage, and after public opinion was firmly behind the bill. In fact, her views on same-sex marriage prior to 2010 were largely unknown. The closest she had come to revealing anything on the subject came during her historic 2007 presidential run. When asked if she would support the right of homosexual couples to marry, she said that she had not made up her mind; and that, in any case, this was a matter for the Congress to decide.

Several factors, however, can be cited to explain Argentina's emergence as a gay rights trailblazer in Latin America and the global South. For starters, the country meets the two most-noted preconditions for societal support for gay rights, especially same-sex marriage: a high level of social and economic development and a low level of religiosity.[10] According to the 2014 United Nations Development Index, among Latin American nations, Argentina places second (after Chile) in overall levels of development; and it is a very close race between the two countries, with Chile receiving an overall score of 0.822 (and a global ranking of forty-one); versus Argentina's score of 0.808 (and a global ranking of forty-nine).[11] Both countries make the cut of "very high human development," the highest in the survey, the only two in Latin America to do so.

As for religion, although Argentina is overwhelmingly Catholic, Argentine Catholics are not fervently so.[12] According to the Pew Research Center, 43 percent of Argentines regard religion as "a very important part of their lives," more than in Chile and Uruguay, with 42 percent and 28 percent respectively; but far fewer than in Brazil, with 72 percent. Argentina also ranks near the top among Latin American nations in the percentage of the public that does not attend church regularly. Only 20 percent of Argentines attend church at least once a week, behind Chile and Uruguay, with 19 percent and 13 percent, respectively, and miles ahead of Brazil and Mexico, with 45 percent each. Argentina ties Chile in second place (after Uruguay) in registering the lowest rating in the "religious commitment index" in Latin America. Additionally, the percentage of Protestants in Argentina, 15 percent, is lower than the Latin American average of 19 percent, and almost half the percentage of Brazil, with 26 percent. This last bit of data is relevant because public opinion surveys show that Catholics are more accepting of homosexuality than Protestants.[13]

Also notable about Argentina is the composition of the party system. There are no Catholic-backed parties in Argentina like the Christian Democratic parties of Chile and Venezuela; and neither one of the nation's two leading parties, the Peronists and the Radicals, considers abortion and homosexuality defining political issues. Much of this is traced to a long history of separation of church and state in Argentina that is rooted in a strong anticlerical tradition. Argentine anticlericalism dates back to at least the late 1880s, when liberal politicians stripped the Catholic Church of many of its official functions and introduced civil marriage and compulsory secular education, while allowing the church to retain its constitutional status.[14] Moreover, there is nothing comparable in Argentina to the clout that Evangelicals exert over the Brazilian Congress or the influence of Catholic groups like Opus Dei over conservative parties in Mexico, Chile, and Colombia.

Yet another factor favoring gay rights in Argentina is the judicial system. Since the reformation of the Argentine constitution in 1994, Argentine jurisprudence has become one of the most liberal in Latin America.[15] The reformed constitution strengthened the independence of the judiciary, expanded social rights, banned almost all forms of discrimination, and granted constitutional status to all international agreements to which Argentina is party, including human rights accords. The revamped constitution also allows citizens to file suit against government officials for violations of statutorily or constitutionally defined rights (through the *amparo* recourse), which has freed many federal and provincial judges to rule in favor of gay rights.

Ultimately, however, it was the smart advocacy by gay rights organizations that mattered most to the success of gay rights in Argentina. As shown in this analysis, the success of this advocacy did not depend upon conventional standards of social movement strength, such as membership levels, financial resources, mobilization capacity, and access to the political system. Indeed, by these standards, the Argentine gay movement should be regarded as weak. Discussing the Argentine gay movement of the mid-1990s, one study noted that "though Argentina's gay pride demonstrations are among the largest in Latin America, the movement is far from able to fill the Plaza de Mayo—the measure of success of Argentinean social movement since the days of General Perón."[16]

Instead, success hinged, first and foremost, on the crafting of the campaign for gay rights, especially the engagement with international gay rights ideas and the adaptation of these ideas to the domestic environment. Framed broadly as a human rights crusade, the Argentine gay rights campaign aimed not only to eradicate antigay discrimination in the law but also to fundamentally transform societal attitudes toward homosexuality. It entailed, among other things, legitimizing gay rights under universal human rights principles rather than Argentine law, folding gay rights organizations into Argentina's large and influential human rights community as a means for accessing the political community, and linking, through a variety of public relations schemes and political alliances, ending antigay discrimination to Argentina's democratic aspirations.

Argentina's successful gay rights campaign did not spring out of thin air. As seen in this chapter, Argentina has Latin America's richest history of organized activism around the issue of homosexuality. This history predates Stonewall, and with the coming of democracy in 1983 it provided rich fodder for "framing" strategies to advance gay rights.[17] Argentine activists also drew inspiration from the international gay rights activism to which many of them had been exposed to while in exile in Europe and the United States, especially the shift away from "sexual liberation" and toward "social integration," as well as from the example set by the local human rights movement. The latter provided gay activists with a ready-made playbook of strategies that evoked the local political and cultural context, such as shaming strategies, aggressive litigation, and media campaigns to influence public opinion.

HOMOSEXUALITY AND STATE FORMATION IN ARGENTINA

Argentina decriminalized homosexual relations in 1886, in keeping with the prevailing fashion in Latin America to emulate France's Napoleonic Penal Code of 1810. Yet in Argentina, as in all of the Latin-Iberian countries that were influenced by the Napoleonic Penal Code, including Brazil, Mexico, and Colombia, laws remained in the books that could be used to prosecute homosexuals on indecency or immorality charges. Pablo Ben's analysis of the Argentine state's response to male homosexuality from the 1880s to the 1930s notes that "countries that did liberalize sexual legislation did not put an end to the policing of men who had sex with other men. Liberal legislation only made the policy-making milder."[18] Morality laws in the books could still land gay men (and sometimes women) in trouble for engaging in activities deemed scandalous, disorderly, and offensive.

Indeed, even as the Argentine government undertook efforts to decriminalize homosexuality, it simultaneously initiated a massive campaign to eradicate homosexual behavior. The campaign had the support of the courts, the medical establishment, the Catholic Church, and the psychological-psychiatric community, the largest in the Spanish-speaking world and outside of Europe. All of these sectors in society were of the view that homosexuality posed a direct threat to the family and the state.[19] Undergirding this early repression of homosexuality in Argentina was the issue of immigration, which conjoined state building and homosexuality in Argentina in ways that are probably unique in all of Latin America. It is estimated that between 1870 and 1914, Argentina's population ballooned from about two million to eight million, of which close to one-third were foreign-born. This produced anti-immigrant sentiments unlike any other in Latin America and even more extreme than that of the United States, another quintessential immigrant society.[20]

Young and male were the dominant characteristics of the foreign population of turn-of-the-century Buenos Aires—in 1895, two-thirds of the immigrant population of the city were men; in 1914, nearly four-fifths of Buenos Aires' male adults were foreigners.[21] This booming population of mostly male immigration was encouraged by the fastest growing and most advanced economy in Latin America in the early part of the twentieth century, a development driven by a massive export-led boom. According to one account, "For 80 years after 1850, the Argentine economy experienced a period of export-led growth with few parallels in history."[22] But immigration was also eagerly pushed by the Argentine politicians who "refounded" the Argentine Republic with the Constitution of 1853, who were of the belief that a large population was essential for fulfilling the country's potential for *grandeza* (greatness). "To govern is to populate," was a common refrain of the era.[23] The refounders of the Argentine Republic were also of the view that a huge influx of European immigration would also work to "improve the national stock."[24]

But things clearly did not unfold as planned. As Jorge Salessi notes in his work on homosexuality and criminality in Argentina, the vast majority of immigrants were not the kind dreamed up by those eagerly promoting immigration. He notes that "by 1900, the immigration that had been imagined by the Argentine ideologues of the mid-nineteenth century as suburban and white (preferably Anglo-Saxon) had in reality become an immigration of a large and visible group of foreigners, mainly Italian and Spaniards, many of whom were young males without traditional family ties and often from the poorest areas of their home countries."[25] Mariano Plotkin's analysis of the emergence of psychiatry in Argentina notes that "once welcomed as a coveted seed for the country's civilization, by the 1910s immigrants were seen as instigators of class and social conflict. At the beginning of the century, citing 'scientific evidence,' nationalists argued that uncontrolled immigration would degrade the national race by incorporating large number of degenerates into society."[26] Plotkin adds that immigrants constituted a "large proportion of patients in mental hospitals" and that the image of the "crazy immigrant" became "an important element in Argentine popular culture."

An issue of particular concern to state officials, psychiatrists, and an expansive and influential "positivist movement" devoted to dealing with the great dilemmas facing Argentine society was the rise of the so-called *mala vida* syndrome—literally, the profligate life; figuratively, the seedy underworld—and its connection to immigrants and homosexuals.[27] Scholars such as Richard Cleminson have described the inhabitants of the *mala vida* (the so-called *malvivientes*) as "products of a transition from a rural to urban society, decentralized to centralized and mainly agricultural to industrial capitalist world and they consisted of groups that had not been successfully integrated into this new order, such as beggars, gamblers, thieves, prostitutes, and homosexuals."[28] According to Cleminson, it was the phenomenon of immigration that made the *mala vida* syndrome more acute in Buenos Aires than in other large Hispanic metropolises where the syndrome was spotted, such as Madrid and Barcelona.

Eusebio Gómez's *La mala vida en Buenos Aires* (1908) theorized that the *mala vida* syndrome was driven by immigrants from certain racial groups, "especially Latin races beset by tendencies toward homicide, murder, and infanticide."[29] For him, male prostitutes were motivated more by money than by sex, and for that reason they were all predisposed to thievery. In making such arguments, Gómez and others drew a gendered distinction between male and female prostitution. While the former was believed to be motivated by a desperate environment that would force men to overcome their scruples, the latter, according to the popular view of the time, "was the consequence of biological flaws that led to moral insanity."[30] Another notable criminologist of the era, Francisco de Veyga, founder of the influential journal *Archivos de Criminología, Medicina Legal y Psiquiatria*, viewed homosexuality, or "sexual inversion," as it was known then, as less an inborn condition than a product of a perverse environment linked to criminality. Salessi's summary of Veyga's theories about "sexual inversion" notes that "Veyga criminalized all sexual inverts and disseminated the notion that all men living on the margins of society were homosexuals."[31]

A key objective behind the pseudoscience about homosexuality purveyed by criminologists such as Gómez and Veyga was to encourage state regulation of homosexuality. Salessi reports that between 1870 and 1914 "a positivist bureaucracy" comprised of "state officials, physicians, psychiatrists, lawyers, criminologists, educators, writers and politicians" developed an "intense preoccupation with the study and definition of medico-legal categories of homosexuality, uranism, sexual inversion, and pederasty" intended to shape public policy toward homosexuality.[32] Like in Germany, the United States, and France, this bureaucracy preoccupied itself with "the homosexual as it might be a peculiar insect, scientifically classifying and dissecting him or her for public inspection."[33] The driver behind this "preoccupation" with homosexuality, according to Salessi, was the "homophobic ideology of homosexual panic" triggered by "a crisis of modernization," a preoccupation that was legitimated by the work of notable criminologists such as Gómez and Veyga.

There was no consensus on what form state regulation of homosexuality would take, however. For some, it entailed police crackdowns in the public spaces that male prostitutes frequented, and a ban on prostitution. For others, like many in the positivist movement, regulating homosexuality entailed reforming the penal system, and prisons in particular, not because homosexuality was a crime (it was not) but because, as seen already, homosexuality was linked to pathologies such as criminality. As argued by Ricardo Salvatore's study of the positivist legacy on the Argentine prison reform movement of the 1920s, the positivists added "a psychological dimension" to the interpretation of crime since each delinquent presented a combination of anomalies reflecting the influence of environment, inheritance, and personal psychological development.[34] This kind of thinking turned prisons into "clinics where specialists, through observation of individual cases, were able to perceive current social problems."[35]

A more active role for the state in regulating homosexuality would come with the advent of the so-called *década infame* (infamous decade), 1930–1943. This was a period of considerable political, economic, and social upheaval ushered in by the domestic repercussions of the Great Depression, including, most notably, a massive wave of rural migration to Buenos Aires fleeing the poverty of the countryside. It is estimated that the population of Buenos Aires swelled from 1.5 million in 1914 to 3.5 million in 1935, mainly due to rural emigration.[36] Lacking much in the way of economic opportunities, Depression-era Buenos Aires became a heaven for lascivious activities, especially prostitution. And for the first time since homosexuality was decriminalized, and as part of the aforementioned "homosexual panic," the state began to regulate same-sex sexual activity. This regulation came in the form of the *edictos policiales* (federal police decrees). Although in place since the late 1800s, the *edictos* had rarely concerned themselves with matters of homosexuality or sexuality. Rather, these edicts dealt with issues such as "the possession and carrying of arms, drunkenness in the public sphere, disorder and scandal, balls, vagrancy, playing cards, the behavior and circulation of minors, and the celebration of carnival."[37] In fact, prior to the 1930s, the closest the police edicts had come to regulate sexuality concerned two issues: "female prostitutes standing in front of brothel windows in order to attract men in the streets" and "men saying obscene words to women who passed by."[38]

The newly strengthened *edictos*, especially the *edicto de escándalo*, allowed for the detention and arrest for any number of "immoral" behaviors, including flirtatious language, cross-dressing, public acts of affection by members of the same sex, and men dancing together in bars. A new law banning *casas de cita* (bordellos), the Law of Social Prophylaxis (1936), was also enacted. For decades, the bordello culture had been a thorn in the side of the government and had given Buenos Aires a terrible reputation abroad, since many of the city's bordellos depended largely on foreign women, many of them brought to Argentina by force. Donna J. Guy's fascinating account of the state's attempt to regulate prostitution in Argentina during the early part of the twentieth century notes that "the very name Buenos Aires caused many a European to shudder."[39] But there was also a homophonic component to the closing of the bordellos, since, as noted previously, the government and much of the scientific community were of the view that the economic desperation of the times was forcing men into prostitution.

Homosexuality under Peronism and Its Aftermath

With the rise to power of General Juan Domingo Perón (1943–1955), who brought the masses to the forefront of politics, the infamous decade came to pass. On the surface, Peronism seemed like a welcome change for homosexuals over the previous regime. Against opposition from the Catholic Church, the new government lifted the ban on bordellos, which meant that homosexuals could find places where they could congregate. Perón's second wife, Eva Duarte de Perón, or "Evita," a political force to be reckoned with in her own right, also did her part to advance a climate of tolerance toward homosexuals by publicly embracing openly noted homosexuals, like actor and fashion designer Paco Jamandreu, whom Evita had met during her time as an actress, and Miguel de Molina, an openly gay flamenco dancer-singer nicknamed La Miguela, who took refuge in Buenos Aires in 1942 as he was fleeing political persecution in his native Spain. He was subsequently expelled from Argentina in 1943 for immoral behavior but was allowed back into the country in 1946 thanks to Evita's influence. He died in Buenos Aires 1993 without ever returning to Spain.[40]

But Peronist Argentina was not a friendly place for homosexuals—quite the contrary. For one thing, Perón's relegalization of prostitution was loaded with homophobia. As Guy points out, the Peronist government was of the view that the legalization of female prostitution could be beneficial in terms of preventing healthy males from being perverted by homosexuality.[41] Guy adds: "As prudery increased, so did homophobia, the fear of homosexuality. Rather than acknowledge that heterosexual values were being repressed, many believed the changed emphasis was the result of increased homosexuality caused by the closed bordellos." Thus, by the 1950s, "The disappearance of the bordellos, added to homophobic anxieties, led many to recollect the days of legalized prostitution with nostalgia."[42]

Equally homophobic, if not more so, was the overarching project of Peronism, which blended masculinity, nationalism, and working-class pride. From its very inception, the Peronist regime regarded homosexuals, or *amorales*, as "a deviation from the normal heterosexuality that was promoted by the regime and its many social institutions." These institutions emphasized rigid gender norms for females and males as well as the nuclear family as the linchpin of society.[43] In 1946, Domingo Mercante, a key ally of General Perón and governor of Buenos Aires province, enacted a law denying homosexuals the right to vote, a law that remained on the books well into the 1980s, mainly because it was virtually unenforceable. Nonetheless, it is suggestive of the extent to which public authorities excluded homosexuals from the political arena and society at large. In 1951, a change in the military code specifically prohibited homosexuals from enlisting in the armed forces.

In factories and offices, Peronist culture made life for homosexuals, and anyone suspected of being one, rather difficult. "From the house to the job, and from the job to the house," was a popular Peronist slogan that stressed the ideal lifestyle of the Argentine male worker. Young men who were unemployed, who liked to socialize after work, or who resisted being part of a heterosexual family unit, whether homosexual or heterosexual, came to be seen as a threat to the "familism" being affirmed by the Peronist administration and the Catholic Church. Increasingly, the so-called youth problem, which was exacerbated by a host of social and economic factors—from limited educational opportunities, to the inability of the labor market to absorb all the young males seeking employment, to the decision of young couples to delay marriage because of the expense of setting up a home—led the government to view military solutions as the answer for dealing with this problem. This led to the harassment of homosexuals in the streets, bars, and parks of Buenos Aires. A report from the daily *La Prensa*, a Peronist mouthpiece, of December 30, 1954, proudly informed readers that "the police had arrested in one night more than four hundred homosexuals in Buenos Aires."[44]

Peronism's golden age came to a screeching halt in 1955 with the military's ousting of Perón from power, with the support of the business community and the Catholic Church, which feared that Perón was on a path toward radicalizing society. Perón's populist policies had nationalized a good share of Argentina's industry, granted women the right to vote, and legalized divorce, which caused him to be excommunicated by the Vatican. The anti-Peronist coup, which declared an outright ban on Peronism, ushered in the presidency of Arturo Frondizi of the Radical Party, in power from 1958 to 1962. Best remembered for its "modernization" schemes intended to turn Argentina into a "developed" nation, the Frondizi era aimed to end "the social chaos and cultural decay that Peronism allegedly represented."[45]

In contrast to Perón's working class-centric policies, Frondizi's policies posited the middle class as the ideal of respectability and stability; in both cases, however, the government was compelled to undertake morality campaigns that, intentionally or not, contributed to a climate of hostility toward homosexuals. To execute its morality campaign, the Frondizi administration allied itself with a host of conservative organizations. Prominent among these groups was the Argentine Patriotic League, an anti-labor organization that organized "morality squadrons" to "clean squares, public transportation, and other public spaces" in Buenos Aires, with the aim of helping the police patrol the city during the day, and the National Council for the Protection of Minors, which, among other morality activities, patrolled Buenos Aires cinemas, nightclubs, and dancing bars after ten o'clock at night to inspect for the presence of minors.[46]

Frondizi was removed from power in 1962 by the military after he lifted the ban on Peronism, believing, rightly, that the ban was undermining political stability. Purporting to be acting to end economic stagnation, after 1962 the military grew more assertive in politics, culminating with the imposition of the military dictatorship of Juan Carlos Onganía (1966–1973), the so-called Argentine Revolution.[47] For some historians, however, the driving force behind the assertion of military power during the 1960s was not the economy but rather the radical social transformations afoot in Argentina.[48] Of particular concern to the military was the embrace by the middle class of psychoanalysis as a belief system around which to organize life and solve life's problems.[49] As contended by Cyrus Stephen Cousins, "The rapid social and cultural changes during the 1960s eroded the position of the family as the basic social institution and encouraged the emergence of psychoanalysis. Individual freedom and self-fulfillment replaced old values linked to familial and personal responsibility."[50]

Under the Onganía dictatorship, social life was "curtailed as the state became increasingly repressive and used police forces to control moral issues such as dressing codes, extra-marital sex, youth culture, etc. In this context homosexuality was deemed a risk to the social system and persecuted."[51] Stephen Cousins's summary of the policies of the Onganía dictatorship suggests the extraordinary level of intrusion that the state exerted on the life of ordinary citizens:

> The 1966 morality campaign attempted to prevent the spread of leftist ideologies and immorality by targeting the young middle-class men and women representing the "modern youth." The police arrested youth caught necking in cars or mingling together with the opposite sex on street corners. Spotlights installed to illuminate the city's park benches supposedly prevented "immoral" public displays of affection. The General Inspection Division ordered clubs to improve their lighting and conducted daily inspection of places in which rock-and-roll bands played. They also closed down popular cinemas and well-known theatres. Police forces raided the Maipo and Nacional cabarets (equivalents of the Lido in Paris) and reported errant husbands to their wives.

THE FLH AND THE POLITICS OF GAY LIBERATION

It was in the context of increased policing of the private sphere that organized gay activism began to appear in Argentina as part of society's challenge to the dictatorial order imposed by the Onganía dictatorship. In November 1967, Nuestro Mundo (Our World), a group comprised of ordinary workers affiliated with the postal union, was formed.[52] According to historian Osvaldo Bazán, the founding members of Nuestro Mundo "were a group of five or six gay males who shared three distinct traits: they were young, educated, and had affiliations with the political left."[53] Bazán adds that the founders were "very confused about what it meant to be a homosexual, and shared little in common with modern gay rights groups. In fact, many of the founding members believed that they had some sort of mental or health disorder (which was a popular belief at the time), and, in part, created the group to help bring about a solution."

Despite the left-wing leanings of its founders, many of whom were affiliated with the Argentine Communist Party and the Peronist Party, Nuestro Mundo never articulated a gay rights agenda beyond wanting gays to be left alone. Héctor Anabitarte, a trade unionist with ties to the Communist Party widely credited as the founding father of Nuestro Mundo, notes: "We were not intellectuals or ideologues and our demands were more reformist than revolutionary."[54] He adds that "our objective was to stop the repression of the Onganía regime, especially the harassment of gays in the streets, in the public restrooms, the public parks." In sum, this was a demand for "negative" rights.

In any case, Nuestro Mundo's leaders were not welcomed into the world of Argentine left-wing politics. The group was shunned by all left-wing organizations, and its leaders, including Anabitarte, were expelled from the Communist Party. This action was in line with the treatment of gay leaders by left-wing organizations across Latin American countries and reflected the Marxist view of homosexuality as a symbol of bourgeois decadence. Bazán cites the case of a member of Nuestro Mundo who traveled to Moscow in 1971, hoping to further his knowledge of Communist beliefs and practices. When the Argentine visitor asked Russian Communist leaders if they accepted gays into their ranks, the Russian leaders replied, "There are no gays in Russia; we have a way of dealing with homosexuals."[55]

Nuestro Mundo leaders' knowledge of gay activities outside of Argentina was quite limited. Anabitarte stresses that the organization's origins and politics had nothing to do with developments outside of their country, such as the May 1968 protests in Paris or New York's 1969 Stonewall Riots. "We were not aware of any movement outside of Argentina," he notes.[56] But Nuestro Mundo members were nonetheless familiar with the plight of homosexuals in other countries, especially in those countries with which Argentina shared close cultural, economic, and political affinities and links, such as Spain. According to Anabitarte, "We were especially concerned about the situation of homosexuals in Spain, who were suffering mightily under Franco's homophobic rule; this kept us in touch with gay activists there, especially Armand de Fluvià, the founder of Catalonia's gay rights movement."[57]

In August 1971, Nuestro Mundo joined ten other existing gay groups, including the lesbian organization Safo, the student organization Eros, the anarchist group Bandera Negra, the Catholic group Emanuelle, and faculty and students from the University of Buenos Aires to create the Frente de Liberación Homosexual (FLH). The emergence of this new organization, as argued by the cultural critic and gay activist Flavio Rapisardi, signaled a dramatic transformation for Argentina's nascent gay rights movement.[58] Within a relatively short period of time, what was born as a small group comprised of ordinary workers in the humble suburbs of Buenos Aires had been transformed into a movement with concerns about the plight of sexual minorities worldwide. The new movement had a large and eclectic membership that included artists, intellectuals, university students, and was housed in some of the most fashionable quarters of Buenos Aires.

A host of local and international events contributed to the auspicious climate that birthed the FLH, including the 1959 Cuban Revolution, the 1968 Paris protests, the 1969 Stonewall Rebellion in New York City, and Argentina's own Cordobazo, a civil uprising that began in Córdoba in May 1969 against the Onganía dictatorship and that eventually forced the military into calling for elections and accepting the return of General Perón from exile in Spain. Fronting the FLH was a small cluster of gay male intellectuals of great renown, including the novelist Manuel Puig (of *Kiss of the Spider Woman* fame), who financed the first issue of *Homosexuales*, the FLH's inaugural political and ideological manifesto; Néstor Perlongher, who was active with the organization prior to his exile in Brazil, where he gained international renown as a poet and anthropologist; and the journalist and essayist Juan José Sebreli.[59]

The FLH's creation would become the first concerted effort by Argentine gay activists to put their country on the vanguard of international gay rights politics. Perlongher recalls in his memoirs that the organization essentially functioned as a conveyor belt for transporting to Argentina the activist energy unleashed by New York's Stonewall Rebellion and its offspring, the Gay Liberation Front (GLF). He writes: "In August of 1971, a group of intellectuals inspired by the *Gay Power Americano* gave birth to the FLH of Argentina."[60] Like New York's GLF, Argentina's FLH worked to advance civil rights for gays even as it questioned the nature of sexual identity and the value of the assimilation of gays into mainstream society. "We don't have to liberate the homosexual; we must liberate the homosexual in everyone," was Eros's provocative slogan.[61] At the core of the struggle for liberalization was breaking down conventional social constructions of gender; consequently, for the FLH the open display of effeminacy by gay men and of masculinity by lesbians was regarded as "positively subversive."[62] Yet it was France's Front homosexuel d'action révolutionnaire, formed in Paris in 1971, the same year as the FLH, that became the model for the FLH. This reflected a long-standing tradition of Argentine intellectuals emulating European trends, paired with the anti-imperialist leanings of the FLH leadership and its sympathy with the Cuban Revolution.

The FLH was also broadly concerned with civil rights, being the first civil society organization in Argentina to petition the government to abolish the *edictos policiales* on the grounds that they were unconstitutional. Advancing women's rights and the rights of other minorities were other concerns for the FLH, generally from a Marxist perspective. According to the group's manifesto: "The struggle against the oppression that we suffer is inseparable from the struggle against all other forms of social, political, cultural and economic oppression."[63] A case in point was the Grupo Política Sexual, an autonomous movement within the FLH founded by Perlongher, which combined sexual liberalization, feminism, Marxism, and psychoanalytical studies to pursue change in the discriminatory male hierarchy that members believed existed in Argentina.

Despite a robust embrace of Marxism, the leaders of the FLH were rejected by most left-wing organizations. Perlongher recalls with regret that at rally in protest of Pinochet's coup in Chile in 1973, "the leftist groups went out of their way to keep their distance from the gays."[64] It certainly did not help that FLH members were bold enough to call the Left on its overt homophobia. According to a policy statement from the organization:

> We homosexuals are a segment of society that suffers from a form of discriminate and specific repression, one that originates in the interests of the system itself and is being internalized by the majority of the population, including some segments that pretend to be revolutionary. In this sense, many of the forms of anti-homosexual prejudice remain intact, disguised as political criticisms. As an example, it is put forth as an objection that homosexuality is a product of decadent capitalism. But societies that were not capitalist or decadent, like the Incas, practiced and praised it.[65]

Nonetheless, Bazán notes that many in the FLH leadership persisted in seeking an affiliation with the Peronist Party, believing in the utility of a political affiliation and in the capacity of the politically diverse Peronist movement to accommodate a wide range of social movements.[66] An estimated one hundred FLH activists took part in the 1973 celebration held at the Plaza de Mayo to mark the inauguration of Peronist leader Héctor Cámpora as caretaker president until new elections were convened (the elections that would allow for Perón's return to power). The activists carried a banner that read: "Love and equality will reign one day."[67] But these actions of support for the Peronist movement were not reciprocated given the prevailing hostility toward homosexuals within the party. At Perón's homecoming party in 1973, the FLH was among the many civil society organizations that greeted the leader at the Buenos Aires airport carrying banners and signs, yet the presence of FLH members was not welcomed by other Peronist organizations and triggered a wave of "homophobic slurs and chants degrading their sexual orientation."[68]

The most obvious explanation for the hostility directed toward the FLH was the very strong homophobic streak that has traditionally run through the Peronist movement, owing largely to the movement's strong working-class roots, which permeated most, if not all, Peronist institutions. Homophobia was most pronounced within the Confederación General de Trabajadores (better known as the CGT), the country's largest trade union and a key reservoir of Peronist culture. But it also extended to many of Peronism's social and political organizations and movements. Bazán reports that the Montoneros, the urban guerrilla movement that flourished during the late 1960s and early 1970s, and by far the most extremist of Peronism's left-wing movements, are thought to have condoned and even encouraged violence toward homosexuals.[69] This behavior places the Montoneros in the same company as other Latin American left-wing guerrilla movements in their harsh treatment of homosexuals.[70]

Ironically, the 1973 elections that returned Perón to power and that marked the promise of a more open society signaled the beginning of the end for the FLH. Much to the chagrin of his left-wing supporters, Perón began his term trying to appeal to the Right as he sought to isolate left-wing extremists such as the Montoneros, an effort that demanded severing ties with many left-wing groups, especially those deemed "radical." This campaign against the radical Left intensified after Perón's sudden death in 1974, which was accompanied by a surge of right-wing paramilitary activity, and the rise to power of his third wife, Vice President Isabel Martínez de Perón, also known as "Isabelita." During her brief and chaotic presidency, the oppression of the radical Left was extended to groups like the FLH, with some of the organization's leaders reportedly tortured or murdered.[71] With the coming of military rule in 1976, the FLH decided to self-dissolve, with the top leaders choosing to flee to Spain and Brazil, from where they denounced the situation in Argentina under the name of "the FLH in exile."[72]

The FLH's dissolution meant a multiyear pause in organized gay activism in Argentina and the silencing of an important voice within Argentine civil society. With the passing of the FLH came the end of *Somos*, Latin America's first gay magazine. Published between 1973 and 1976 (eight issues altogether), the magazine dealt with a wide range of domestic and international issues of interest to the gay community, from denouncing police brutality toward the gay community, to reporting on the repression of homosexuals in Chile by the Pinochet regime, to warning just before the 1976 coup about a military plot to "exterminate the gays, hippies, and drug-addicts," whose increased visibility in Argentine society was attributed to "an international Marxist plot."[73]

A new low for repression of political and civil liberties in Argentina arrived with the coming of another military regime in 1976. The military regime in place between 1976 and 1983, and headed by General Jorge Videla from 1976 to 1981, was notable, above all, for its systematic assault on civil society, with the aim of eradicating political dissidents, especially labor leaders, journalists, students, academics, and generally anyone considered to be Marxist or a left-wing sympathizer.[74] This "dirty war" was effectively conveyed in the official name of the regime—El Proceso de Reorganización Nacional—a name that conjured the sentiment within the military that a wholesale reorganization of Argentine society was needed to correct whatever was wrong with the country.

The scope of the terror imposed by the new regime is legendary, at least to those familiar with Latin American politics or aware of the major instances of human rights violations in the twentieth century. It included a vast network of secret prisons, torture chambers, and concentration camps—including the infamous Escuela Superior de Mecánica de la Armada, today transformed into a museum honoring the memory of victims of state terrorism; practices such as throwing the drugged out bodies of prisoners from planes into the ocean as a means of "disposing of the evidence"; stealing the babies of pregnant female prisoners and giving them to military officers for adoption; and widespread complicity by the Catholic Church in sanctioning and assisting in the persecution of "enemies" of the state.

According to the official report of the Comisión Nacional sobre la Desaparición de Personas (CONADEP), which became a runway international bestseller under the title of Nunca Más (Never Again), ten thousand Argentines disappeared under military rule. Human rights activists have long rejected that official figure as too low, putting the actual number of disappeared at thirty thousand. But the official numbers are suggestive enough in demonstrating that the violence inflicted by the military in Argentina between 1976 and 1983 has no peer in the South American context. As reported by Alfred Stepan in his comparative analysis of military politics in Brazil and the Southern Cone: "On a per capita basis, for every person who disappeared or died in official custody in Brazil, ten died or disappeared in Uruguay, and over three hundred died or disappeared in Argentina."[75]

Regrettably, Nunca Más does not name a single person detained or disappeared because of his or her sexual orientation.[76] This glaring omission prompted Carlos Jáuregui, a prominent gay activist exiled in France during the military dictatorship and future leader of Argentina's post-transition gay rights movement, to complain that "the gays are the disappeared among the disappeared."[77] Jáuregui's own account of the military's repression of homosexuality, provided in his book *La homosexualidad en la Argentina*, includes the following explosive passage:[78]

It is difficult to ascertain if anyone disappeared because of being homosexual. There is no information; nor, regrettably, will there ever be. We know that the assassins were very careful in covering their tracks. But we strongly believe that among the thousand of comrades who disappeared victims of state terrorism were a few hundreds that were homosexual. This statistic does not appear in the report of the National Commission on the Disappeared but one of the members of the Commission confirms of the existence of at least four hundred homosexuals in the tally of horrors. This member added that the treatment given to homosexuals was analogous to that given to the disappeared Jews: especially sadistic and violent.

Jáuregui died, at age thirty-eight, without providing any evidence to back up his charge of four hundred gay killings. But gay activists routinely cite the charge of four hundred killings to make the case for the "systemic persecution" of gays by the old regime.[79] This has given Jáuregui's charge something akin to "official" recognition; indeed, the charge is often noted matter-of-factly as something that is beyond questioning, in large part because, as Ben notes, "Jáuregui has become such an icon of homosexual rights in Argentina."[80] After his death, a plaza in the Buenos Aires neighborhood of Constitución was named after Jáuregui, and August 20, the day of his death, is recognized as national day of sexual diversity activism. More recently, Jáuregui's charge of four hundred gay killings has appeared in several scholarly analyses of gay rights politics in Argentina, usually in connection with the rise of gay rights legislation, further burnishing the charge's popularity and credibility.[81]

Gay historians, however, have recently begun to question the veracity of Jáuregui's claims and so far have concluded that there is no evidence to support them. Santiago Joaquín Insausti, an Argentine scholar working on a history of the FLH, has done the most exhaustive research on the subject of gay repression under military rule.[82] He notes, for starters, that it would be difficult to establish a concerted effort by the military government to target homosexuals since many of the members of the FLH who were arrested, tortured, and even made to disappear were also active in left-wing organizations, making it difficult to ascertain if they became a target of the military regime because of their sexual orientation or because of their political activities.[83]

In support of this point, Insausti adds that while the disappeared were housed in the "clandestine" circuit of detention, this was rarely the case for homosexuals, who were more likely to have ended up in either the "contraventional" circuit or perhaps even in the "penal" circuit, alongside thieves, sex workers, and other lawbreakers. In any case, Insausti adds that "there are no references in either state archives or the records of human rights organizations about the persecution of individuals on the basis of their sexual orientation, especially of the scale suggested by gay activists. He adds that an interview with Graciela Fernández de Meijide, one of the last surviving members of CONADEP, confirmed that the commission's review of some nine thousand filings of human rights abuses by the military did not include any claims about the detention or persecution of individuals because of their sexuality. All of this said, Insausti is quick to make this affirmation: "I am certain that the number of homosexuals and transvestites killed by the Argentine state far exceeds the 400–500 claimed by Jauregui," but he adds: "that tally would cover the period since the first Peronist government."

Despite the intensity of the debate over the number of gay casualties inflicted by the military, there is little debate about the overall climate of hostility and violence toward gays that prevailed in Argentina under the military regime. The intense anti-gay sentiment of the regime was foreshadowed in a 1975 editorial in the far-right military magazine *Cabildo* with the title of "To Finish-off the Homosexuals." Among other things, the article blamed Marxism for "utilizing homosexuality for corrupting the people" and called for the creation of "morality brigades to sweep neighborhoods looking for gays to round them up and kill them." This editorial, according to Insausti, was "an inflection point" for gay activists. In the months that followed publication of the editorial, which were accompanied by increasing repression of all political activities, the FLH stopped all of its activities and went into hiding.[84]

Historical reconstructions of the period of military rule are in sync with much of what is discussed above. As reported by Bazán, the alienation, repression, and demonization of the dictatorial years pushed gays into what he refers to as a "double clandestine existence," since gays had to contend not only with the hostility and violence of the political regime but also with the homophobia of Argentine society and many of its institutions, including the Catholic Church, which is widely thought to have aided the military in repressing the gay population.[85] One of the few places where gay men could meet with some degree of safety was public bathrooms, usually those located in public parks, a choice of meeting place that Bazán argues was symbolic of how far out of public sight the military had driven the gay community.

Bazán's contentions find considerable resonance in the oral histories collected in *Fiestas, baños y exilios* (parties, bathhouses and exiles), Flavio Rapisardi and Alejandro Modarelli's densely documented account of gay life under military rule.[86] This work describes how the shutting down of the gay community —in the form of gay bars, restaurants, bookstores, and discotheques—during the 1960s and 1970s pushed the gay community into conducting its social life in an almost completely clandestine existence. In the environment of repression created by the *razzias* (police raids), blackmail, and extortion, sexual desire persisted; in fact, it thrived, as bathhouses, public bathrooms, train stations, and even a dormitory at the police station of Casa Rosada (the presidential palace) became places where resistance and pleasure would coexist.

Historians have identified at least two particular instances when the military regime targeted the gay community, especially male homosexuals. The first instance came around the time of the 1978 World Cup, which was held in Argentina two years following the military coup (and which Argentina won, allowing the military to try to shift attention away from the massive human rights violations that were rapidly becoming apparent at home as well as abroad). Targeting gays became part of a "cleansing" campaign that preceded the tournament, and which according to some accounts included members of the federal police "sweeping the streets in search of homosexuals" and "savagely beating in public view those resisting arrest."[87]

The second instance occurred between January 1982 and January 1983, during the twilight of the military government, when a former member of the FLH and seventeen additional gay males were murdered. This wave of antigay violence came in the wake of a pronouncement by the paramilitary group Comando Cóndor, which spread its terror throughout South America and beyond, that it intended to "wipe out the homosexuals."[88] Other reporting of this killing rampage notes that of those murdered, most were "tortured and executed in their own homes," and that the police never found the perpetrators.[89]

This level of antigay repression and violence suffered under "El Proceso" is certainly among the worst experienced by any Latin American society under right-wing military rule. Worse than under any other dictatorial regime in the region, save, perhaps, the possible exception of the repression imposed on homosexuals by the Castro regime in Cuba after 1959. Brazil, whose politics during the 1960s and 1970s mirrored those of Argentina, provides a contrasting example. Although for the entirety of military rule in Brazil (1964–1985) homosexuals were subjected to police harassment, and even imprisonment, an overall tolerance of homosexual activity (and even some degree of gay activism) prevailed as well.[90] In fact, as seen later, many gay organizations and publications were actually born in Brazil during the twilight years of the military regime, which gave the country something of a leg up over Latin American nations in starting the gay rights movement in the posttransition era.

So why so much violence directed at homosexuals, especially male homosexuals, in Argentina? At some level, antigay violence cannot be divorced from the long and dark history of state violence in Argentina, going back to the colonial period, especially the violence directed at elements deemed alien, foreign, or different. Scholars of the formation of the Argentine state, such as Nicolas Shumway, have highlighted the role of violence in the refounding of the Argentine Republic in the nineteenth century, as suggested by the appeal of the Inquisition and the Crusades to the founding fathers.[91] More directly related to our concern is the widespread characterization of the Argentine state as possessing a distinct *machista* orientation almost from its very inception, and as suggested by its macho generals and dictators, most notably Juan Manuel de Rosas (1835–1852). Diana Taylor writes that "Rosas perfected ... the model for the 'macho' nature of authoritarianism that characterizes later manifestations of *nationalismo*, an ultraconservative, antirevolutionary, Catholic movement that has played a dominant role in the Argentine armed forced throughout much of the twentieth century."[92]

Historians of homosexuality in Argentina are more inclined to highlight a broader range of societal factors.[93] Ben notes that the social transformations of the 1930s and 1940s are key to understanding what happens to homosexuality during the 1950s and 1960s. He notes that the rise of a vast working class with middle-class aspirations that spread into the suburbs of Buenos Aires created social conditions under which all sexual minorities came to be seen as "suspect and dangerous."[94] According to Bazán, antigay violence in Argentina reflects the deeply engrained homophobia among the state and some societal actors, such as the Catholic Church and the medical establishment, all of which have traditionally regarded heteronormativity as the natural order of things and anything that deviates from that as a direct threat to the nation. He observes that throughout Argentina's history "gays have always been seen as wrong: as a sin by the Catholic Church, as an illness for the doctors, and as a crime for the state."[95]

Whatever its root causes, the military's behavior toward homosexuals dealt a severe blow to the Argentine gay community that persisted well into the democratic period. The marginality and indeed obscurity that gays were forced into under the old regime helps explain why during the last years of the military dictatorship, when civil society was gearing up for the return to democracy, and groups such as students' associations, women's groups, and a bourgeoning human rights movement began to demand for a return to democracy, as well as for accountability for the crimes of the military regime, gays were largely invisible. Bazán notes that despite the sense that the collapse of the dictatorship was imminent and democracy was around the corner, "the gay community had no central core, and no one was demanding that gays be represented in the plans to examine the human rights transgressions of the military."[96] It would take the formal collapse of the old regime and the return of exiled gays from Europe and the United States for gays to begin to assert themselves politically and revive what was once Latin American's most thriving gay community.

THE CHA AND THE POLITICS OF SOCIAL INTEGRATION

Argentina's decisive defeat at the hands of the British in the 1982 "War of the Malvinas," an ill-conceived attempt by military officers to drum up support for the military regime by boosting nationalism, accelerated the collapse of military rule and put the country on the path to democracy. As noted by journalist Mabel Bellucci, whose reporting provides one of the few published firsthand accounts of gay activism in the earliest days of the new democracy, no other group in Argentine society showed greater joy than the gay population about the advent of democracy. She reports that on election day (October 30, 1983) "hundreds of gays" gathered at the Palladium discotheque to watch the election returns, and that when Raul Alfonsín of the Radical party was announced as the winner, there was "dancing, hugging, and a general air of happiness."[97] This euphoria had little to do with ideology or party affiliation, a point underscored in Rapisardi's reporting. "The gays that flooded the urban core of Buenos Aires to celebrate Alfonsín's victory did not do so by carrying the red and white flag of the winning party, but by unabashedly strutting their stuff, believing that the dawn of a new era was upon them."[98]

Yet the support that the gay community offered Alfonsín was not devoid of political intention. As was the case for many liberals and progressives around the time of the transition, many in the gay community were drawn to Alfonsín's political message. He made human rights and political accountability (which he linked to his family background—his father, an immigrant from Spain, was a passionate supporter of the Republicans during the Spanish Civil War and a foe of General Francisco Franco) the centerpiece of his political platform by pledging to seek truth and justice for the victims of the dictatorship. Alfonsín was also seen by many gays, as well as by many ordinary Argentines, as the best prospect for changing politics as usual in Argentina. During the 1970s, he had been one of the few politicians from either the Right of the Left who dared to criticize the military dictatorship, earning him the reputation of a political maverick. Unlike Peronist politicians, Alfonsín refused to strike bargains with the military that would have accelerated the transition to civilian rule in exchange for political amnesties with respect to human rights violations. Moreover, as noted by Rapisardi, gays were "spooked" by Peronist discourses throughout the electoral campaign that privileged "national identity" over individual rights.[99]

Gay Politics during the Democratic Transition

The first attempt to organize gays in the new democracy occurred in 1982, just before the formal collapse of the military dictatorship. Dubbed the Coordinadora de Grupos Gay, this was a loosely organized network of some eight organizations. "Heated debates on struggle strategies" crippled this organization from its very start.[100] A smaller but better-defined organization, the Comunidad Homosexual Argentina (CHA), founded in 1984, would endure and eventually prosper. Its early leaders comprised a small cluster of intellectuals, lawyers, and journalists, including Carlos Jáuregui, the organization's first president, César Cigliutti, its current president, and Marcelo Ferreyra, currently director of the Buenos Aires–based Latin American office of the International Gay and Lesbian Human Rights Commission. The CHA remained the only official gay organization in the country for the first eight years of the new democracy. It was also the first gay organization in Argentina to be granted legal status by the state.

As with the case of the rise of the first gay rights organization in Argentina, Nuestro Mundo, in 1967, state repression of homosexuality was the main driver behind the emergence of gay rights organizations in the new democracy. Interviews with the leaders of the CHA suggest that both the formation of the organization and its human rights roots evolved, first and foremost, from the harsh social and political environment facing the Argentine gay community during early years of the new democracy. "We thought that democracy would guarantee our basic rights but it rapidly became crystal clear that this would not be the case," recalls Cigliutti.[101] Indeed, although democracy's return to Argentina brought about the restoration of political freedoms, the social climate for gays remained downright inauspicious as gays continued to be persecuted, stigmatized, and marginalized. The main enforcer of antigay repression in the new democracy was minister of the interior Antonio Tróccoli, "who was a firm believer that homosexuality was an illness."[102] To lend legitimacy to his views, Tróccoli was fond of citing the Pan American Health Organization, which in 1984 still listed homosexuality as a mental disorder.

A review of police and newspaper records of the early years of democracy in Argentina concludes that "gays were the predominant victims of police repression against sexual dissidents, and murders publicized in the press, while symbolic violence prevailed in the case of lesbians."[103] Between December 20, 1983, and March 21, 1984, under the Ley de Antecedentes (Criminal Records Act), 21,343 people were arrested for "background checks," the majority of them homosexual males. After being detained, the men were often threatened with being outed to their relatives and employers or blackmailed in exchange for money or a confession of their homosexuality. A bribe of $50–$100 would usually be required for release without an official record. Bars and restaurants catering to homosexuals were required to pay bribes to the police's "morality brigades" to prevent police harassment of their gay clientele. Granting the police virtual carte blanche to harass and imprison gays for up to ninety days without filing formal charges were the infamous *edictos policiales*, including the *edicto de escándalo*, which prohibited members of the same sex from dancing together in bars and discotheques and showing public signs of affection. Little wonder that among the CHA's earliest publications, the magazine *Sodoma*, one finds articles such as one titled "And this was Democracy?" It makes the point that for homosexuals "there was much continuity between the old military dictatorship and the new political regime."[104]

In fact, it was the *edicto de escándalo* that the police employed on March 21, 1984, to justify arresting some three hundred males at the discotheque Balvanera. The mass arrest was followed by days of protests by patrons in front of the club. Unsurprisingly, some gays in Argentina have taken to referring to this episode as Argentina's own Stonewall Rebellion. But gay activists are careful not to draw any direct comparisons to the American experience of 1969. Enrique Rojas, an ex-FLH member, recalls that after the 1984 raid of Balvanera "there was no Stonewall; there was no gay power."[105] Nonetheless, just weeks after the Balvanera raid, on April 17, 1984, a politically diverse group of some 150 gays and lesbians gathered at the bar Contramanos to form the CHA. Only a handful of them, however, felt comfortable in making their faces known to the public.

As was also the case of Nuestro Mundo, no major political party from the left or the right wanted anything to do with the CHA. According to Cigliutti: "The Argentine political parties did not have nor did they afford a space for us to raise our issues and even less space for us assert our rights."[106] Of the ten existing left-wing parties in the new democracy, only the small and very far left Trotskyite organization Movimiento al Socialismo (MAS) offered explicit support to the CHA. This was, however, an affiliation that the CHA sought to shirk. It has been reported that the CHA attempted to hide the support offered by the MAS. Rapisardi notes an interesting incident in which the CHA magazine *Vamos a Andar* ran a picture of a public demonstration in which the CHA had participated that erased the banner of the MAS, which in the original version appears directly behind the CHA's own banner.[107]

Until the early 1990s, when the CHA was successful in securing legalization, after a long legal and political battle, the organization was shunned by the state. This shunning made the organization fearful of running afoul with the law. For years after its creation, a sign hung in the CHA's Buenos Aires headquarters warning those under age twenty-two "to leave immediately," as the organization was afraid that its leaders would be arrested "for trying to corrupt minors."[108] Understandably, for much of the 1980s and even into the 1990s, the Argentine gay movement looked with envy at its Brazilian counterpart, which by then was enjoying full legality and even the backing of a major political party with presidential aspirations, the Workers' Party. Lamenting the political picture for gay rights organizations in Argentina in the 1980s and early 1990s, in contrast to the situation in Brazil, a study of Argentine gay activism of the era notes: "There is no equivalent in Argentina to Brazil's Workers' Party, which has forged a working relationship with a broad range of social movements, including the lesbian and gay one. In Argentina, power historically alternates between the Radical party and the Justicialistas (Peronists), neither of which has indicated much support on issues relating to sexuality."[109]

Needless to say, the absence of support from the political system made for a very trying early existence for the CHA in its early years. Those years, according to Cigliutti, were "a touch-and-go situation; and it was not clear for several years if the organization would make it."[110] Membership in the organization reached as high as three hundred in the mid-1980s, although membership was rather loose then—the organization essentially consisted of forty to fifty core activists. Funding for the organization was strictly donation-based; there were no sponsors or supportive organizations. "We were really on our own. We would do the rounds of clubs like Contramano and Balvanera asking for donations from the patrons," recalls Cigliutti.[111]

The Primacy of Human Rights

As far as its politics were concerned, the CHA was unlike any other gay rights organization that had come before it, either in Argentina or in Latin

America. The organization's dominant characteristic was the centrality of human rights in its rhetorical, political, and operational orientations. According to Cigliutti: "All the political and legal conquests for the gay community that we have achieved in Argentina have been fundamentally defended from the standpoint of human rights."[112] Such a comprehensive conjoining of human rights and sexuality was an important departure for human rights politics in Latin America. Prior to the 1980s, the employment of human rights discourses in Latin America was the exclusive domain of those protesting the military's torture, kidnapping, and disappearance of political dissidents.

Bringing sexuality into human rights debates also made the CHA into an international gay rights pioneer. Ironically, we have to go back to the era before the 1948 Universal Declaration of Human Rights to find gay rights organizations whose activism is as closely associated to human rights as that of the CHA—such as the Scientific Humanitarian Committee, the world's first gay rights organization, formed in Berlin in 1897 and closed by the Nazi regime in 1933; and Chicago's Society for Human Rights, the United States' first gay rights organization, created in 1924 and shut down by political pressures soon thereafter.[113] Both organizations sought to end the criminalization of homosexuality, alongside enlightening the public about homosexuality by stressing the humanity of homosexuals and encouraging them to fight for their freedoms.

Human rights were prominently showcased in the CHA's founding motto: "The Free Exercise of Sexuality Is a Human Right."[114] Human rights also featured prominently in the organization's constitutional charter. Approved on May 20, 1984, the CHA charter explicitly states the goal of the organization as "positing ourselves among human rights organizations" and joining other human rights organizations in the country that recognized the universality of these rights.[115] In its early policy documents, the CHA made human rights a central component for ending legally sanctioned discrimination against homosexuals. A document published in *Boletín de la CHA* on September 8, 1985, noted: "Our only commitment is the struggle for human rights in Argentina; bringing dignity to homosexuals is only one component of that struggle."

In June 1986, a human rights division was created within the CHA devoted to advancing the notion that "sexuality and human rights are intrinsically linked and that Argentina's human rights aspirations could not be fulfilled as long as homosexuals continued to be repressed, marginalized and victimized, and to coordinate activities with other human rights organizations and emerging human rights apparatus within the Argentine government."[116] Throughout the late 1980s, the CHA's human rights commission organized a series of conferences with titles such as "Sexuality and Human Rights," "Human Rights in Everyday Living," and "Human Rights in Argentina." These conferences and other informational activities had the dual purpose of raising awareness about the organization and boosting its recruitment efforts by promoting, in the words of one analyst, "the realization of sexual identity through an ideological matrix focused on human rights." This realization implied "a rite of passage" to become "a homosexual militant," by which individuals underwent a "reconstruction of individual identity under non-stigmatized parameters, informed by political commitment."[117]

The CHA's robust embrace of human rights and the humanization of gays was part and parcel of a broader strategy to incorporate gays and lesbians into the mainstream of Argentine society. This effort entailed prioritizing social integration over sexual liberation, a rising trend in international gay rights activism.[118] The goal of "mainstreaming" has led some observers to categorize the CHA as "integrationist"[119] and, less charitably, as "assimilationist."[120] Mainstreaming was premised on showing gays as ordinary people living ordinary lives and, as such, deserving of the same rights afforded to anybody else. This goal was pursued by the CHA through an aggressive media strategy to promote *darse a conocer*, or self-outing, which Jáuregui regarded as the gay community's "most potent resource" to advance its goals.[121] Jáuregui promoted these views in newspaper articles and television appearances.

Not surprisingly, social integration went hand in hand with showing gays and lesbians as having no signs of difference in either clothing or behavior from ordinary heterosexual men and women. This stood quite in contrast to the FLH, which, as seen previously, prized sexual marginality and welcomed gender nonconformity in clothing and behavior, as well as visibility for gays in all public spheres. The very physical appearance of the CHA's leadership underscored a desire to stress conventionality, ordinariness, and a desire to blend in. According to Ferreyra, Jáuregui was ideally suited as the face of the new organization and was able to completely erase the radical image of gay activists left behind by the FLH: "Carlos was blond, very masculine in appearance, and most importantly, professional, educated, and affable."[122]

The CHA's emphasis on social integration and mainstreaming meant that the organization would originally be suspicious of American concepts such as "gay pride" because of its obvious association with "gay liberation." CHA leaders believed that erasing stereotypes about homosexuals by educating the public through media campaigns and working directly with public officials to ease harassment of gays were more effective ways to end antigay discrimination than a public display of homosexuality. As observed by Diego Sempol: "The CHA talked about 'homosexual dignity,' stressing adherence to universal humanistic values, as opposed to 'gay pride,' which was understood as unwanted promotion of group distinctions."[123]

To support its mainstreaming agenda, the CHA also sought to remain politically independent. This meant, above all, skirting the traditional far-left affiliation of previous gay rights organizations in Latin America, even though much of the leadership of the CHA shared broad left-wing sympathies, from Peronism to Communism. Instead, the organization emphasized political autonomy and connections to other groups in civil society, especially human rights organizations. Driving this desire for political independence was the belief that support for homosexuals in society should cut across the political spectrum. "Nobody should be against homosexuals," Jáuregui said the magazine *Libre* in June 19, 1984.[124]

Past political experience also enhanced the CHA's desire for political independence. Jáuregui was very sensitive to the perils of political affiliations, especially with the Peronist Party, in light of the experience of the FLH. In the same interview with the magazine *Libre* in which Jáuregui emphasized the importance of political autonomy, he went on at some length about the difficult association between the FLH and Peronist organizations during the early 1970s, which he labeled "a mistake." He noted that:

> The FLH openly supported Peronism, and it was well received. In time, however, the world turned upside down and the Montoneros began defending themselves against the Peronist right by chanting: "We are not faggots, we are not queer; we are revolutionaries, we are soldiers of the FAR [Frente Revolucionario Armado] and Montoneros." The FLH gave all of its support and that is how they were rewarded.

Among the many reasons for the CHA's conjoining of human rights and the struggle for integration the most obvious is the rise in prominence of human rights in the political culture of Argentina's new democracy. This was a direct consequence of the wanton disregard for human rights by the outgoing military regime. Powered by societal demands for accountability for the extrajudicial war waged against political dissidents by the old military regime, including the world-famous Las Madres de la Plaza de Mayo, the group of mothers and grandmothers demanding justice and accountability for their disappeared children, the human rights movement during the years of democratic transition succeeded in turning Argentina from "a pariah state" to "a protagonist in international human rights politics."[125] Born rather quietly during the worst excesses of the military dictatorship in the late 1970s, the human rights movement rapidly grew into the most formidable force within civil society by the time of the democratic transition in 1983. As noted by sociologist Elizabeth Jelin, "At first almost in hiding and unseen, then becoming steadily more visible, gaining step by step in relevance and central- ity, the movement and the issues it raised gradually came to occupy a signifi- cant position in the public arena."[126]

As noted previously, much to the disappointment of the gay commu- nity, the national commission on the disappeared, the CONADEP, failed to report on the repression of homosexuals during the dictatorship. But, as seen in the next chapter, the emergence of human rights to the fore- front of politics in the new democracy under the Alfonsín administration nonetheless allowed gay activists many opportunities to fold the history of their own repression under the military regime into the narrative of crimes against humanity of the old regime, to incorporate themselves into the human rights community (a struggle in its own right, given the homophobia prevalent in several human rights organizations), and to engage with the state's expanding human rights bureaucracy to advance their demands for gay civil rights. Indeed, the repression of homosexuals under military rule in Argentina, although contested by historians, would eventually emerge as a key feature in the larger narrative of the human rights abuses of the military period, and a legitimating factor in the debate over same-sex marriage in 2010.

Less apparent about the roots of the CHA's activist agenda was the political orientation of a brand-new generation of Argentine gay leaders whose formation as gay activists was strongly informed by their experi- ence abroad. This experience had exposed these new activists to a post- sexual liberation activism that was less idealistic and more pragmatic than earlier waves of Argentine gay activists. Although the CHA's early leader- ship drew on the surviving leaders of the FLH (the most notable being the writer Zelmar Acevedo), it was members of the exiled gay community who began to dictate the organization's programmatic agenda upon returning to Argentina around the time of the transition. Especially notable is that many CHA members had spent time in France, where by the mid-1980s gay activists had come to embrace the claim that "the rights of homosexu- als were human rights" and had begun to press European supranational institutions, such as the European Court of Human Rights, the European Economic Community (the precursor to the European Union), and the Council of Europe, into embracing this idea.[127]

Among the gay exiles who had spent time in France and fell under the influence of French gay politics, the most prominent was Jáuregui. As president of the CHA from 1984 until 1987, when he became the organization's first secretary for human rights, Jáuregui exerted the most influence over the organization during its formative years. It is noteworthy that Jáuregui had no previous affiliation with any gay group in Argentina; in fact, he had no activist past to speak of prior to his return to Argentina in 1982. He had spent the years of military dictatorship in exile as a graduate student in medieval history in France, where he was exposed to new trends in gay activism. In particular, Jáuregui found much inspiration in Michael Foucault's theories about homosexuality, from which he derived ideas about increasing societal acceptance of homosexuality that relied on showcasing the ordinary humanity of gays and lesbians.

According to Bellucci's biography of Jáuregui, while in France Jáuregui not only decided to become a gay activist, he also sketched the future of gay activism in Argentina. Bellucci cites a letter Jáuregui wrote to a friend (Patricia Narváez, one of the first female members of the CHA), and later published in the magazine *La Maga* in August 1996, recounting Jáuregui's first experiencing witnessing a gay pride march in Paris in the early 1980s:

> I cried like never before when I saw my first gay march. I saw it by chance in the Latin Quarter. I said to myself that if I ever return to Argentina I had to work on something like this. I had no experience in political activism. But I was certain that I had discovered something that I really wanted to do. So I put my scholarly investigations aside and devoted my life to gay militancy.[128]

An even more inspiring experience was the march Jáuregui attended in his first Parisian spring in May 1981 to celebrate the victory of Socialist President François Mitterrand in the presidential elections. For that occasion, around ten thousand homosexuals took to the streets of Paris, clearly visible as gay men and women and without fear of reprisals from the police, joined by a multiplicity of civil and human rights organizations. As recounted in Bellucci's biography of Jáuregui (quoting Jáuregui's own words):

> The main driver behind my decision to become a gay activist was the demonstration of May 1981. From that moment on, I began to think that we had to do something similar in Argentina. Here in France I was being witness to how to live in a free society. It was incredible for me to discover that it was possible to organize a community, seeing that behind that march was a clear political movement.[129]

Other Argentine gay activists had spent time in Spain, where they absorbed changing gay rights trends in an environment not that dissimilar from Argentina's. Following the demise of Generalissimo Francisco Franco's dictatorship in 1975, Spanish gay activists were finding "a new space between pragmatism and the utopia." While veteran revolutionary organizations insisted on rejecting insider politics, a host of new "reformist" groups showed a clear sympathy toward a different kind of interaction with existing polity members.[130] Groups such as the Coordinadora Gay y Lesbiana de Cataluña and the Colectivo Gay de Madrid, both created in 1986, "broke with the liberationist tradition" of the Movimiento Español de Liberación Homosexual, founded in 1971, while the Franco regime was still in place. These groups introduced "a new understanding of gay and lesbian protest, anchored in a redefinition of the role of the individual participant (activists that replace militants), in the establishment of links of solidarity between politicised and non-politicized homosexuals (community politics), and in the implementation of pragmatism as the dominant guiding principle of outward political activity."[131]

Even less apparent in informing the CHA's orientations was the political learning that CHA leaders drew from the first wave of gay rights activism. This point speaks powerfully to the importance of the historical roots of the gay movement in Argentina in the development of gay rights in the democratic period. While respectful of the legacy of the FLH, CHA leaders were openly critical of the FLH's revolutionary past, "a period of madness" in the eyes of some CHA leaders, with regard to both sexual liberation and radical economic change. Both were deemed dangerous liabilities. In their view, the FLH's attempt to liberate gays by subverting gender norms, attacking the "heterosexual patriarchy," and embracing Marxist solutions for ending societal oppression had undercut the appeal of the organization and accelerated its demise by offending Argentina's bourgeois values. Moreover, CHA leaders were convinced that in the new democracy, attempts at promoting sexual liberalization would have a similar, negative consequence by turning off potential allies of the gay movement within civil society and the political establishment. Of particular concern to CHA activists was that a reputation for radicalism would harm the possibility for the organization's incorporation into Argentina's prestigious human rights community, which the CHA and its leadership regarded as critical to both the organization's survival and its activism.

In contrast to the radical, Marxist-infused politics of the FLH, human rights and mainstreaming arguments opened up space for collaboration with other actors in civil society, like the business community and the more progressive members of Argentina's religious community. This more measured approach also had the benefit of unlocking access to the legal and political system, something that had proved quite elusive to the FLH. In forging ahead with its vision, the CHA believed that it could reinvent the mission of the FLH by charting a new gay rights agenda that was more reformist than revolutionary, but still sought to radically transform society.

Controversies, Cleavages, and Dissent

Predictably, the CHA's emphasis on human rights, social integration, and political autonomy invited controversy and even outright dissent. The most visible opposition came from the old, leftist gay guard, which saw in many of the newcomers, like Jáuregui, a blatant disregard for the legacy of the FLH. For these old hands, such as Perlongher, the absence of an anticapitalist, Marxist discourse and a revolutionary spirit within the CHA, suggested clearly by the embrace of a human rights-based discourse, was disheartening. There were also those who saw the FLH as an unrealistic model for the gay community in the 1980s but still believed that the CHA would benefit from an affiliation with the Peronists, such as Carlos Grasso, an early CHA member. Grasso eventually split with the CHA and attempted to create a gay group within the Peronist Party. The now-defunct Grupo de Jóvenes Gays y Lesbianas Construyendo Nuestra Sexualidad pointedly rejected the idea that gays were like anybody else. As self-identified intellectual inheritors of the FLH, this group placed "renewed importance on gay liberation" and valued marginality, emphasizing "that the rights-based discourse does not accord any value to difference. The group was also critical of what it termed "the mainstream movement," which it charged with "making short-term concessions in exchange for tolerance rather than adopting a longer-term perspective."[132]

Controversy and dissent were also prevalent within the CHA itself. Women, in particular, represented a particular challenge to the organization.[133] A key issue was the lack of representation of women within the organization's top leadership and the corresponding frustration that many women felt about being pushed to the margins in the decision-making processes of the organization. According to Bellucci's recollection of the origins of the CHA, at the time of the founding of the organization, in April 1984, only two women were part of the organization, Maria Teresa De Rito and her girlfriend Rosa, "and both had secondary roles in what was essentially a men's club." Both came to the CHA from the Peronist labor movement and self-identified as "homosexual and not 'feminist,'" and were "more cognizant of their oppression as lesbians than as females." Indeed, the identity of lesbian within the CHA was rare, and this became an issue in its own right. According to Fabiana Tuñez, an early activist within the CHA, the majority of women in the CHA identified themselves as "gay or homosexual": "We were very few, the ones who self-identify as lesbian." A related sore point for self-identified lesbians was that the early pronouncements of the CHA tended to identify its membership exclusively as "homosexual" and avoided direct references to "lesbian." In "La situación homosexual en la Argentina" (1985), the CHA's first public statement on the purpose of the organization, there are no references to lesbians but rather to "the homosexual population." In noting her frustration with the CHA's male leadership, Tuñez recalls that "there was no point in fighting because we accepted that the males had the power; they had the power of the voice, and they had the power of the money."

Some sectors of the lesbian movement were also uncomfortable with the CHA's overwhelming focus on human rights. This concern was not so much a critique of the idea of human rights. Rather, the critique noted that the inherent liberal, universalism of human rights tends to obfuscate the uniqueness of the discrimination faced by homosexual women. As explained by Elisabeth Jay Friedman, there is a gender critique in the way in which feminist lesbians criticize human rights. "It is easier for gay men to assimilate a patriarchal society by gaining liberal rights than it is for lesbians, who not only challenge gender norms, but also male dominance in general through their activism and their relationships."[134]

The role of women within the CHA began to change by the late 1980s, triggered by internal self-criticism, such as an editorial in Boletín de la CHA of 1985 written by María Paz and titled "Y nosotros cuando?" (When do we get our turn?). The essay bemoaned the state of women within the CHA by noting: "We have to come into the light. . . . In discussions of homosexuals, only men are mentioned, very rarely is the focus on women. Many women have left the organization, they have thrown in the towel." That same year, 1985, the group Mujeres de la CHA (Women of the CHA) was formed by seven women activists with the purpose of debating the double oppression that gay women felt: first as women and then as lesbians. To that end, the group organized meetings and conferences on the unique challenges faced by lesbian women and on the idea of uniting men and women in the battle against homophobia. Essays on these subjects began appearing more often in CHA publications, such as Informativo Mensual de la CHA and Vamos Andar. In fact, Vamos Andar opened a section specifically devoted to lesbian readers. By the mid-1990s, women were making significant headway within the CHA. Mónica Santino, vice president of the organization between 1993 and 1996, notes that by 1992 women occupied eight of the twelve slots in the CHA's governing board, and that women were involved in most if not all decision-making aspects of the organization.[135]

The CHA's strong emphasis on social integration and seeming discomfort with "lesbians" also put the organization directly at odds with the transsexual and transvestite communities, which by the late 1980s were becoming quite visible in Argentina. The accepted wisdom is that from its very founding the CHA was outright hostile toward both. Bellucci's interview with Belén Correa, founder of the Asociación de Travestis de Argentina, reveals the apparent discrimination against the transvestites within the national gay movement that the CHA was attempting to lead. "On the door of the gay club Contramano (where the CHA was conceived) there was a sign that read transvestites not allowed. During the first, second, and third gay pride marches (in the 1990s), we had to fight not only the heterosexual community but also the 'classic' gays and lesbians."[136]

As noted in the next chapter, internal tensions and divisions within the CHA, paired with the stress of the continuing repression of homosexuals by the state well into the new democratic regime, and the new challenges posed by the AIDS epidemic, would eventually take a tremendous toll on the organization. All of this contributed to several organizational breakdowns, some notable splits, and a near-death experience. But out of the CHA's growing pains emerged a stronger and more diverse gay rights movement, one strong enough to revolutionize both the gay community and the nation as a whole.

CHAPTER 4

Human Rights and the Argentine Gay Rights Campaign

On March 2, 1992, the Comunidad Homosexual Argentina (CHA) was granted *personería jurídica* (legal or official status), a requirement for any organization wanting to lobby the government, to receive state grants, and to raise funds.[1] This action came nearly a decade after the advent of democracy in Argentina, and in the wake of a protracted political and legal struggle that went all the way to the Argentine Supreme Court. Securing legal status for the CHA became the launch pad for the expansion of the gay rights movement in Argentina. It also set the stage for a stunning string of gay rights victories in the posttransition era, including, most notably, same-sex marriage and adoptions in 2010. More importantly, at least for the purposes of this study, the legalization of the CHA is emblematic of how gay activists in Argentina went about realizing their objectives in the new democratic regime. As it pursued legalization, the CHA displayed an impressive arsenal of strategies, drawing largely from the playbook used by the Argentine human rights community. These strategies included aggressive litigation, pressure tactics designed to shame public officials, media campaigns intended to influence public opinion, and, most suggestively, perhaps, reinforcement from abroad.

Timed to coincide with the advent of the administration of Peronist president Carlos Saúl Menem, the second of the democratic period, the CHA's petition for legality was submitted to the Office of the Inspector General in early 1990. It reflected the organization's desire to publicly engage the state and civil society in advancing civil rights for gays and lesbians, much the same way in which Argentine exiled activists had experienced gay activism in Europe and the United States. In a terse decision issued on July 12, 1990, the government squelched this desire for openness and legality. In denying the petition, Inspector General Alberto González Arzac noted that the activism of the CHA "was not compatible with the conception of the common good, as an expression of the public or general interest," and that legalization of the CHA would amount to recognizing a "hybrid third gender," adding that "homosexuality, according to the National Academy of Medicine, is a deviation of the normal sexual instinct that impedes the formation of the family and actually directly threatens the family."

After the government's rebuke, the CHA decided to try its luck with the courts. On November 22, 1991, the Supreme Court ruled, in a vote of six to two, that the CHA's appeal lacked merit, noting that the constitutional right to free association was not violated since the CHA could continue to operate as a "civic association." More importantly, however, the court determined that "the constitutional rights to freedom of expression and association were circumscribed by the state's need and duty to uphold public morals and the common good," a potentially devastating blow to the CHA and the evolution of gay rights in Argentina. For the government this was a pyrrhic victory, however, if there was ever one. Only months after winning at the Supreme Court, the Menem administration dramatically reversed itself and legalized the CHA. Prompting the reversal was a year long international campaign intended to pressure and shame Menem for his refusal to legalize the CHA. By the time the CHA was legalized, the issue had become one of the biggest political headaches for the new administration.

For much of 1991, CHA activists, working in concert with foreign gay rights organizations, picketed Argentine embassies and consulates in Europe and the United States to pressure the government into legalizing the organization. The most high profile of these demonstrations was held in February 1991 in front of the Argentine consulate in New York, organized by the CHA in collaboration with ACT UP's New York chapter. The demonstration attracted considerable attention in the Spanish-speaking media, and drew some sixty activists, with some wearing a strip of pink fabric around the heads in the style of Las Madres de la Plaza de Mayo, while others covered their heads completely in a manner reminiscent of the protests against the Dirty War. Among the most notable cardboard signs on display was one showing ACT UP's slogan Silence = Death, in Spanish, inscribed onto the Argentine flag. Another one showed *Mafalda*, the world-famous Argentine cartoon, demanding recognition of the CHA with a typically stern expression. The demonstration was followed by a media campaign in the Buenos Aires newspapers paid for by ACT UP, which highlighted the CHA's struggle for legalization as part of Argentina's commitment to human rights.

Pressure on Menem reached its peak during a November 1991 seven-day trip to the United States that was intended, according to the *New York Times*, to "enhance the image of Argentina as a close friend to Washington and attract billions of dollars in loans and investment to rebuild Argentina's struggling economy." Instead, due to the endeavors of gay activists at home and abroad, the trip became a major irritant for the Argentine president. A CHA official, Rafael Freda, managed to obtain Menem's schedule (usually not announced in advance) and, ably aided by an Argentine activist working at the San Francisco–based International Gay and Lesbian Human Rights Commission, lined up American gay rights organizations to show up basically everywhere Menem went, including ACT UP, the Metropolitan Church (a Protestant gay denomination), the International Lesbian, Gay, Bisexual, Trans and Intersex Association, the United States National Lesbian and Gay Task Force, and the World Congress of Gay and Lesbian Jewish Organizations.

At a New York press conference that Menem expected would burnish his "prestige," he was confronted with protestors carrying blown-up photographs of AIDS patients chained to their beds at a hospital in Buenos Aires, of homosexuals murdered or tortured by the Argentine police, and of three Argentine gay males who had been given asylum in Canada after claiming that, because of their sexuality, they feared for their lives. A speech at Columbia University's School of International and Public Affairs that Menem intended to serve as the basis for a discussion of trade and investment opportunities in Argentina instead turned into a debate about discrimination against sexual minorities in Argentina. A former member of the CHA active with ACT UP Americas asked Menem: "How democratic is Argentina if a minority group does not enjoy the right of free and legal association?"

Menem's answer stunned the audience, and especially the activists: "Dear friend, Argentina is over the issue of establishing legal recognition of the CHA." Before reaching Washington to address a joint session of Congress, Menem's aides were already in touch with CHA officials in Buenos Aires to inform them that Menem intended to legalize the CHA upon his return home and to ask the organization to call off its dogs. No official reason was given for Menem's change of heart about the CHA, but according to CHA activists, the protests were imperiling the realization of something that the president cared a great deal about: improving the image of Argentina abroad and, more specifically, projecting a new image of Argentina as a modern, First World nation.

As seen in this chapter, the determination, resourcefulness, and ingenuity that led to the legalization of the CHA reflected nearly a decade of experience by CHA activists in battling the Argentine state, building extensive ties to domestic human rights groups, and working in concert with foreign gay rights activist networks. Less apparent is that by 1992 the CHA had patiently laid down the groundwork for crafting the campaign for gay rights as a human rights crusade. This crafting process entailed utilizing human rights as a rhetorical device for humanizing homosexuals and legitimizing gay rights. It also involved putting society front and center in the struggle for gay rights, and, as suggested by the framing literature, creating multiple "frames" intended to facilitate acceptance by the public of homosexuality and of the notion of gay rights, to mobilize gays into action, and to disarm the foes of the gay community.[2]

Crafting a successful gay rights campaign in Argentina hinged not only on the skills of activists and their ability to come across as credible advocates of their cause, but also on the surrounding political environment in which this campaign was constructed. This point underscores the importance of "frame resonance," which stresses that successful framing strategies must evoke symbols prevalent in the culture at large in order for these strategies to have their desired psychological impact.[3] In this respect, as shown next, the overall framing of the campaign for gay rights as a human rights crusade in Argentina got off to a very auspicious start in the new democracy given the emphasis that the Raúl Alfonsín administration, of the Radical Civic Party gave to human rights. Gay activists were able to capitalize upon this human rights emphasis to relaunch gay activism after the hiatus imposed by the military dictatorship, to begin to raise the issue of antigay discrimination in the context of human rights abuses under the old regime and the new democracy, and to gain admission into the political community.

THE ALFONSÍN YEARS, 1984–1989

Among the Latin American nations that undertook to democratize during the 1980s, Argentina stands out for the extent to which it adopted human rights as its guiding framework for consolidating democratic governance. This was largely dictated by the strength of the local human rights movement, which was propelled to national and international prominence by the massive scale of human rights abuses of the departing military regime.[4] Argentina's posttransition human rights movement was fronted by Las Madres de la Plaza de Mayo, the group of mothers and grandmothers that began to demand answers from the military regime about the whereabouts of their children and grandchildren that had been made to "disappear" while under the custody of the state.[5] Initially dismissed as *las Locas* (the crazy ones), Las Madres eventually grew into the most influential group in Argentine civil society and played a significant role in bringing together a coalition of human rights organizations that defended the "traditional rights of the person—life, liberty, and personal security."[6]

Undoubtedly the greatest achievement of Argentina's posttransition human rights movement was to put pressure on the government to undertake prosecution of members of the old military regime on human rights violations; a first for a Latin American government. This was also the first time since the landmark Nuremberg International Tribunal (organized by the United States and Britain at the end of World War II to bring justice to Germany's Nazi regime) that the world had witnessed a war crimes prosecution.[7] Argentina's military trials, which commenced on April 22, 1985, following the completion of the report by the truth commission, which the Alfonsín administration used to file charges against the military regime, became a defining moment of the new democracy. Testimony was heard from some eight hundred witnesses, most of whom recounted unspeakable crimes and offenses. The trials succeeded in convicting all the major players of the old regime, including the former head of the junta, Jorge Videla, who received the maximum sentence allowed by the law: life in prison.

Crafting a Gay Rights Campaign

The prominence of human rights in Argentina's new democracy provided a golden opportunity for launching the human rights-inspired gay rights activism of the CHA, even though the Alfonsín administration never acknowledged that the notion of human rights extended beyond the political crimes committed by the military regime, and that by and large it ignored the existence of the CHA. For starters, the Alfonsín administration's attention to human rights abuses allowed gay activists the opportunity to highlight the repression and violence inflicted on the gay community by the military at the very time when the nation was focused on matters of state repression and violence. To those ends, the CHA devised an inaugural public relations campaign intended to make the Argentine public aware of the repression and violence against homosexuals in Argentina at the hands of the military, and of the continuing repression of homosexuals in the new democracy, as well as to introduce the CHA to the Argentine public.

For its first-ever media campaign, paid for with money raised "from passing a cup in places where gays congregated, like clandestine bars," and published in the daily *Clarín* on May 28, 1984, the CHA employed the slogan "With Discrimination and Repression There Is No Democracy."[8] The advertisement argued that "there will never be a true democracy if society permits the existence of marginalized sectors and the methods of repression are still in place." It concluded by noting that more than 1.5 million Argentine gays are "preoccupied with the national situation" and that "they experienced with the rest of the nation the hard years of dictatorial rule." The point of the advertisement was to "question the democracy of the period" in light of the continuing human rights abuses of the gay community.[9] Moreover, in making the connection between democracy and antigay discrimination, the CHA invited the public to connect the suffering of the gay community under military rule with that of the rest of Argentine society while also aiming to incorporate ending antigay discrimination into the nation's democratization agenda. This early media campaign was a textbook case of "injustice framing."

Early media strategies by the CHA also included the public self-outing of several CHA officials with the intention of demonstrating how the repression of the time affected ordinary gays and lesbians, a notable example of "motivational framing." On May 23, 1984, CHA president Carlos Jáuregui and another CHA member, Raúl Soria, a "fake boyfriend," declared their homosexuality by being featured with their arms around each other in a cover story of the national magazine *Siete Días* with the title "The Risk of Being Homosexual in Argentina." Among the subjects covered in the article was the harassment of gays by the police and the discrimination that gays faced in the workplace, universities, housing, and government agencies for no reason other than whom they chose to love. Success was achieved on at least three key fronts.

The unprecedented act of self-outing prompted many gays and lesbians to do the same, motivated by the fact that "never in the history of Argentina had anyone given his or her face for the cause of gay rights."[10] Moreover, the *Siete Días* cover story signaled the start of a shift in how the Argentine media dealt with the issue of homosexuality. A May 28, 1984, article in *Clarín* about gay rights, human rights, and democracy was one of the first sympathetic treatments of homosexuality in Argentina to appear in a mainstream publication. By the early 1990s, it is reported that stories about homosexuality in the media were jettisoning "a sensationalistic and stigmatizing tone" and adopting "a more respectful tone," by telling stories of the everyday lives of gays and lesbians as well as by denouncing acts of discrimination.[11] Self-outing, or "letting people know," also changed the image of gays in society and this, in turn, contributed to facilitating societal acceptance of homosexuality. According to Analía del Franco, general director of the polling firm Analogías: "A turning point in people's perception of gays (which traditionally has veered toward a caricature) was when they began to view them as ordinary people, with jobs, feelings, etc. . . . Once people began to relate to gays as ordinary people, they concluded that they are just like me."[12]

The prestige and legitimacy that the Alfonsín administration accorded human rights also enhanced and accelerated the CHA's desire for incorporation into the human rights community as a means for accessing membership into the body politic. Alongside organizing the truth commission and ordering the prosecution of the military on crimes against humanity, the Alfonsín administration pursued a host of policies intended to raise the profile of human rights, such as grants for fledgling human rights organizations and the creation of new bureaucracies within the state to monitor human rights compliance, like the Ministry of Human Rights, whose job it was to secure compliance with human rights conventions. As seen previously, from the very onset of democracy, the CHA sought membership in Argentina's large and influential network of human rights organizations by adopting an unabashed human rights identity. But securing incorporation into the human rights community proved to be a struggle in its own right.

Journalist and feminist activist Mabel Bellucci notes that "while some human rights leaders embraced the CHA at a personal level, such as Laura Bonaparte of Las Madres de la Plaza de Mayo, this was not the case of the human rights community as a whole, with most human rights organizations seeing gay activists as extraterrestrial and regarding their involvement with gay issues as a detriment to their own cause."[13] It was also the case that the human rights community did not initially welcome the introduction of sexuality as part of the dialogue on human rights. CHA president César Cigliutti recalls that "at the inception of democracy not a single human rights organization supported the CHA as a legitimate human rights organization, and none of them regarded sexuality as an appropriate subject in the field of human rights, but we persevered—we went to all the marches convened by the human rights organizations with our CHA flag and banners, and we also joined Las Madres on their weekly demonstrations at the Plaza de Mayo, and slowly we came to be accepted by the human rights community and our struggle was folded into their struggle."[14]

Perseverance paid off. An early step toward acceptance into the human rights community came on September 20, 1984, when a CHA delegation attended the public ceremony held in the historic Plaza de Mayo where the CONADEP delivered its final report to President Alfonsín. This, the first public outing for the CHA, was a bittersweet moment for gay activists, given the report's silence on the repression of the homosexual community under the military regime. As noted in the previous chapter, the report is mum on the repression of homosexuals because the commission members could not ascertain if gays had been targeted because of their political affiliations or because of their sexual orientation. Another important step arrived in March 1986, for the commemoration of the tenth anniversary of the military coup, convened by Las Madres. Under the banner of "Justice and Punishment for the Guilty," the CHA marched alongside other human rights organizations. In May 1987, the CHA was invited for the first time to join a roster of nine "historic human rights organizations" to chart the course of future strategies for the human rights movement as a whole. This event came in the wake of the first of four *carapintadas* rebellions, the series of mutinies by army officers upset with the government's prosecution of the military on human rights abuses.

In the ensuing years, the incorporation of gay rights organizations into Argentina's large network of human rights organizations would be formally recognized. CHA officials became active participants in the reviews conducted by the United Nations Human Rights Council on the condition of human rights in member states, especially the "universal period review," which takes place every four years. CHA officials were also part of the process of civil society consultation that took place around the reform of the Argentine constitution in 1994, which led to, among other things, a stipulation that granted all international agreements signed by Argentina the status of domestic constitutional law, including the 1948 Universal Declaration of Human Rights, and the 1969 American Convention on Human Rights, also known as the Pact of San José, which Argentina ratified in 1984 and is overseen by the Inter-American Commission on Human Rights. Making these agreements a reference point of policy and jurisprudence was a priority for all human rights organizations in Argentina during the process of constitutional reform, including the CHA.

In folding itself and its struggles into the Argentine human rights community, the CHA adopted many of the features and strategies of this community. For one thing, the CHA avoided affiliations with the party system, resulting from a strong desire to be "nonpartisan," a desire anchored in the belief that gay rights transcend political divisions. The CHA, much like other human rights organizations, also cultivated close relations with the state's expanding human rights bureaucracy created by the Alfonsín administration to monitor human rights conditions and to coordinate human rights efforts between the government and human rights organizations.

In 1984, CHA officials began periodic meetings with Eduardo Rabossi, sub-secretary for human rights at the Ministry of the Interior, to discuss the state of the gay community in Argentina.[15] The most urgent issue discussed with Rabossi was police abuse and violence toward gays at the hands of the Ministry of the Interior, led by Antonio Tróccoli, who, according to Cigliutti, imposed a "moralistic brigade mentality within the police."[16] In 1986, CHA president Alejandro Salazar accepted a human rights position within the Ministry of the Interior.

Following the trend modeled by other human rights organizations of prioritizing litigation to achieve their ends, the CHA created a legal division, the first of its kind for a gay rights organization in Latin America, devoted to collecting and filing charges of human rights abuse perpetrated against the gay community and providing free legal advice and services to those detained by the police. The CHA legal strategy was born out of the repression to which the gay community was subjected in the early years of democracy, including, most notably, the arrest of CHA president Jáuregui in 1985 for participating in a peaceful demonstration. He appealed his detention (and won), which inaugurated a pattern of gay activists seeking to advance their rights through the courts. This "success" emboldened the organization to fight discrimination not only in the everyday life of the gays and lesbians, but also the symbolic discrimination enshrined in Argentine law. Underscoring the latter point was a law in the province of Buenos Aires that barred gays from voting, though (for obvious reasons) this provision was virtually unenforceable. The law was unearthed by the CHA's legal team as part of their scouting of all legal discrimination against gays in the books.

Finally, the CHA, like other human rights organizations, was invested in publicizing the crimes of the old regime. The overarching goal of this endeavor was to raise awareness about the repression that the gay community endured from 1976 to 1983, with the intention of memorializing the victims and enhancing the prospects for justice and accountability. To highlight this repression, gay activists have tended to depict the old regime not only as a ruthless killing machine of homosexuals, but also as "genocidal state," a charge common to the Argentine human rights community. These efforts are more than self-evident in Carlos Jáuregui's *La Homosexualidad en la Argentina*. Published in 1987, only a few years after the founding of the CHA, the book charts Jáuregui's journey as a gay activist alongside tales of repression of Argentina's gay community at the hands of a murderous political regime. The book's most famous passage is the unproven charge of four hundred killings by the military regime.

The advent of Carlos Saúl Menem's administration, in July 1989, ushered in one of the most challenging periods for the gay rights movement in the posttransition years; this, in turn, forced the coming of a more rights-oriented agenda. Unlike the previous administration, the Menem administration seemed quite disinterested in human rights, which dealt a blow to the CHA's strategic prioritizing of human rights. A silver lining of the period, however, was the new trends in international gay activism coming to Argentina from the United States and stemming primarily from the battle against HIV/AIDS. Ironically, the Menem administration, through its refusal to legalize the CHA and its inept response to the AIDS epidemic, would play a direct role in the successful exportation of these trends to Argentina. Both strengthened the connections of Argentine gay rights groups to their counterparts in the United States.

To be sure, the decline of human rights policies began well before Menem came to office. Despite a firm commitment to justice and accountability on the part of President Alfonsín, in the end he was only able to attain "partial justice."[17] In the face of several military rebellions that directly threatened the stability of the new democratic regime, and confronting the prospect of a judicial backlog of military prosecutions that could potentially paralyze the judicial branch, the Alfonsín administration ultimately settled on a delicate balance between justice and peace by passing laws that limited the extent and scope of human rights violations. In 1986, the Ley de Punto Final (Full Stop Law), which stipulated that any charges not filed within sixty days would not reach trial, went into effect; and in 1987 the Ley de Obediencia Debida (Due Obedience Law), which allowed amnesty for lower-level military officers who could claim a defense that "they were only following orders from their superiors," was enacted.

But Menem was outright dismissive of human rights. In October 1989, he issued a presidential pardon to two hundred military officers, including Leopoldo Galtieri, a former president and army general, intended to end military prosecutions once and for all. He justified this action as necessary to shore up the stability of the new democracy. The human rights community, including the CHA, broadly interpreted these actions as an attempt to undermine the community by shutting down the channels used to demand retribution against and accountability from the old regime. According to Las Madres leader Rene de Epelbaum, Menem's pardons were "mock justice."[18]

Overt hostility toward homosexuality was another characteristic of the new administration. Gays and lesbians were certainly made to feel unwelcome within the Menem administration and all Peronist institutions, a point stressed by Menem himself, who proudly boasted that "there are no militant gays and lesbians in my party."[19] He was also in the habit of ridiculing homosexuals, even in public.[20] The Menem administration also clashed with gay activists over the CHA's request for legal recognition. As seen previously, Menem turned down the request for legalization, a decision reaffirmed by Argentina's Supreme Court, before dramatically reversing himself a year later, after he was subjected to an international shaming campaign.

The CHA's legalization in 1992 opened the floodgates for a dramatic expansion of the Argentine gay rights movement, one of the few bright spots for civil society under the Menem administration, whose neoliberal economic policies drove a stake through the heart of the trade unions and other popular movements.[21] New organizations, such as the Sociedad de Integración Gay-Lésbica Argentina (SIGLA), founded by two former CHA members, Rafael Freda and Alfredo Manes, began to challenge the CHA's hegemony over the gay movement and to give the CHA some competition for international foreign aid. Only the second gay rights organization in Argentina to attain legal status, SIGLA questioned the CHA's programmatic priorities, especially the lack of a more straightforward approach for advancing civil rights protections for sexual minorities.

Lesbian groups also experienced something of a boom during the Menem years, with the rise, among other groups, of Convocatoria Lesbiana, Las Lunas y las Otras, and Lesbianas a la Vista. While for the male-oriented organizations like the CHA the AIDS issue was the driving concern, lesbian groups were focused on feminism and gender discrimination. Irene Ocampo, a journalist and lesbian-feminist activist from Rosario, and cofounder of the group Las Safinas de Lesbianas Feministas, notes: "For some feminist and lesbian groups, it was a priority to develop an activism that was closer to the defense of the human rights of lesbians and that put a spotlight on the many ways in which the hetero-patriarchy oppresses not only lesbians, but also transsexuals and the intersex."[22] Also new to the era were groups like Travesti Unidas and Asociación Travesti Argentina, which sought to advance acceptance of the transvestite and transgender population, and Iglesia de la Comunidad Metropolitana, the Argentine branch of Metropolitan Church USA.

More important, perhaps, the Menem administration showed considerable ineptitude, and even callousness, in the face of the HIV/AIDS epidemic. Public officials first detected the HIV virus in Argentina in 1982, and by 1993, the number of people infected in Argentina had reached an estimated one hundred thousand, putting the country third in South

America in the overall number of infections, behind Brazil and Colombia.[23] Yet it was not until 1990, under national and international pressure, that the Argentine Congress approved a national AIDS law. Described be some analysts as coming "too late" and "half-hearted," the law emphasized that individuals have the right to make their own decisions concerning treatment of the illness, physician-patient confidentiality, nondiscrimination against virus carriers, and information and education on all aspects related to AIDS and its transmissions.[24] In 1994, another AIDS law was enacted requiring all healthcare providers to cover AIDS treatment and compelling the Ministry of Health to cover medical costs for those unable to do so on their own.

The 1990 law was accompanied by the creation of a national AIDS program, intended to develop national strategies for fighting HIV infection. These strategies, however, left a lot to be desired. Influenced by the Vatican, the Argentine Conference of Bishops, and the World Council of Churches, the Menem administration's AIDS policy reflected negative stereotypes about homosexuals and ignorance about how the epidemic was spread.[25] Archbishop of Buenos Aires Antonio Quarracino spoke for many within the Catholic establishment when he referred to homosexuals as "a dirty blemish on the face of the nation" and called for them to be "segregated."[26] Gay activists responded with a legal stunt by suing the cardinal for his inflammatory comments. The suit was never heard in court, but it "prompted discussions about discrimination and acceptance of sexual minorities in the media."[27]

For years into the epidemic, the Menem administration promoted Pope John Paul II's "condemnation of promiscuity" in its publicity to prevent HIV infection and opposed the free distribution of condoms and frank discussion of how the HIV virus was transmitted.[28] This approach led to some serious missteps in the government's efforts to contain the epidemic in Argentina. In 1991, when opposing the free distribution of condoms, the executive director of the government's AIDS policy, Dr. Alfredo Miroli, argued that "the benefits of condoms did not justify the State's expenditures." In June 1996, it was reported that Argentina risked losing a $20 million loan from the World Bank for AIDS patients as a result of the Ministry of Health's refusal to promote the use of condoms and clean syringes. According to the ministry, the Bank's condition "affected the State's policy." It was not until 1998 that the Ministry of Health (with support from the World Bank) began to finance AIDS prevention campaigns.

Thus it fell mainly on the CHA to shoulder the responsibility of educating the Argentine public about HIV/AIDS, aided financially and programmatically by international organizations and NGOs, including the Norwegian Red Cross, the American Foundation for AIDS Research, Human Rights

Watch, and Canada's Civil Liberties Association. By the late 1980s, the CHA was devoting all of its energy and resources to STOP-SIDA, Argentina's first AIDS prevention campaign, and to establishing links with groups in the healthcare sector to provide treatment for those affected by AIDS. The organization's newsletter *Vamos a Andar*, traditionally a venue for educating the public about homophobia and antigay discrimination, rapidly shifted its focus to AIDS education and prevention. According to Cigliutti, the CHA "had no choice but to focus all of its energy on the AIDS crisis. For many gays AIDS was a double crisis: they had the virus and they were being blamed for the epidemic."[29]

Importing American-Style Activism

By the early 1990s, drained of its financial resources and experiencing a severe case of leadership fatigue, the CHA stopped its AIDS-related programs and, for a short while, suspended operations. A nearly crippling blow to the organization was the departure of several of its founders, including Jáuregui, Cigliutti, Ferreyra, and the writer Alejandro Modarelli, to form Gays por los Derechos Civiles ("Gays DC"). Established in 1991, this new gay rights group was very keen on taking the CHA's gay activism beyond the all-consuming issue of AIDS, which by 1991 had become the sole focus on the CHA, as well as becoming a more inclusive organization than the CHA by aiming to represent all sexual minorities, especially those facing marginalization within the LGBT community, such as transsexuals and transvestites. "The origin of our struggle is the dream for all types of freedom," was Gays DC's motto.

In recalling the roots of the split, Cigliutti acknowledges "questions of power and personal rivalries among the top leaders."[30] Nonetheless, Cigliutti characterizes the separation as "never hostile" and as born out of the frustration that he and others shared about the CHA having become "too big and weighed down by bureaucratic processes. So it was with a heavy heart that some of the original members were forced to leave." He admits, however, that the CHA was divided over the issue of transsexuals and the role they played in the fight for gay rights. Ultimately, Cigliutti notes, "The split was purely based on Gays DC's wanting to do business more effectively." In recalling the split, Modarelli echoes Cigliutti when observing that "the CHA was no longer conscious of the changes afoot in the international front."[31]

Implicit in the recollections of Cigliutti and Modarelli was the desire to infuse Argentina's gay rights activism with the activism that the HIV/AIDS crisis had unleashed in the United States. This desire, notes Pablo

Ben, a former member of the CHA in the early 1990s, is underscored by the "American-sounding name given to the organization."[32] In particular, Gays DC aspired to emulate ACT UP, an organization whose protests and provocative acts of civil disobedience were setting the standard for gay activism across the United States and much of Western Europe. Making ACT UP especially attractive to gay activists in Argentina was the special connection the American group had to Argentina.

As seen previously, CHA activists had worked closely with ACT UP's New York branch as part of the transnational effort that led to the legal recognition of the CHA, an effort that former CHA official Freda notes "ACT UP activists adopted as one their own."[33] Recalling the tremendous influence of ACT UP in Argentina during the early 1990s, at the height of the AIDS epidemic, Freda adds that ACT UP had a powerful impact on Argentine gay activists, not only because its protest and legal activities were redefining international gay activism but also because ACT UP was willing to join the fight for gay rights in Argentina. He recalls ACT UP's funding of an effort, Comisión para Ayudar a la CHA (Commission to Help the CHA, or "CACHA"), which paid for newspapers ads in support of the CHA's mission and provided tactical expertise to local activists on how to achieve their goals.[34]

Despite its brief existence (the group closed shop in 1996), Gays DC reinvented gay activism in Argentina. The group embraced a more ambitious gay rights agenda than was typical of the CHA, such as asking Congress to change the civil code to allow for state recognition of same-sex relationships and to enact antidiscrimination legislation to protect those battling HIV/AIDS (these petitions went nowhere since no one in the Congress was willing to support them). Additionally, in contrast to the CHA, Gays DC sought more direct engagement with the political system, the congressional parties in particular, something that the CHA had by and large avoided. Some felt that direct political engagement was needed to effectively deal with antigay discrimination and to advance a more vigorous civil rights agenda. As noted by Ferreyra in 2008 when justifying breaking the CHA's long-standing tradition of keeping itself at a distance from the political parties: "In reality, we were not certain about engaging in a dialogue with the political parties, but since we spoke so much about rights it was indispensable that we had to relate to the parties since the lion's share of our demands had to go through the Congress, the legislature."[35]

Gays DC also pursued a more aggressive approach to litigating antigay discrimination. This was very much in the style of American HIV/AIDS legal clinics, which by the 1980s began suing private companies on discrimination charges. Gays DC was pivotal to a major legal victory on behalf of an individual dismissed from his employment because of his HIV/

AIDS status, although this victory happened after the organization was no longer active. In October 2002, a court forced two companies—ELMA (Empresa de Lineas Marítimas) and Prefectura Naval Argentina—to compensate the victim. This was the first recognized case of discrimination in the workplace related to AIDS in Argentina and in all of Latin America. Gays DC also intensified the legal fight against the police ordinances that allowed the police to harass, detain, and prosecute anyone (but usually sex workers, transvestites, and homosexuals) for things like cross-dressing, and public display of affection by same-sex couples.

Finally, Gays DC introduced an American-style and pride-focused gay activism to Argentina. Modarelli recalls that "we planned the first pride parade in Buenos Aires, with opposition from the CHA, which at the time was still focused on the idea of dignity."[36] Attended by all the existing gay organizations, Argentina's first gay pride parade (or march as it is generally referred to in Argentina to underscore the political nature of the event), was staged on July 2, 1992. Headed by Jáuregui and other notable gay personalities, the march drew some five hundred participants, many of them wearing masks due to the climate of the times, and followed the trajectory of all the great public demonstrations in Argentine history: from the Plaza de Mayo to the national Congress.

According to Bellucci, Buenos Aires' first gay pride march represented a novel way for the gay community to make itself noticed, for stressing the importance of coming out, for attracting media attention, and for projecting the growing politicization of the gay community.[37] The march also provided a venue for attacking the Menem administration's opposition to the legalization of the CHA and its inattention to the HIV/AIDS crisis, and for calling for action to move the gay rights movement forward, in other words, a "prognostic frame." As Bellucci reports, Buenos Aires' first gay pride marches had a strong "anti-Menem" orientation. Many gay activists opposed Menem's neoliberal economic policies, and almost all were appalled by his response to the AIDS crisis. But for the participants the march was also an inflection point, with many activists demanding a more straightforward civil rights agenda for the gay movement from leadership.

In 1997, Gays DC was folded into the CHA when Cigliutti assumed the presidency of a struggling CHA. But the legacy of Gays DC would live on, beginning with the transformation of the CHA itself. One of the key changes of the revamped CHA was to downsize the organization by allowing only serious activists to have a say in the organization's activities. The intention was to make the organization more nimble in its everyday operations and more effective at lobbying the government and accessing the judiciary. More important, however, was delineating a new mission for the organization. While the CHA would continue educating the public about ending antigay discrimination and promoting the social integration of gays into mainstream society based on core human rights demands, it would also seek to emerge as the nation's forefront organization for advancing the civil rights of the gay community.

Capitalizing on Constitutional Reforms

An unexpected boon for gay civil rights during the Menem era came as a result of the reformation of Argentina's constitution in 1994, the first revision since the nineteenth century.[38] The reform of the constitution originated in the Pact of Olivos, a set of extraordinary political bargains between Menem and the leadership of the leading opposition party, the Radicals. At the heart of the pact was Menem's desire for a second term, which was then prohibited by the constitution. But amending the Argentine constitution requires convening a constitutional convention agreed to by two-thirds of the chambers of the congress. Menem could comfortably get the convention approved in the Senate, but not in the Chamber of Deputies. Thus, in exchange for the Radicals' agreeing to support a change in the constitution that allowed Menem to run for re-election for a second term, Menem consented to a host of constitutional reforms that in retrospect provided numerous and unprecedented political opportunity structures for gay activists to advance their policy objectives.

Among the many changes and innovations introduced in the 1994 constitutional convention, the most consequential for gay rights was the granting of political autonomy to the Federal District of Buenos Aires. Indeed, save for the possible exception of allowing for the re-election of the president of the nation, the granting of autonomy to Buenos Aires was the most consequential for national politics of all the constitutional reforms introduced in 1994. Almost from the moment of the creation of the Autonomous City of Buenos Aires, which granted the residents of the Argentine capital the right to elect their own chief executive and to enact their own laws, provided that these laws did not contravene the national constitution, the city had emerged as a local-level laboratory for the political and legal strategies that gay activists would later employ to make gay rights, including same-sex marriage, a reality at the national level.

Following the example of several Scandinavian and Northern European countries, which began to legislate gay rights in the early 1990s, gay activists wasted no time to pressure the newly elected city legislature in 1996 into enacting legislation banning antigay discrimination, with the first opportunity for doing so provided by the drafting of the city's new constitution. To that end, gay activists capitalized on some of the personal connections that they had made with several members of the city council during the early years of democracy, like Enrique Rodríguez, who worked with Cigliutti at the Ministry of Labor to lobby in favor of the ban. They also worked with civil rights and human rights organizations, journalists, and academics to coordinate the message that discrimination on the basis of sexual orientation was a human rights violation. Despite all of these efforts, and much to the chagrin of gay activists, the constitution's first draft failed to ban discrimination based on sexual orientation.

In challenging this oversight, gay activists staged a protest that blended foreign influences inspired by ACT UP with homegrown strategies derived from the Argentine human rights movement. Chief among these strategies were *escraches* (literally screeching), consisting of accosting someone at their place of work or residence in order to publicly humiliate them. This strategy was pioneered in 1995 by HIJOS (Sons and Daughters for Identity and Justice Against Oblivion and Silence), an organization created to raise awareness about the issue of the disappeared. Initially used to target officers who were spared human rights prosecution for their participation in the Dirty War, the strategy has been adopted by numerous other social movements in Argentina and other parts of the Spanish-speaking world, including Spain.

On August 27, 1996, some twenty gay activists stormed the building where city council members were meeting armed with blown-up photos of former CHA president Carlos Jáuregui, who had died of AIDS the week before.[39] The activists, accompanied by members of the press, tracked down the members of the commission responsible for writing the new constitution and shamed them for speaking the language of human rights while ignoring the blatant human rights violations against the gay community. Then, meeting individually with each member of the city council, gay activists argued that a human rights charter that did not incorporate protections for sexual minorities failed to meet the city's aspiration of adhering to human rights standards. The activists' core demand was not that the members of the city council had to advance "gay rights" but rather that the council was compelled to protect the human rights of gay people. Success was unqualified. When the law was finally approved on August 30, 1996, unanimously and in homage to Jáuregui, Buenos Aires became the first Latin American city to ban antigay discrimination. Article 11 of Buenos Aires' new constitution reads:

It is acknowledged and guaranteed the right to be different. There will be no admission of discrimination that segregate people for reasons or pretexts of race, ethnicity, gender, sexual orientation, age, religion, ideology, opinion, nationality, physical traits, psycho-physical, social, economic or any other kind of circumstance that would suggest distinction, exclusion or restriction.

A new constitution banning antigay discrimination proved to be a powerful catalyst for future actions intended to end antigay discrimination in Buenos Aires and Argentina as a whole, beginning with a renewed effort by the CHA's legal department to abolish the infamous *edictos policiales*. This cause was first undertaken by the FLH in the 1970s and later adopted by Gays DC in the early 1990s. Success finally came on March 4, 1998, when the *edictos* were formally abrogated. In the end, the edicts fell in a rather anticlimactic fashion through a reformation of the City of Buenos Aires' civil code intended to put the code in line with the city's new constitution and its protections for individual freedoms. Nonetheless, the formal end of the *edictos* was hailed by the media as "a sign of progress in the establishment of a new constitutional order for the City of Buenos Aires."[40] Remnants of the edicts, however, would manage to survive in federal ordinances intended to protect the "social order" until at least 2003 when Minister of Interior Aníbal Fernández, armed with a ruling by the Inter-American Human Rights Court, compelled provincial governors to enact reforms to completely abolish the edicts.

The CHA also continued to press city officials on its treatment of the gay community's weakest and most marginalized members. In June 1998, the organization's lawyers made a splash in the media when they condemned the forced and violent removal by the federal police of the residents of the Aldea Gay (Gay Village), a Buenos Aires shantytown populated by several hundred people, including gays, transvestites, and teenagers forced to leave their homes because of their sexuality. The rationale used by the government to justify the forced relocation of the village's residents was rather ironic: to build the Parque de la Memoria, a public space that honors the memory of the disappeared under the military regime.

ECONOMIC CRISIS AND THE "QUEERING" OF BUENOS AIRES, 1999–2003

Another milestone for gay civil rights in Argentina arrived with the enacting of a civil unions law for same-sex couples for the residents of Buenos Aires in 2002. France's law of civil solidarity pacts, enacted by the French Parliament in 1999, provided the impetus for the pursuit of a similar law in Argentina. According to Pedro Paradiso Sottile, the CHA's legal coordinator,

"The French civil solidarity pacts showed the way for how to advance gay rights without having to adopt the institutions of heterosexual society."[41] He adds that the significance of the civil unions law in Argentina was "monumental—the law marked a before and after moment for the gay rights movement in Argentina by changing the environment in favor of rights for our community."

Introduced by CHA leaders with the backing of several left-wing legislators on August 28, 2001, the bill for civil unions was debated and approved by the Buenos Aires City Council on December 12, 2001. Mayor Aníbal Ibarra subsequently signed the bill into law, allowing it to come into effect in March 2002. This ordinance represented the first time that a jurisdiction in Latin America granted any kind of legal recognition to same-sex couples. The law granted same-sex couples in the Argentine capital living together for at least two years marriage-like benefits such as pension benefits, health insurance, and hospitalization visitation rights. CHA president Cigliutti and CHA secretary Marcello Suntheim, who were joined in partnership on July 18, 2002, inaugurated the law. Working in tandem with the CHA, other Argentine cities and provinces were soon to copy the Buenos Aires example, including the province of Rio Negro, the city of Villa Carlos Paz, and the city of Rio Cuarto.

According to the received wisdom, Buenos Aires' city officials came to legislate same-sex unions as a consequence of Argentina's plunge into economic despair during 2001–2002. What caused the plunge, "one of the most harrowing economic crises in Argentina's history,"[42] remains contested among students of Argentine politics—the excesses of Menem's neoliberal policies of the 1990s, fixed exchange rates, especially the pegging of the Argentine peso to the American dollar, and the lack of competitiveness of the Argentine economy, are but a few of the most notable explanations. Whatever the root cause of the crisis, within six months the economy had all but collapsed. Growth contracted by about a third (setting the GDP level back by almost a decade), the banking system was in tatters, the unemployment rate had soared to 22 percent of the active population, and one and a half million people had been driven into the rolls of the so-called new poor. Unable to reach an agreement with its international creditors, including the International Monetary Fund, Argentina defaulted on a $US 90 billion debt obligation, at the time the largest default for any country.

Equally severe was the crisis's toll on politics. Between October 2000 and August 2002, two presidents and five different ministers of the economy resigned. First to go was President Fernando de la Rúa of the Radical party, the former head of the Autonomous City of Buenos Aires, who had replaced Menem in 1999. He was forced to resign after he ordered a state of emergency that only served to aggravate the situation. On December 20–21, 2001, clashes between the police and demonstrators resulted in several people getting killed, precipitating the fall of de la Rúa, who, in one of the most indelible images of the crisis, fled the presidential palace (Casa Rosada) by helicopter.

In linking the economic collapse to the same-sex civil unions bill, many observers have made the point that denying civil rights to the gay community as the economy was in a free fall seemed pointless and even heartless. As noted bluntly by historian Osvaldo Bazán, "When people are eating out of garbage cans it really does not matter if you are gay or not."[43] CHA activists have offered a similar perspective by noting that the economic crisis created auspicious conditions for demanding state recognition of same-sex unions, given that the crisis engendered a political climate that was very receptive to claims of justice. "The year 2002 became the year of protests," recalls Sottile, and this happening provided a hospitable environment for gays to raise issues of fairness since the protests "brought out in Argentina the idea of social justice."[44] He adds that "due to the collapse, civil and social rights were brought to the public's attention and politicians were forced to pay special attentions to the demand of the people, who were obviously quite unhappy."

The reality of how the 2002 civil unions law came into being, however, is considerably more complex. In the end, the civil unions law hinged on persistence, compelling arguments, and clever strategizing. Gay activists, led by the CHA, were relentless in lobbying and pressuring city councilors to act. When CHA officials made their presentation to the City of Buenos Aires Human Rights Commission—the first step in the process of approval for the civil unions bill proposal—they brought the media along, an action that proved prescient. As recalled by Cigliutti, "The human rights commission was timid about considering the project at all. But with all the media around, they had to." More suggestive, still, when the commission appeared hesitant about acting on the proposal, gay activists unleashed a series of actions intended to shame the legislators. "We did *escraches* and the legislators got so scared that they had one of the longest sessions in recent history—almost eighteen hours, uninterrupted, from 1:00 p.m. to 6:00 a.m. the following day," recalls CHA secretary Suntheim.[45]

Gay activists also had to convince the city legislators that they had the authority to legislate family law in the first place. One of the principal arguments against the civil unions ordinance raised by some of the more conservative members of the city council was whether the council had the legal standing to legislate this issue. In their view, the issue of civil unions belonged in the national Congress rather than in the city legislature because this was a "family matter," and, as such, it had to be in accordance with the national civil code. By raising the technical issue of "standing," opponents of the measure were hoping to either preclude consideration of the measure altogether or to have the measure transferred to the national Congress, where it was sure to face a far less friendly reception, and perhaps no consideration at all.

In characteristic fashion, gay activists countered with points that stressed humanity over legality. When presenting the civil unions proposal to the legislators, gay activists highlighted the need for city officials to enact legislation that was "respectful about human rights" as well as the "importance of being tolerant toward different ideas, ideologies, sexual orientation, and ethnic and racial differences."[46] More suggestively, gay activists noted that the issues at stake with the civil unions ordinance pertained not to "family" but to "affection," "love," and "sexuality," and even "the rules of relationships."[47] They argued that civil unions would address the injustices being perpetrated upon same-sex couples whose relationships were not being recognized by the state, like the inability of same-sex couples to access the social benefits conferred to heterosexual couples, such as receiving the pension of a deceased partner or visiting a sick partner while convalescing at a hospital, while fostering "greater social cultural acceptance of the effective, erotic bonds between people of the same sex."

Gay activists were also quite astute and pragmatic in crafting the civil unions legislation. Seeking to avoid a perception of the law as "gay legislation," the drafters of the law agreed to include heterosexual couples. Clearly, this was generally seen as a gesture intended to broaden the appeal of the ordinance. But according to Suntheim, including heterosexuals as part of the legislation was about self-protection, a reflection of long-standing distrust on the part of gay activists of the state around matters related to homosexuality. "To create a civil union law just for gays is to create a blacklist—a register for homosexuals. Given the history of this country under the dictatorship in the 1970s, that's very dangerous."[48] In response to concerns by lawmakers that the civil union law would create a slippery slope down to marriage, gay activists insisted that civil unions, not marriage, was their ultimate goal as long as civil unions provided the same rights. Indeed, gay officials argued that they preferred civil unions to marriage. They viewed civil unions as "more progressive than marriage because civil unions free couples from excessive state regulations over their relationships."[49]

Before the bill's final vote, gay leaders met individually with the members of the council. These meetings were aided by the personal connections that gay activists had forged with the city legislators in the struggle to ban antigay discrimination. Especially useful to gay activists were those legislators, like Daniel Bravo, who had a personal connection to human rights (his father, Alfredo Bravo, a prominent human rights activist, was kidnapped and tortured by military), or who themselves were known for their human rights activism, such as María Elena Naddeo. As might be expected, the most reticent members of the council were those with religious objections. To bring them along, gay activists by and large avoided arguments about morality and instead deliberately stressed the council's commitment to advancing human rights, a cause now enshrined in the city's constitution. These arguments persuaded even the most devout Catholics in the council to support the bill. Recalling her vote for the bill, Alicia Perrini noted: "I have long been linked with the Church. But for me it was a question of dignity, equality, and rights. These people are asking for human rights and we have to give it to them."[50]

Another argument employed by gay activists with the legislators was that Argentine society, and the residents of Buenos Aires in particular, had already come on board with the idea of extending recognition to same-sex relationships, aided by evidence provided by editorials from major papers, public opinion surveys showing broad public support for the bill, and testimony from notable jurists. This evidence included a *Clarín* editorial describing the law as a "big step toward a constitutional democracy" and an expression of the city's commitment to "tolerance, pluralism and participation,"[51] and an endorsement from Graciela Medina, a judge known for her advocacy of LGBT rights, having ruled for the first time in Argentina in favor of extending benefits to a same-sex couple, and a legal advisor to the CHA. Medina's views were echoed by testimony from members of the law faculty of the University of Buenos Aires.

The Advent of the "Pink Economy"

A surprising development that followed the civil unions law was ushering in a "gay market" that made gays more visible than ever before, that brought gay culture into the mainstream, and that raised the political clout of the gay community. To jumpstart the economy, the government devalued the national currency by nearly 75 percent, which paved the way for the emergence of Buenos Aires as South America's new gay Mecca, a title long held by Rio de Janeiro. With what was once the most expensive city in South America suddenly a bargain for tourists, gay activists and Buenos Aires city officials devised a plan to make the Argentine capital a hot spot in the international gay-friendly tourist circuit by hosting such events as the international gay world cup and the international gay tango competition. In a short time, as observed by *The Economist*, the influx of "pink money" into Buenos Aires had become "a pillar of the city's economy."[52] According to 2007 estimates, 20 percent of all tourists in Buenos Aires were gay—300,000 a year—and they spent some $600 million.[53] It is thought that these figures have doubled since gay marriage became legal in 2010, with the growth in popularity of Buenos Aires as a "destination" wedding among same-sex couples around the world.[54]

Since the recovery of the Argentine economy, which began well before same-sex marriage became legal, the gay market has been strengthened as many businesses, especially those linked to tourism—airlines, restaurants, hotels, and retail stores—are nowadays eager to stress their gay-friendliness. More important in helping solidify the gay market is the entry of corporate behemoths of the information age such as Google, Motorola, and Apple into the Argentine economy. These corporations are known in the United States for offering gay-friendly benefits such as domestic partner benefits for same-sex couples and employment protection for transgender workers (well before these benefits were mandated by the government) and for sponsoring gay pride parades.

Such progay policies spread rapidly throughout the Argentine economy, as did direct business appeals to the gay community, spurred by the creation of the Argentine LGBT Chamber of Commerce, which is modeled after the American LGBT Chamber of Commerce. In making the pitch for why businesses should target homosexuals in their advertising, gay leaders in Argentina have made the familiar argument that gays have more disposable income than straights. "The gay market has more money to spend. There are families without children and families with few children and this impacts how spending decisions are made," according to Pablo de Luca, president of Argentina's LGBT Chamber of Commerce.[55]

To be sure, not every sector of the gay community in Argentina is either accepting of or a participant in the gay market and the commercialization of homosexuality. The gay market is certainly oriented toward the middle class at the domestic level and especially toward affluent gay males as it relates to tourism. This explains the rise of a small but not insignificant alternative gay community, affiliated with antiglobalization movements (many of whom rose to prominence after the 2001 economic implosion). It organizes its own counterprotest gay pride march in Buenos Aires (*la contramarcha*) intended to highlight the diversity of the gay community and its solidarity with transvestites, transsexuals, sex workers, drug users, and others who, according to sexual rights activist Alejandra Sardá, do not fit in "democratic, gay-mecca Argentina."[56]

An era of unprecedented cooperation between gay activists and the Argentine state arrived with the advent of the Néstor Kirchner administration in 2003, widely credited with stabilizing politics and the economy after the 2001 crash. Gay activists certainly welcomed the renewed attention to the issue of human rights granted by the new administration. Kirchner entered office noting: "We absolutely reject the identification between governance and impunity."[57] In keeping with that creed, Kirchner was quick to signal his support for efforts to revive the prosecution of military and police officers responsible for the Dirty War. Among other things, Kirchner repealed a de la Rúa administration decree barring Argentine judges from complying with foreign requests for the extradition of those suspected of human rights violations. He also endorsed bills passed in the Congress to annul the amnesty laws enacted by the Alfonsín and Menem administrations, as well as the decision by the Supreme Court in 2005 that declared unconstitutional the amnesty and presidential pardons given to the military.

More important to the advancement of gay rights was that, in response to the massive wave of mobilizations triggered by the economic meltdown, Kirchner introduced a "social justice" agenda that included direct dialogue with civil society organizations. In pursuit of this policy, in 2004 Minister of the Interior Fernández invited CHA officials to discuss how to expand civil rights for gays. The importance of this moment, according to Sottile, was twofold. "First, it was a symbol of the Kirchner administration reaching out to the gay community—and not the other way around since Fernández initiated contact—acknowledging that we mattered. Second, it put the CHA in contact with Fernández, who has proven to be one of our most important allies in our fight for human rights."[58]

Almost from the onset, conversations between the Kirchner administration and CHA leaders bore impressive results. CHA leaders were successful in enticing the Kirchner administration to support Brazil in its effort to introduce a 2003 resolution on "Human Rights and Sexual Orientation" to the United Nations Commission on Human Rights that called for the protection of the human rights of all persons regardless of their sexual orientation. The resolution was broadly denounced by the Vatican, which urged nations, especially those with Catholic-majority populations, to reject it. But Argentina took the unusual step of separating itself from the Vatican. Minister of Foreign Affairs Rafael Bilsa informed the Vatican that Argentina supported the resolution as part of its global support for human rights. Sottile argues that this break with the Vatican was important because it signaled that the government intended to pursue an agenda "independent from the Vatican" with respect to gay rights. An early sign of this stance came in 2006, when the government announced plans to end the ban preventing homosexuals from serving openly in the military.[59]

The Kirchner administration also brought gay activists into the drafting of the report of the National Plan Against Discrimination, a comprehensive review of the situation of all social groups in Argentina. Sponsored by the United Nations High Commission on Human Rights, it focused on those groups most likely to be discriminated against: women, immigrants, indigenous groups, and LGBT people.[60] The report's lengthy section on "sexual identity" summarized the history of the gay movement in Argentina, noting that "the Dictatorship fostered the disappearance of these movements whilst creating a scenario of persecution against Argentinean homosexuals," including "thousands of cases of police persecutions and tortures" and the "struggle by gay rights organization to incorporate issues of sexual identity into the agenda of human rights organizations." The report recommended enacting a same-sex civil unions law modeled on Buenos Aires' civil unions law to remedy discrimination against same-sex couples.

Even greater cooperation between gay activists and the government arrived in 2007 with the election of Cristina Fernández de Kirchner, Néstor's wife, as Argentina's first elected female president. Fernández de Kirchner's rise to power benefited tremendously from the popularity of her incumbent husband, who left office (after a single term) as "the most popular outgoing president in modern Argentine history," largely because of his success in reviving the country's economy.[61] Fueled largely by a competitive exchange rate and soaring commodity prices, Néstor grew the economy by 9 percent between 2003 and 2007, leading to a vast improvement in living standards. Unemployment and poverty rates were halved: unemployment fell from 20 percent in 2002 to 9 percent in 2007, while poverty rates fell from nearly 50 percent to 27 percent.

In August 2008, the social security administration began allowing same-sex couples that had lived together for at least five years to collect the pensions of their deceased partners, the first federal law affecting same-sex couples. This law was the culmination a decade-old struggle by CHA officials that was launched with a lawsuit involving Alfredo Pascale, a retired hairdresser whose claim to inherit the pension of his partner of forty-seven years had been denied by the government. Working in concert with the legal clinic of the University of Palermo, CHA lawyers took the case all the way to the Supreme Court. Following a landmark victory, the Fernández de Kirchner administration recognized the right of surviving gay partners to inherit the pension of their deceased partners provided that they could prove cohabitation for at least five years.

In February 2009, the national Congress passed a new military code that abolished a decades-old ban on gays serving in the armed forces, abolished capital punishment, and brought the military into the federal justice system. Gay activists hailed the lifting of the ban preventing gays from serving openly in the military as a milestone in the country's history. According to Sottile, this was "an institutional decision on the part of the Kirchner government to change the climate with respect to human rights and the democratization of the armed forces; a great symbolic action because the very organizations that were notable for the prosecution and murder of sexual minorities were now accepting of these same people."[62]

The Rise of the Marriage Equality Movement

There were limits to the Kirchners' support for gay rights, however. Néstor did not speak publicly about the CHA's 2005 proposal to extend Buenos Aires' civil unions law to the rest of the nation, which probably sealed the fate of that proposal. And Cristina was not, prior to 2010, the passionate advocate for LGBT rights that she is today. Although she came into office as the most socially liberal Peronist politician in history—given her support for contraceptives and gender quotas—during her historic 2007 campaign she remained largely mum on the issue of same-sex marriage. Her only comment on the subject was a radio interview she gave during the 2007 presidential campaign in which she noted that "it is in the free will of all men and women in Argentina to choose their sexuality," but also noted that "it is not an issue on which I have to express myself."[63]

Lack of support from the executive branch did not deter activists from pursuing their plans for state recognition of same-sex relationships. Same-sex marriage, in particular, was given a massive boost on July 3, 2005, when Spanish Prime Minister José Luis Rodríguez Zapatero signed same-sex marriage into law, making Spain only the third country in the world to do so. The impact of this foreign event, which was broadcast live in Argentine television and made the cover of all the local papers the following morning, on local activists cannot be overstated. According to María Rachid, the lesbian-feminist activist who led the fight for same-sex marriage: "The arrival of marriage equality in Spain in 2005 was a momentous occasion for us in Argentina. Before 2005, marriage equality existed only in a handful of places—Holland, in a few American states, and in South Africa, countries very different from Argentina; consequently, its approval in Spain, a country culturally similar to Argentina, both with a very strong Catholic Church, meant that it was also possible to do this in Argentina."[64] Bruno Bimbi, a journalist for the daily *Crítica* and Rachid's media director and chief strategist, notes that "Spain gave us the push we needed. . . Spain is the country that gave us our language and most of our traditions, it is the land of our grandfathers and our great-grandfathers."[65]

On June 28, 2006, within months of Spain's historic decision, a new group laser-focused on bringing same-sex marriage to Argentina emerged on the scene: the Federación Argentina LGBT (FALGBT). This organization's emergence constitutes the clearest and most compelling example of the role of local groups in transporting international gay rights trends and adapting them to the domestic environment. Esteban Paulón, the organization's current president, recalls: "We drew on Spain's experience with marriage equality—we saw the possibility of the marriage equality law passing in Argentina because of similar social structures. We immediately got into contact with LGBT groups in Spain, analyzing their strategy and applying them to our situation."[66]

Not surprisingly, the FALGBT fashioned itself after the Federación Estatal de Lesbianas, Gays, Transexuales y Bisexuales (FELGBT), the main gay rights group involved in the legalization of same-sex marriage in Spain. Alongside other Spanish gay NGOs, such as the Fundación Triángulo, the FELGBT provided financial support and political expertise to its Argentine offspring. Nowhere was this external influence more evident than in the FALGBT's insistence on same-sex marriage over same-sex civil unions. This insistence on marriage was conveyed in the slogan "Los mismos derechos con el mismo nombre" (The same rights with the same name), which anchored the campaign for same-sex marriage in both Spain and Argentina.

More suggestive still is that the Argentine activists' insistence on same-sex marriage reflected the evolution of Spanish gay politics. In the late 1990s, Spanish LGBT organizations rejected legislation proposed by the conservative administration of José María Aznar that would have given same-sex couples in Spain most of the rights associated with marriage, believing, in the words of former FELGBT head Beatriz Gimeno, "that if you do the smaller thing first, then you have to open the debate again, mobilize people again."[67] In her travels to Argentina, Gimeno held strategy sessions with local activists and progressive politicians. She strongly advised them against lowering their ambition, advice that FALGBT leaders took to heart. In the first meeting that FALGBT activists had with Minister of the Interior Fernández, on August 3, 2007, they asserted that "if the government does not support marriage equality, we will continue to seek refuge in the courts, and to work through the congress, the media, and the streets.

And if a civil unions bill is introduced in the Congress we will publicly oppose it on grounds that it is segregationist and discriminatory."[68]

Before it could succeed in its core mission, the FALGBT had to overcome a schism within the gay community over marriage. Between 2007 and 2010 this schism erupted into a veritable fratricidal war. Key differences in strategy and background between the leadership of CHA and the FALGBT underpinned the schism. Before the FALGBT came onto the scene, the CHA was already at work on the extension of Buenos Aires's same-sex civil unions law to the nation as a whole. Largely a reflection of the weakness of the gay movement outside Buenos Aires, attempts to copy the civil unions law in several other provinces had proved unsuccessful. To back the national civil union bill, in 2005 the CHA rolled out an elaborate media campaign focused on individual stories of same-sex couples and their struggles to be a family rather than on the abstraction of gay civil rights. One notable story concerned Martín Farach and Andrew Colton, a gay couple, and their five-year-old twins Lucas and Julia, who identified themselves as a "a regular, boring family, like any other."[69] The couple became a media sensation and were featured prominently in newspapers, including the conservative daily *La Nación*, alongside testimony from family experts "who stressed that what is important is the fulfillment of maternal and paternal functions, and not the gender of the person fulfilling them, thus tacitly endorsing adoption by same-sex couples."[70]

A sense of pragmatism also informed the CHA's favoring of civil unions over marriage. For many of the organization's leaders, marriage seemed an overreach that might trigger a backlash against the gay community. Civil unions, by contrast, enjoyed the support of conservative legislators, if only as a means for thwarting the momentum of the same-sex marriage bill. Moreover, although CHA president Cigliutti had married his partner (CHA secretary Marcello Sunthein) in Spain in January 2008, arguing that the absence of same-sex marriage in Argentina was forcing him to marry abroad (Cigliutti and Sunthein were able to marry in a European Union country because Sunthein holds both Argentine and German citizenship), many in the CHA leadership were ambivalent about the institution of marriage. This ambivalence reflected the debate about whether gays should adopt a heterosexual institution in which to encase their relationships or instead develop institutions of their own. "We are not happy with the institution of marriage," notes Sottile. "We wanted less government and church interference in the personal lives of people. Thus for us civil unions were more inclusive, more free, and with less entanglements and regulations."[71]

The CHA was also less than happy with the intervention of outside forces in the marriage debate in Argentina, which added an element of contention with the FALGBT. Tellingly, CHA officials declined to meet with the delegation from Spain brought by the FALGBT to assist in the battle for same-sex marriage, and chided the FALGBT for relying on foreign assistance (more than a bit ironic considering the CHA's long history of relying on reinforcements from abroad). As noted by Sottile, "The Spanish groups had a very clear agenda. It was marriage or nothing; that was their condition for working with Argentine gay groups." This intervention, according to Sottile, smacked of colonialism. "The independence of Argentina—politically, economically, and socially—is something that we take very seriously—and being told what to do did not sit well with us."

For the FALGBT, by contrast, civil unions were an unacceptable proposition. "There was no reason for perpetuating inequality and injustice," according to Rachid, who headed the FALGBT in its infancy.[72] She adds that, for her organization, "it was nonnegotiable that there would be two different kinds of institutions recognizing homosexual and heterosexual relationships." Defending her position, Rachid notes that when she was criticized by the CHA for overreaching in her ambition, she replied: "We stand for marriage equality, you [the CHA] stand for civil unions, but these positions do not have to undermine each other—quite the contrary. If marriage equality is not possible, you can carry on negotiating civil unions, and that will be a step in the right direction." Rachid, however, could barely hide her contempt for the CHA, even when attempting to praise the organization. "The CHA is an important organization; they have a great history in Argentina. But it is an organization of gay males—lesbians and transsexuals occupy secondary positions in the leadership."

The FALGBT's insistence on marriage or nothing reflected not only a firm belief among its leaders, especially Rachid, in equal rights but also a background that was quite radically different from than that of CHA leaders. Born in 1974, Rachid has no ties to the historic struggles for recognition under the old regime and the trying years of democratic transition. She is also a US-educated lesbian-feminist activist with a background in women's reproductive rights; quite the contrast to the male-centric world of the CHA. In 1998, she founded La Fulana (Spanish for an anonymous woman) to combat discrimination against lesbian and bisexual women as well as to raise the profile of lesbians within the gay rights movement.

In the end, the FALGBT prevailed over the CHA and other skeptics of marriage equality within and outside the gay community. By the time congress began to debate in earnest the issue of same-sex marriage, in 2009–2010, the gay community was firmly united behind the same-sex marriage bill, with the CHA putting its considerable network of contacts and lobbying experience drawn from past gay rights battles, especially

Buenos Aires' 2002 civil unions ordinance, on behalf of marriage equality. This was very much a triumph of idealism over pragmatism. According to Bimbi, whose job as the FALBGT's communications director entailed rallying the gay community behind the idea of marriage equality, the FALGBT embraced the quixotic nature of its struggle. Its guiding principle was "let's be realistic and ask for the impossible."[73]

Winning the Same-Sex Marriage Battle

In pursuit of marriage equality, the FALGBT undertook a multi-pronged campaign that operated on political, legal, and public relations fronts and that engaged, almost simultaneously, the legislature, courts, government, civil society, media, and public at large. Almost nothing was left to chance. The effort began in earnest in 2007, when FALGBT leaders persuaded Deputy Eduardo Di Pollina of the Socialist Party and Senator Vilma Ibarre of the Popular and Social Encounter Party (affiliated with the governing party) to introduce bills in their respective chambers to legalize same-sex marriage. The bills were doomed to failure—only twenty deputies and one senator endorsed them—if only because 2007 was a presidential campaign year.

In 2009, another same-sex bill was introduced in the congress. This was the same bill the FALGBT had introduced in 2007. The bill was quite simple. Like Spain's same-sex marriage bill, which served as a blueprint, Argentina's same-sex marriage bill entailed a small change in the portion of the civil code concerning marriage by changing the words "man and woman" to the neutral "contracting parties." Success was far from assured, however. The bill entered congress amid considerable uncertainty, following the government's loss of control of the Chamber of Deputies in the 2009 mid-term elections. Gay activists were also acting without explicit support from the government and its governing coalition, Frente para la Victoria. And even if President Fernández de Kirchner could be persuaded to support the bill, it was far from certain that she could rally her multiparty coalition on its behalf. For many Peronist social conservatives, especially those from rural areas, same-sex marriage was "an example of Buenos Aires imposing its decadent, city values upon the 'real Argentina' of farms and villages."[74]

Another factor was the still-powerful Catholic Church, which quickly became the face of the opposition to same-sex marriage. In April 2010, in a document titled "On the Unalterable Good of Marriage and the Family," the Plenary Assembly of Argentina's Conference of Bishops branded same-sex marriage an attack on the natural family: "The union of persons of the same sex lacks the biological and anthropological elements intrinsic to marriage and family. Same-sex unions lack the conjugal dimension and the possibility for the creation of new life."[75] In conjunction with this official announcement, representatives of the Catholic hierarchy paid private visits to the legislators to remind them of "their grave moral duty to oppose the bill." In June 2010, sensing momentum for the same sex-marriage bill, the Catholic Church upped the ante. In a letter to the Carmelite Nuns of Buenos Aires, in which he asked the nuns to pray for the legislators, Buenos Aires archbishop Jorge Mario Bergoglio, Argentina's top Catholic official, came down hard on the same-sex marriage bill, characterizing it as "a plan to destroy God's plan. It is not about a mere legislative project (this is only a tool) but rather a move by the father of lies who seeks to confuse and trick the children of God."[76]

Church officials tried but were mostly unsuccessful in mobilizing the faithful against the same-sex marriage bill. The most important protest against the bill took place on July 13, 2010, on the eve of the final vote, in front of the National Congress building. The orange-themed protest, attended by some sixty thousand people, featured children dressed in orange and carrying orange balloons and chants of "Kids have a right to a mom and a dad."[77] This was an impressive turnout, but it pales in comparison to the five hundred thousand people who took to the streets in Madrid on June 17, 2005 to express their opposition to the legalization of same-sex marriage. One of the largest protests in Spain in the post-Franco era, it was led by the Spanish Catholic hierarchy.

In retrospect, the Argentine Catholic hierarchy probably overplayed its hand and ended up doing more harm than good to the effort to derail the same-sex marriage bill. As noted by political observer Thomas Dollar, "This overt ecclesiastical pressure probably backfired. Argentina is a secular state, and past Church interference in civic affairs has bred a strong current of anti-clericalism." He adds that "the Church hierarchy has been tainted by its complicity in the repression of dissidents under the former military regime" and that "having Cardinal Bergoglio as the front man for opposition to gay marriage conjured up these bad memories."[78] Sociologist Juan Marco Vaggione notes that Bergoglio's letter to the nuns "triggered strong reactions by the press and the legislators." Once it became public, "The letter caused some citizens and politicians who formerly identified with the Church's official stance to distance themselves from it."[79]

Vaggione adds that the Catholic hierarchy's heavy-handedness also triggered a counterresponse from progressive Catholic clergy that allowed many Catholics to feel at ease opposing the church hierarchy. He notes that the pronouncements in favor of gay marriage by the progressive clergy allowed legislators and even deeply religious Christians "to think, define, and act differently from what the ecclesiastical hierarchy proposes by constructing Catholicism as a heterogeneous tradition with respect to sexuality."[80] In May 2010, twelve priests from Córdoba province endorsed the gay marriage bill and also gay adoptions—one of the most controversial aspects of the proposed bill, stating that "Jesus never condemned nor mentioned homosexuality" and "that all biblical revelation points toward focusing on love without any type of exclusion." Two months later, a group of eighteen priests from the Quilmes Diocese of Buenos Aires province published a document denouncing the "climate of intolerance, and in many cases of attitudes truly worthy of the worst Crusades, motivated by troubling biblical, philosophical, and anthropological fundamentalism," an obvious rebuke to Bergoglio's pronouncements against the gay marriage bill.

To counter opposition from the church and other conservative forces, gay activists enlisted a number of powerful allies within the government to exert pressure on the legislators. María José Lubertino, the director of the Instituto Nacional contra la Discriminación, la Xenophobia y el Racismo (INADI), a government agency located within the Ministry of Justice and Human Rights that monitors discrimination in Argentina and one of the oldest allies of the gay community, going all the way back to the banning of anti-gay discrimination in Buenos Aires in 1996, was an early and unwavering supporter. Her office submitted a letter to the Chamber of Deputies that argued that the same-sex marriage bill "intended to remedy the denial of human rights to people because of their sexual orientation."[81] She also opened doors to gay activists throughout the state.

Another key source of support within the government was Aníbal Fernández, now in the very influential position of Chief of the Cabinet of Ministers. By 2010, he was on record as favoring same-sex marriage and adoptions, having declared his support for both on the cover of *Crítica* in June 2009. In strategy sessions with gay activists, especially Rachid and Bimbi, Fernández noted that although he was "fully on board with the idea of same-sex marriage" it was the activists' job "to create the conditions that would facilitate support from the government." He also advised them to do extensive polling on the issue beyond greater Buenos Aires to gauge the level of support for same-sex marriage across the nation, and to see where they needed to work to increase support.[82]

Gay activists were also successful in bringing major civil society organizations to support their campaign. A joint letter to congressional legislators signed by seventy-three separate human rights organizations, headlined by Las Madres de la Plaza de Mayo, argued that "the new law needed to be adopted in order to end the restrictions of rights derived from marriage, like inheritance, the treatment of conjugal assets, custody of children, adoption and widow's pensions and other benefits."[83] For that reason, the human rights groups rejected the civil union proposal put forth by the opposition as an alternative to same-sex marriage. "Denying marriage on the grounds of sexual preference is a form of discrimination prohibited by the national constitution, and creating a separate institution is a flagrant violation of human rights." The letter echoed numerous private statements in support of the bill from prominent human rights activists, like Estela Carloto and Tati Almeyda, and from legal scholars such as Monica Pinto, Alberto Bovino, and Gustavo Arballo, and a statement by the Supreme Council of the University of Buenos Aires, the nation's leading higher education institution, that urged the Congress to extend the right to marry to gays as a human rights matter and in keeping with the Argentina's human rights tradition dating back to military trials of the 1980s.

Rabbi Daniel Goldman, head of Argentina's largest synagogue, testified to the congress that in the Jewish faith "the concept of family is ever-evolving, so family models, across time, can be modified."[84] Goldman's testimony, which was echoed in statements in support of same-sex marriage by mainline protestant churches (Lutheran, Anglican, and Methodist) served to blunt the negative views of Evangelical pastors Rubén Salomone and Rubén Proietti, representing major Evangelical and Pentecostal confederations. They observed, respectively, that "when you go against God's law the nation begins to disintegrate" and "that the marriage of a man and a woman is the only formula for the perfect psychological development of children."

More surprising was the success of gay activists in rallying support from the country's trade union movement, historically a reservoir of homophobia. Hugo Moyano, the truck-driver head of the Confederación General de Trabajadores (CGT), Argentina's largest workers' confederation, speaking to radio host Oscar González Oro, noted that he was for marriage equality because "gay people are honorable and serious people, and I have met worse heterosexuals." The CGT as an organization called on the legislators to enact marriage equality without delay. Commenting on this support by the CGT, Cigliutti noted that the CHA began to cultivate relations with the trade unions, well before 2010, while working on the extension of healthcare and surviving partners' benefits to same-sex couples.[85]

FALGBT activists also secured international partners to put pressure on the legislators. The Chamber of Deputies' Committee on Family, Women, Children and Youth heard oral testimonies from a Spanish delegation that included individuals from the organizations involved in the legalization of same-sex marriage in Spain. The delegation, headed by Pedro Zerolo, the

Spanish lawyer and gay activist widely noted as the father of Spain's marriage equality movement, testified that "Argentina deserves to arrive at the point of equality.[86] The Spanish delegation further argued that, as had occurred in Spain, extending the right to marry to same-sex couples would entail a big step toward social modernization and the recognition of the dignity and human rights of homosexuals. Freedom to Marry, the main organization pushing for same-sex marriage in the United States, urged the Argentine Congress to take the historic step of extending the right to marry to gay couples, noting the importance of the symbolism coming from an overwhelming Catholic nation.

Concurrent with the introduction of the first same-sex marriage bill in the national Congress, in 2007, the FALGBT launched a legal strategy to attain what gay activists termed "egalitarian marriage." Domestic and international factors encouraged this legal strategy, such as the arrival to the Supreme Court after 2003 of several justices, including Eugenio Raúl Zaffaroni, with ties to the gay and human rights communities, and the 2004 decision of the high court of the Commonwealth of Massachusetts declaring unconstitutional a ban on same-sex marriage. In 2007 Rachid filed a *recurso de amparo* for the right to marry her partner, Claudia Castro, which contended that the existing ban on same-sex marriages violated her constitutional rights, a claim summarily denied.[87] Undeterred, in 2009, gay activists brought together more than sixty same-sex couples to petition the government for marriage licenses. Their intention was to flood the courts with suits and force the Supreme Court to consider the issue of same-sex marriage.

These efforts began bearing fruit by 2010, with some court rulings finding a constitutional right to marry in the Argentinian Constitution and in the international human rights agreements that Argentina was a party to, such as the Inter-American Charter of Human Rights. On November 12, 2009, Judge Gabriela Seijas ordered the city of Buenos Aires to recognize the marriage of Alejandro Freyre and José Maria Di Bello, who had sued the city for failing to recognize their union as a marriage. To the surprise of many, conservative Buenos Aires Mayor Mauricio Macri, a businessman turned politician, chose not to appeal the ruling. Instead, he lauded the decision as "an important step because we must learn how to live in freedom without hurting the rights of others." He added that the decision was the outcome of "an important internal" debate to "improve the liberties of the citizens."[88]

Just before the wedding was to take place another judge revoked the earlier ruling. This was a temporary setback, as Freyre and Di Bello managed to be married in the world's southernmost city, Ushuaia, in Tierra del Fuego province, after they received the blessing from the province's governor, thus becoming Latin America's first married homo-sexual couple. In explaining her decision, Governor Fabiana Rios said that gay marriage "is an important advance in human rights and social inclu-sion and we are very happy that this happened in our state."[89] On July 2, 2010, just weeks before the final congressional vote on the gay marriage bill, several media outlets reported that the Supreme Court was ready to declare unconstitutional articles 172 and 188 of the civil code that pre-vented same-sex couples from marrying. Weighing heavily on the Supreme Court was the desire to bring Argentine law in line with the expanding international conception of human rights, as reflected in the constitutional amendment of 1994 that afforded constitutional status to all international agreements signed by Argentina.

Gay activists also unfolded a massive media campaign with the goal, according to Bimbi, of *ganar la calle* ("to win the streets."). "If a sector of soci-ety is demanding its rights it needs to show itself and make its case."[90] As part of this effort, Argentina's best-known public figures from the worlds of politics, media, business, and entertainment were recruited to make pub-lic statements in support of marriage equality. More often than not, these statements employed heterosexuals as proxies for the gay community to explain that gay people's desire for marriage was rooted not in arguments about the law but in their desire to partake in an institution that was avail-able to everybody else. Among those participating in the campaign were Senators Rubén Giustiniani and Vilma Ibarra, former Buenos Aires Mayor Aníbal Ibarra, banking executive Carlos Heller, journalist Luis Majul, singers Ignacio Copani and Liliana Herrero, dancer Julio Bocca, trade union leader Hugo Yaski, and the heads of all the major human rights organizations.

Gay activists also coordinated a torrent of sympathetic media articles about gay marriage, which helps explain why, save for the editorial page of the right-wing *La Nación*, press coverage of the gay marriage campaign was overwhelmingly positive. These articles, penned by the country's leading journalists, were promoted via social media to create a sense of inevitabil-ity about gay marriage. One of the most influential articles was written by Ricardo Kirschbaum, editor-in-chief of *Clarín*, the nation's most widely read paper. His column for the paper, published as a letter to the reader just days before the final vote in congress, asserted that "gay marriage needs to be approved in Argentina."[91]

The most talked-about support for marriage equality in the media, how-ever, came from the soap opera *Botineras*, a sports comedy broadcast on Telefe, Argentina's most popular television network. The comedy featured a storyline (co-written with gay activists) that incorporated a strong mes-sage about marriage equality. It centered on Flaco, a soccer player who decides to reveal his homosexuality before the media outs him. When confronted by a journalist who wants to know Flaco's views on same-sex marriage, he replies: "It is natural to be respectful, and what alters the natural order is, it seems to me, to deny the rights to those who are the same." Flaco's teammate, who is straight, comes to his defense by noting: "We are part of a community. It seems to me you cannot stand on the other side and speak. We are all equal." The storyline also featured a gay kiss between Flaco and his boyfriend that rocketed *Botineras* to the top of the TV ratings.

Last but not least, gay activists used the debate about same-sex marriage to resuscitate old claims about the state's past treatment of homosexuals. Around the time the debate over same-sex marriage began to heat up, in 2009 a slew of articles began appearing in the national media about the history of homosexuality in Argentina stressing the pain and suffering endured by the gay population, with titles like "Victims without Names" and "The Struggle Continues."[92] This effort to highlight and amplify the victimization of gays played well into an increasingly popular narrative of Argentina as a "genocidal state" whose roots go back to the founding of the nation in the nineteenth century.[93] According to historian Pablo Ben, the CHA and other gay rights organizations in Argentina understand that being a victim of the "bad dictatorship" is crucial in today's political environment. Consequently, the claim about the "gay *desaparecidos*" say more about present-day politics than about past realities."[94]

The Presidential Endorsement

The first big test for the same-sex marriage bill came on May 5, 2010, when the Chamber of Deputies voted on the bill. In keeping with tradition, in anticipation of the vote gay activists reached out to every legislator, demanding to know where they stood on the bill, and usually in the presence of someone from the press. They also mobilized long-time allies of the gay rights movement within the Chamber, such as Juliana Di Tullio, and their staffers to underscore the importance of the vote to the advancement of democracy and human rights in Argentina. The vote was a resounding victory: 126 in favor, 110 against, and 4 abstentions. The bill then moved to the Senate, where it faced an uncertain future, as most senators did not reveal their intentions until the last minute. Moreover, this is a more conservative body, since the Argentine Constitution allows for three senators to each province, meaning that small and rural provinces have the same number of senators as large ones, such as Buenos Aires.

Yet momentum was certainly in the direction of approval, if only because of the staunch support that the bill received from Fernández de Kirchner, who up until then had remained on the sidelines (this was not the case of her husband, who voted for gay marriage as a member of the Chamber of Deputies). But after she endorsed the bill, she put her reputation on the line and employed her considerable political skills to get the bill across the finish line. She imposed significant discipline within her Peronist coalition when she instructed its senators not to fall for attempts by conservative politicians, prompted by the Catholic Church, to put the issue of gay marriage to a national referendum. She also warned against a proposed compromise on same-sex marriage by agreeing to the creation of same-sex civil unions, which reportedly was secretly endorsed by Archbishop Bergoglio once passage of the gay marriage bill seemed imminent.[95]

Most notably, however, Fernández de Kirchner used the bully pulpit to justify her support for same-sex marriage as "a human rights imperative" and to question the democratic credentials of those opposing the bill. Responding to those who wanted to put the issue of marriage to a national referendum, she noted that leaving the fate of the rights of a minority to the whim of the majority was "unbecoming for a democratic society." Civil unions, she argued, "would stigmatize the gay population as second-class citizens."[96] Aiming squarely at Bergoglio, she noted her disapproval of the tone of the debate: "It is very worrisome to hear of such expressions as an attack on God's plan and a devil's project, things reminiscent of medieval times and of the Inquisition."[97] Cleverly, during the final Senate vote she left the country (for China) on a trade mission and took with her a number of Peronist Senators who for political reasons wanted to skip the vote, thereby helping the bill in its final vote.

Fernández de Kirchner's support for the same-sex marriage bill, which was undoubtedly pivotal to the bill's passage in the Senate, remains a subject of intense speculation. The conventional view is that her actions were an act of political opportunism rather than an act of political courage, a view especially common among the opposition. "Kirchner doesn't care about the rights of the gay community," said opposition leader Elisa Carrió of the Coalición Cívica party.[98] Implied in Carrió's comments was that the president's support for gay marriage was a cynical ploy designed to improve her standing in anticipation of the 2011 elections, especially by appealing to urban and more educated voters, a point stressed in the domestic and foreign media.

Fernando Laborda, a critic of the Kirchners at the daily *La Nación*, wrote that "the Kirchners' militant attitude in favor of homosexual marriage is a naked political ploy since in their many years in power they had never concerned themselves with this issue and did not even raise it during the 2009 electoral campaign."[99] Laborda's comments were echoed in *The Economist*, which argued that the politics of gay marriage changed once the president's governing coalition lost its congressional majority in 2009:[100]

> The Kirchners were looking for a controversial bill they could force through the legislature to prove the government could still get its way, and they settled on gay marriage as the best candidate. The topic would unite their leftist base, and enable them to demonize opponents of the measure—particularly the Catholic Church, with which they have long tense dealings—as retrograde bigots. Although several opposition senators pushed for a civil union instead, which would not include adoption, the Kirchners made it characteristically clear the battle would be all or nothing.

Gay activists offer a more charitable take on the president's support for same-sex marriage, even as they recognize some political motivation. According to the CHA's Sottile, support for same-sex marriage allowed Fernández de Kirchner to recast herself as a social progressive in the eyes of civil society after the attacks she endured for the "war" her administration waged against Grupo Clarín, the media conglomerate that owns newspapers and television stations, including the daily *Clarín*, a frequent critic of the administration.[101] Rachid, today a Buenos Aires city councilor and the recipient of many accolades for her efforts on behalf of the LGBT community, such inclusion in *El País* 100 most important people in Latin America and the City of Buenos Aires Distinguished Personality in Human Rights Award, sidesteps political motivation in the president's actions. "I agree with the president that the same-sex marriage law is not a victory for the government or any particular political party, but rather for society, and especially for those fighting for equality and human rights."[102]

In the end, however, Fernández de Kirchner's support for the gay marriage bill rested on the fact that it was good politics, given the popularity of the bill among ordinary Argentines. In the months leading to the congressional vote, public opinion polls were suggesting an approval rate approaching 70 percent.[103] In symbolic fashion, the public's strong support for gay marriage brought the story of gay rights in Argentina full circle, since this development appears deeply rooted in the CHA's early human rights activism, as well as in the belief that the public's eventual acceptance of homosexuality is premised on the public's ability to relate to the homosexual community as ordinary people, a point made by several analysts in the wake of the enactment of the same-sex marriage law. According to pollster Analía del Franco, who worked closely with gay activists in designing polls and focus groups to test how the public would respond to same-sex marriage, the public's support for same-sex marriage mirrors "the country's strong human rights tradition." To this clear reference to the work of gay activists, she adds that "the fight against the military dictatorship had helped propel the gay marriage bill; this is something that comes from way back."[104]

On July 14, the eve of the Senate vote, the heads of the three major voting blocs in the Senate—Frente para la Victoria (which incorporates the ruling Peronist Party), Coalición Cívica, and Grupo Socialista—all gave their blessing to the bill and released their legislators to vote their conscience.[105] In an effort to avoid making gay marriage a wedge issue, Senate leaders organized a press conference that stressed the importance of the vote for fulfilling Argentina's aspiration for a more fair, humane, and equitable society, and noted that the vote arrived on the anniversary of the French Revolution, which "planted the seeds for individuals freedoms and those of society." Gay activists invited to the ceremony urged the senators "to vote with courage, liberty, and information."

On July 15, thousands of people gathered in near-freezing temperatures in front of the Congress building to cheer the law or to pray for its defeat. After deliberating into the wee hours of the morning, the Senate approved the bill by a vote of thirty-three in favor and twenty-seven against. Three senators abstained from voting and nine skipped the vote. The vote was remarkable for the broad support it enjoyed from across the political spectrum. This can be seen, perhaps, as confirmation of the early goal of gay activists of avoiding polarizing the issue of gay rights along ideological lines by choosing or cultivating an affiliation with a major political party.

The bill garnered votes from senators representing some fifteen different political parties and almost every Argentine province. Many senators characterized their support for gay rights as a way to come to terms with the country's turbulent past. Córdoba Senator Norma Morandini of the Civic Coalition drew on her experience as an exile in Spain during the years of military rule to argue that she supported same-sex marriage because the discrimination experienced by the homosexual community was very similar to the oppression imposed by Argentina's dictators decades ago.[106] She noted that "what defines us is our humanity, and what runs against humanity is intolerance." Entre Ríos Senator Blanca Inés Osuna of the Peronist Party noted that "this was not about religion but about the responsibility that democracy owes to discriminated minorities."[107]

Gay activists greeted the vote as a vindication of their human rights struggles. "Today we are a more just and democratic society. And this is something we should all celebrate. And we can be proud to be the first Latin American country to make this progress in human rights," said FALGBT head Rachid.[108] The victory made for an especially festive gay pride parade in Buenos Aires on November 2, 2010. As might be expected, President Fernández de Kirchner was canonized as a gay rights crusader at the parade, which came one week after her husband's sudden death. The president's speech during the signing ceremony of the gay marriage law on July 21, 2010, played loudly on the main stage. That speech was delivered in the Gallery of Latin American Patriots of the Presidential Palace (Casa Rosada), attended by the president's cabinet; members of Congress (including the president's husband, a member of the Chamber of Deputies); heads of the leading gay rights organizations; prominent human rights activists, such as the head of the Madres de la Plaza de Mayo; and judges, provincial governors, and artists, Fernández de Kirchner used the speech to frame the story of the gay rights movement in Argentina as a quintessential struggle for equality for all. She noted: "We are a more equitable society this week than last week," observing that "thousands of Argentines have conquered rights I already had."[109] She added that "the law of marriage equality did not belong to any group in particular but rather to society itself, as part of a progression toward more equality, diversity, and pluralism."[110]

Fernández de Kirchner also linked the struggle for gay rights in Argentina to that of other groups discriminated against in the past, most notably women. In one of the more memorable moments of the ceremony, she pointed to Evita's portrait and exclaimed: "I have no idea how she felt, how she felt when she witnessed the triumph of women's rights (a reference to Evita's successful campaign to give women the right to vote); but here we are." The comparison earned the president the first round of applause from the crowd, including "gay militants who were still incapable of assimilating the shock of being part of a ceremony at the presidential palace."

PART III

Comparative Perspectives

CHAPTER 5

Gay Rights and the Paradox of Brazil

As recently as the mid-2000s, it was obvious which Latin American country was poised to emerge as the region's gay rights champion—Brazil by a long shot.[1] Boosting that impression was the country's reputation as an erotic Eden going back to the colonial period. "Beneath the Equator sin does not exist," wrote Dutch historian Caspar von Barlaeus in 1660 upon returning to Europe from a visit to Brazil.[2] Arguably, Brazil's renown for freewheeling sexuality and hedonism resonates most powerfully in connection to homosexuality, which was decriminalized in 1830, a first for a nation in the Western Hemisphere, shortly after the country gained its independence from Portugal.[3] Underscoring the importance of this history for Brazil, Luiz Mott, an anthropologist at the Federal University of Bahia, and Brazil's foremost gay activist-scholar, observes that "Brazil enjoys an international reputation of being the New World country with greatest freedom for homosexuals."[4]

Many features in contemporary Brazilian culture bolster Brazil's image as a country friendly toward homosexuals and other sexual minorities. Gay characters and plotlines are a staple of the popular *telenovelas* (television soap operas). Transvestite/transgender culture has long been a fixture of Brazilian society, a point marked by Roberta Close, a transsexual female, who after undergoing sex reassignment surgery in Britain in 1989 was chosen by popular acclaim as "Brazil's most beautiful woman." The popularity of Afro-Brazilian religions, especially Candomblé, which commonly feature effeminate or androgynous figures as spiritual leaders also speaks to Brazilians' apparent comfort with flexible gender norms; as does Carnival in Rio de Janeiro, in the eyes of the world the very essence of Brazilian culture. Rio de Janeiro's carnival is famous for men dressing up in women's clothing and taking to the streets without enduring any shame or ridicule, and for a sexual debauchery that since the advent of the AIDS epidemic in the early 1980s has forced city officials to hand out some three million free condoms every year to revelers.

Also revealing is the zest with which Brazilians have embraced contemporary markers of gay culture. By the mid-1990s, the intensity of this embrace had prompted Jackson A., a gay columnist for the influential newspaper A Folha de São Paulo, to declare: "O gueto acabou, querida" (The ghetto is over, darling).[5] São Paulo's Parada do Orgulho LGBT (Gay Pride Parade) is the most compelling evidence of the vibrancy of Brazilian gay culture. Running through Avenida Paulista, the skyscraper-lined thoroughfare that cuts through the very heart of Brazil's largest city and financial center, the parade is the second most popular event in the social calendar of the city (after the Formula One race) and a major tourist attraction. By 2009, the parade was drawing an estimated attendance of three million people, making it, according to the Guinness Book of World Records, the largest gay pride parade in the world. The parade is also a symbol of the economic and political clout of Latin America's largest gay community. Staged at the cost of two million Brazilian reais (US$900,000), paid for by grants from the city and state of São Paulo and national and international multinationals, the 2014 parade was attended by São Paulo Governor Geraldo Alckmin, São Paulo Mayor Fernando Haddad, and Secretary of Human Rights Ideli Salvatti.

"Official" politics have also been tolerant of homosexuality in Brazil, at least since the democratic transition in 1985, which ushered in the first generation of gay-friendly and openly gay politicians in Latin America as well as the first debates on gay rights legislation by a national legislature in the region. These developments are intimately tied to the rise of the Partido dos Trabalhadores (Workers' Party), also known as the "PT," the first political party in Latin America to declare its support for the LGBT community. Since its creation in the late 1970s by former president Luiz Inácio "Lula" da Silva, then the leader of the militant São Paulo trade union movement, the PT incorporated Afro-Brazilians, feminists, environmentalists, indigenous peoples, progressive Catholics, and gay activists in an attempt to harness the full diversity of Brazilian civil society in a unified political movement.[6] Understandably, by the time Lula ascended to the presidency in 2003, Brazil was the best-positioned country in Latin America for a dramatic expansion of gay rights.

That early gay rights promise in Brazil, however, has left much to be fulfilled. Indeed, Brazil's gay rights record is quite spotty, giving rise to an interesting paradox: Latin America's most famously sexually liberal society is also one of the region's most troubled places when it comes to advancing and protecting the rights of LGBT people.[7] There is little doubt that there has been considerable progress in Brazil; enough, in fact, to make the Brazilian gay rights movement "among the most successful in the Global South."[8] In 1985, the Brazilian Medical Association removed homosexuality from its list of disorders (a decision that came years before the World Health Organization took a similar step), and in 1999 the Psychology Federal Council banned reparative treatment for homosexuals. In 1997, the northeastern state of Bahia became the first in Brazil to enact an anti-discriminatory law that covered LGBT people. Fourteen other states and over eighty municipalities have since adopted similar laws. Most significantly, perhaps, is that same-sex marriage was introduced at the federal level in 2013, making Brazil at that time the largest country in the world to allow same-sex couples to marry.

But seen from the vantage point of gay rights developments in other Latin American nations, especially Argentina, the Brazilian experience looks decidedly less sanguine. For one thing, marriage equality in Brazil came later and in a more contentious fashion than in Argentina, a country that, as seen already, is not known for social tolerance for sexual diversity, and where the political environment has been, until fairly recently, very hostile toward gay activists. Furthermore, marriage equality arrived in Brazil via judicial fiat rather than by legislative action, as was the case in Argentina. In fact, since the enactment of a new democratic constitution in 1988, the Brazilian Congress has not enacted any gay rights legislation; not even a law banning discrimination on the basis of sexual orientation, something that has been possible in many Latin American nations, including Ecuador, Colombia, Mexico, and Chile, the last two under conservative administrations. Nor has Brazil seen fit to enact a gender identity law similar to Argentina's, that allows anyone to change gender without undergoing surgery or permission from a judge or a medical doctor.

There is no shortage of explanations for making sense of the Brazilian gay rights paradox. In fact, we are faced with a plethora of explanatory riches. Three factors, all interrelated to some extent, stand out. For starters, there is a virulent strand of homophobia in the culture of Brazil that belies the country's reputation as a paragon of sexual liberalism. The Brazilian religious landscape also features a larger than average percentage of Evangelicals (for Latin America), which surveys find harbor more negative attitudes toward homosexuals than Catholics. These two factors serve to discourage the public from supporting or demanding gay rights while making gay rights a relatively high-risk proposition for Brazilian politicians. Finally, there is a very tough legislative environment, especially a highly fragmented political party system and dysfunctional parliamentary rules. Broad coalitions are required to pass any legislation and small parties have undue influence in vetoing legislation, such as the Brazilian Republican Party, an ardent opponent of gay rights.

In keeping with the study's core argument, however, my analysis emphasizes the crafting of the gay rights campaign as the crucial factor. As in Argentina, human rights claims framed the campaign for gay rights in Brazil. Yet these claims did not have the same impact in Brazil that they had in Argentina. This was to be expected, however, since human rights do not resonate in Brazil in the same manner that they do in Argentina. Indeed, Argentina is almost unique in that regard. Political justice against the military was not a part of the Brazilian transition, despite significant human rights transgressions, and the Brazilian human rights movement, relative to Argentina's, is almost politically insignificant. Brazil also lacks the history of state-sponsored antigay violence that allowed Argentine activists to provoke moral outrage and to tie advancing gay rights to the nation's human rights aspirations.

More important is that in contrast to Argentina, the Brazilian gay rights campaign had the political system rather than society and the culture at large as its main theater of operation. Indeed, seen through the lens of Argentina, the Brazilian gay rights campaign comes across as a political and policy dispute. Lobbying the legislature and collaborating with state agencies with the aim of seeing gay rights legislation enacted into law rather than changing hearts and minds about homosexuality was front and center in the agenda of gay activists. A close partnership between gay activists and the Workers' Party anchored this effort. On balance, the strategy of working through the legislature and the state was a mixed blessing. While it provided gay activists with levels of visibility and access to the state that were the envy of other gay movements in Latin America, it generated very little in terms of actual rights. Moreover, the strategy undercut the ability of gay activists to critically engage the state on issues other than HIV/AIDS and led activists to neglect society as a focus in the struggle for gay rights. This neglect made the struggle for gay rights in Brazil less grounded in society than in Argentina as well as less focused on eliciting public support for gay rights.

More recently, however, a new generation of Brazilian gay activists disillusioned with the PT and frustrated with an increasingly conservative Congress, and inspired by the success of gay rights in Argentina (whose gay rights veterans are now active in Brazil, hoping to recreate their success there), is charting new strategies for the gay community. In so doing, these activists are bringing the Brazilian experience closer to that of Argentina. For one thing, there has been in recent years more of a concerted effort to approach the courts, especially the Federal Supreme Court, whose bold actions in favor of gay rights since 2011 stand in contrast to the temerity of the executive branch and the embarrassing inaction of the legislature. In working through the courts, Brazilian gay activists have displayed considerable skill at framing their demands for equal rights in ways that capitalize on those areas of Brazilian law that call for respect for human rights. Less apparent is the growing recognition of the need to engage with society and the culture more directly with the goal of increasing societal acceptance of homosexuality and sexual diversity more broadly.

THE MYTH OF SOCIETAL ACCEPTANCE

The view that homophobia, or "negative thoughts, feelings or actions toward homosexuals,"[9] exists (and indeed thrives) in Brazil is directly at odds with the country's reputation as tolerant toward homosexuality, a reputation upheld by several academic studies.[10] Yet recent studies suggest that homophobia in Brazil has traditionally been overlooked by scholars. This is suggested by the fact that the very large literature on homosexuality in Brazil seldom focuses systematically on homophobia and that this literature is centered on the more modernized and industrialized parts of country (the southern states and in particular the cities of São Paulo and Rio de Janeiro), thereby missing important regional differences.[11] One of the few studies of homophobia in Brazil, from the late 1990s, focused on the Northeast, one of the least developed parts of the country, found that homophobia is widespread, and that contrary to findings in the United States, "women are slightly more homophobic than men, and that male homophobia is equally directed toward male and female homosexuals."[12]

Polling data about societal acceptance of homosexuality in Brazil more than hint at persistent homophobia in Brazilian culture. A survey of May 10, 1993, published in *Veja*, Brazil's largest newsweekly, which polled two thousand individuals on a wide range of questions related to homosexuality, is quite revealing. The survey showed that 79 percent of those interviewed would be upset if they had a homosexual son or daughter; 56 percent would change their behavior around a colleague if they discovered he or she was gay; 56 percent did not agree that an openly homosexual candidate would ever be elected president; 47 percent would change their voting choice if it were revealed that their favorite candidate was gay; 45 percent would change to another doctor or dentist if they discovered their present one was a homosexual; and 36 percent would not hire a homosexual in their company even if he or she were the most qualified applicant.[13]

Admittedly, the survey is not comparative, so it is hard to see how Brazilian views stand against those of citizens of other nations, but the views elicited are certainly at odds with Brazil's traditional image as a haven of tolerance for sexual diversity. Other comparative survey data, however, do show that Brazil lags behind other democracies when it comes to acceptance of homosexuality. In the 2013 Pew Survey on global views on homosexuality, 60 percent of Brazilians professed acceptance of homosexuality—the same percentage as in the United States—but a smaller proportion than in other countries in the Americas and Western Europe, such as Argentina, Chile, Mexico, Canada, Italy, France, and Spain, which led the survey with an impressive 88 percent of the public professing approval of homosexuality.[14] A 2010 survey on "homosexual acceptance in politics," from the AmericasBarometer, which asked respondents, "Do you approve of homosexuals holding public office?" also shows Brazil with surprisingly low results. Under half (44.4 percent) of Brazilians answered in the affirmative, behind Canada (75.3), Argentina (66.5), Uruguay (62.1), and the United States (62.1).[15]

Society's hostility toward homosexuals in Brazil is underpinned by endemic socioeconomic inequality. Despite its considerable wealth, Brazil is one of the most unequal societies in Latin America, and indeed the entire world.[16] According to the 2010 UN-Habitat Report, Brazil, together with Guatemala, Honduras, and Colombia, has the highest levels of inequality in the region. This inequality accounts for the existence of large pockets of Brazilian society, especially Afro-Brazilians and many of the states in the impoverished Northeast, that, lacking in education and economic opportunities, harbor more negative attitudes toward homosexuals than the population at large, and that tolerate discrimination and even violence toward the LGBT population.

For many decades now, Brazil has been gripped by an epidemic of gay killings. According to Grupo Gay Bahia (GGB), Brazil's oldest gay rights organization still in existence, whose data on gay violence have been employed by the Brazilian government and the US State Department's human rights office to compile reports about violence in Brazil, between 1980 and 2008 there were 2,998 gay killings in Brazil, a figure that the organization calls a veritable "homocaust."[17] Since 2008, according to GGB, violent attacks on the gay community in Brazil have climbed steadily and registered an all-time high of 326 gay killings in 2014, close to one killing per day. This tally, in the view of GGB head Marcelo Cerqueira, does not represent the true dimension of the phenomenon since many gay killings go unrecognized or unreported because relatives of the victims are often unwilling to "out" the victims.[18]

Much controversy surrounds the GGB's data on Brazilian gay killings and the organization's claim that Brazil is "the world's champion of homophobic crimes," based on the calculation that 44 percent of the world's anti-LGBT violence occurs in Brazil. It has been suggested that Brazil is unfairly singled out among Latin American countries because local gay organizations do the best job in the region monitoring antigay violence.[19] The data on gay killings compiled by GGB have also come under criticism for being unscientific, by failing to account for the wider context of violence that exists in Brazil. *Veja* columnist J. R. Guzzo observed in 2012: "In a country that has more the 50,000 murders per year, it is clear that there is no problem with gay violence." He added that "homosexuals are victims of thieves in their apartment buildings and of express kidnapping; they are attacked in the streets, and can be killed with a shot to the head if they made the wrong gesture at the time of an assault—exactly as it occurs to heterosexuals. The real drama for everyone is that murder is a fact of life in Brazil."[20] GGB has also come under heavy criticism for not reporting the names of the victims of antigay violence, so that the motivation behind their deaths cannot be independently ascertained. The organization has defended the practice of anonymity because often those murdered were still in the closet, and revealing their sexual identity would only compound the suffering of those who survive them.

Gay activists and scholars, however, remain undeterred in their view of homophobia as the chief reason behind Brazil's epidemic of gay killings. Mott notes that Brazil's antigay violence cannot be explained away as part of the random acts of violence that plague Brazilian society, casualties of stray bullets or robberies and kidnappings gone array. "This is violence driven by bigotry and is intended to push gays back into the closet. Homophobia can be found across all levels of our culture, and enjoys a sphere of influence that infiltrates everything from popular lexicon to major means of communication and social institutions."[21] He adds that "on the streets, at schools, and in workplaces, when one wishes to antagonize a youngster or an adult, the first insult usually hurled by Brazilians is *veado* [a deer]," slang for gay.[22]

In a similar vein, British anthropologist and longtime resident of Brazil Peter Fry notes the ambiguity of Brazilian sexual attitudes and the way in which these attitudes interact with homophobic violence. He argues that "people unsure of their masculinity find guns and gay-bashing proof of their machismo."[23] Recent acts of antigay violence support these points. In 2008, the president of São Paulo's gay pride association, Alexandre Peixe dos Santos, was gagged, hooded, beaten, and left unconscious at his place of work by an unknown number of attackers. In 2009, a homemade bomb exploded in São Paulo during the city's gay pride celebrations, injuring twenty-one people. In March 2011, in Belo Horizonte, a surveillance camera captured the brutal killing of Priscilla Brandão, a twenty-two-year-old transvestite shot while walking down the street.

THE EVANGELICAL FACTOR

Further complicating the picture for gay rights in Brazil is the religious landscape. It is not that Brazil is less Catholic or less secular than other Latin American countries, or that the state-church divide is less strict. Rather, that Protestants in Brazil represent a much larger proportion of the population than in most of Latin America (26 percent versus 19 percent), and that they play a very different role in national politics. By far the single largest Protestant group in Brazil is the Pentecostal church—according to one study by the Pew Research Center from 2006, eight in ten Protestants in Brazil self-identify as "Pentecostal" or "Charismatic."[24] By 1999, when Brazil's Pentecostal population was estimated at about 15 million, it was already being described as "the largest Pentecostal community in the world."[25]

Brazilian Evangelical leaders are famously homophobic, and they exert considerable influence over the lives of millions of ordinary people. At the megachurches that dot Brazil's largest cities, especially Rio de Janeiro, the epicenter of Pentecostal Brazil, Pentecostal leaders preach "prosperity theology"—a point underscored by the extravagant wealth of Brazil's leading pastors—alongside a steady flow of attacks on the gay community.[26] Their rhetoric feeds the homophobia inherent in the general culture, and this in turn translates into a culture that both tolerates and encourages violence toward LGBT people. In essence, religious rhetoric contributes to a kind of structural homophobia. A case in point is Silas Malafaia, a former head of Brazil's largest Pentecostal church, Assembleia de Deus Vitória em Cristo. In a television interview with journalist Marília Gabriela that made headlines all over Brazil (and that was echoed in a profile of Malafaia in the *New York Times*),[27] Malafaia noted that "nobody is born gay; homosexuality is a behavior. . . . There is no homosexual chromosome; there is only male and female."[28] He added that, when it comes to homosexuality, his attitude is to love the sinner but not the sin. "I love homosexuals like I love criminals and murderers."

To be fair, Pentecostal leaders are no more hostile in their views on homosexuality than their Catholic counterparts, although the antigay comments from the Catholic hierarchy do not seem to generate as much attention and controversy. Dom Eusébio Oscar Scheid, metropolitan archbishop of Florianópolis, once said that "homosexuality is a tragedy. Gays are only half human; if they are human at all."[29] In 2010, around the time when the Catholic Church in Brazil was battling accusations of sexual child abuse, Archbishop Dadeus Grings of Porto Alegre tried to explain away the scandals to the newspaper *O Globo* by arguing that gay rights would pave the way for societal acceptance of pedophilia. "When you start to say that they [homosexuals] have rights, rights to publicly demonstrate, in a short time pedophiles will have rights too," he said.[30]

But Evangelical leaders do appear to have a monopoly on mobilizing the faithful against gay rights. It is hard to think of a better example of the culture war raging in Brazil over gay rights (gay marriage in particular) than the showdown of competing parades that takes place in São Paulo every year. Preceding São Paulo's pride parade is the "March for Jesus," an opportunity for Evangelicals to denounce "the destructive gay lifestyle" and society's willingness to accommodate "the gay agenda." In keeping with its counterpride nature, the parade runs through São Paulo's Avenida Paulista, the main site of the city's pride parade. According to police estimates, the March for Jesus parade draws one million people, fewer than those attending the pride parade but an impressive showing nonetheless.

AN INAUSPICIOUS LEGISLATIVE ENVIRONMENT

The swelling ranks of Evangelicals in Brazil have given them a level of political influence that immediately brings to mind the American Christian Right. David Fleischer, a political scientist at the University of Brasilia, notes that Evangelicals "don't yet have quite as unified an agenda as the Evangelical movement in the United States, but they are growing and are far more effective than the Catholic Church at convincing people to vote one way or another."[31] There is no more compelling evidence of the political influence of Evangelicals in Brazil (or in Latin America for that matter) than the so-called *Bancada Evangélica* (Evangelical bloc).

Operating from the Chamber of Deputies, the lower house of the Brazilian Congress, the Evangelical bloc makes up almost 15 percent of the Chamber. Most of the bloc's members are elected into office under the banner of the Brazilian Republican Party. This party is widely known as the political branch of the Universal Church of the Kingdom of God, an organization that claims a membership of some eight million Brazilians. Together with the *ruralistas*, proagrarian forces opposed to environmentalism and indigenous groups, and the law-and-order caucus, the Evangelical bloc is a testament of the growing clout of conservatives in the Brazilian Congress. By one account from 2013, these three caucuses combined account for 60 percent of the 515 seats in the Chamber of Deputies.[32] As might be expected, conservative caucuses often vote in lockstep, ensuring a steep hill for almost any socially progressive legislation.

Among the priorities of the Evangelical bloc are bringing Protestants on equal legal footing with the Catholic Church and opposing abortion and homosexuality. Over the years, the Evangelical bloc has introduced legislation that stood little chance of passing but that delighted their base nonetheless, such as bills banning public kissing by persons of the same sex and providing federal assistance for those seeking to change their sexual orientation from gay to straight. The main target of their antigay legislative endeavors, however, has been blocking a federal law to ban discrimination on the basis of sexual orientation on grounds that the bill grants special status to gays and that it would impinge on religious freedom.

In promoting its antigay agenda, the Evangelical bloc capitalizes upon the dysfunction of the Brazilian electoral system. Brazil is a textbook case of a "deadlock democracy," a system that generates and rewards a multiplicity of weak parties and individualistic, pork-oriented politicians with little accountability to citizens.[33] A key feature of the system is an open-list system of proportional representation. Intended to enhance democratic representation, it actually works to undermine democratic governance by generating a multiplicity of weak parties while encouraging pork-barrel payoffs, political horse-trading, and corruption. After the 2014 general elections, the number of parties represented in the Chamber of Deputies rose to twenty-eight from twenty-two, and no party has more than 70 of the house's 513 seats, not even the two leading parties, the PT and the center-right Brazilian Social Democratic Party. This makes enacting any legislation, but especially socially divisive laws, an uphill struggle.

A good example of the bizarre politics that the Brazilian political system produces can be seen in the current state of the Chamber of Deputies' Commission on Human Rights and Minorities. Someone sympathetic toward the gay community usually heads the commission, which has historically served as a platform for advocating for LGBT rights. But in March 2013, Marco Feliciano, a Pentecostal pastor and a fierce opponent of same-sex marriage and homosexuality in general, from the Christian Social Party, managed to get himself elected chair of the commission as a result of the horse-trading of posts that is typical of Brazilian parliamentary rules. Feliciano's election outraged gays and liberals, and many in the gay and human rights communities, at home and abroad, have called for his resignation, especially after *O Globo* quoted a book in which Feliciano argued that feminism would turn women gay. "When you stimulate a woman to have the same rights as men, she would want to work, her part of being a mother starts getting diminished. She will either not marry, or keep a marriage, or have a relationship with a person of the same-sex, enjoying the pleasures of a childless union."[34]

In protest of Feliciano's appointment, openly gay Rio de Janeiro congressman Jean Wyllys formed an alternative human rights commission without legislative authority. Undeterred, Feliciano has proposed legislation that would lift the federal ban on "gay conversion" therapy imposed in 1999. He is also involved in the effort to challenge the ruling by the Federal Supreme Court that opened the door to same-sex marriage in Brazil in 2011 by drafting a law would define family, for the purpose of federal law, as the exclusive union of a man and a woman. The law, according to gay activists, has very little chance of passing, but it is "a powerful symbolic threat" that conveys legitimacy to homophobia.[35]

THE ORIGINS OF GAY ACTIVISM IN BRAZIL, 1978–1982

Confronting homophobia in Brazilian culture and battling foes of the gay community, such as the Evangelical bloc, are at the heart of the activism of Brazil's gay rights movement. Its origins are generally traced to the creation in São Paulo of the Nucleo de Ação pelos Direitos dos Homossexuais (Action Nucleus for Homosexual Rights) in May 1978.[36] Organized by students, artists, and intellectuals, the Nucleus's activities included "study and discussion, militancy, services, consciousness raising, artistic activities, and nonverbal expression."[37] Shortly after the group's founding, in an effort to broaden its appeal, the group changed its name to SOMOS (We Are: Group of Homosexual Affirmation). The change was an homage to Argentina's Frente de Liberación Homosexual (FLH) and its magazine *Somos*, both crushed by the 1976 military coup in Argentina. The movement solidified its operations with the first Brazilian Meeting of Homosexuals held in 1980 in São Paulo.

Brazil's delayed development of gay rights relative to Argentina by almost a decade has not gone unnoticed by scholars. According to historian James N. Green, who was active in homosexual political circles in Brazil in the 1970s, this delay may be attributed to the oppression that followed the 1964 military coup. He notes: "Had Brazil not been under the domination of a military dictatorship in the late 1960s and early 1970s, it seems clear that the Brazilian gay liberation movement would have developed somewhat earlier than it did."[38] Green adds that "the years when Argentina's FLH was at its height [the prerevolutionary years that followed the civil uprising of the Cordobazo, 1969–1974], were the worst years of the Brazilian dictatorship (the so-called *anos de chumbo* or years of lead)."[39] The dictatorial regime "suspended constitutionally guaranteed rights, increased press censorship, and stepped up the arrest and torture of those who opposed military rule." This repression did not "specifically target homosexual men and women," but it did create "a climate which discouraged the emergence of a Brazilian lesbian or gay rights movement in the early 1970s."[40]

But several other factors appear to have been at work as well. Fry, another foreign academic involved in launching gay activism in Brazil, notes that the gay community in Brazil in the 1960s was not especially politicized; in fact, it was quite apathetic. "There wasn't really a gay public place so being gay for most people was a very individualistic business. There were clubs, but they were not really into demanding rights, and when activism did start it was pretty amateurish."[41] He adds that the gay community in Brazil was isolated from the outside world, with "few potential activists in exile at the time." Mott offers a different perspective by contending that a common view among local gays is that gay militancy is redundant since there is no discrimination against homosexuals. He notes that gay activism in Brazil has traditionally been hampered by a social climate that does not favor gay militancy given the perception that "if a Brazilian is discreetly gay or lesbian or is aggressively transvestite, s/he won't suffer much discrimination."[42] This point of view, according to Mott, prevents Brazilians from developing a political awareness about the need to join and support gay organizations, as well as to confront gay discrimination in the culture.

Whatever the cause for the delayed rise of gay activism in Brazil, the implications of this delay for the evolution of gay rights are quite apparent. For starters, the absence of early gay rights pioneers in Brazil meant that there would be no jolt to the local gay community by New York's Stonewall riots of the like witnessed in Argentina, which led to the formation of the FLH. Nor would Brazil experience a wave of returning gay exiles of the like experienced by Argentina in the 1980s in the post-transition years, which served to transport international gay rights strategies and politics, since there was no mass exodus of Brazilian gay activists following the military takeover of 1964. All of this is to say that by the time the transition to democracy started in Brazil, there was little in the way of an established tradition of gay rights activism, and much less of an internationally connected cluster of gay activists. As Green observes about Brazilian gay activism in the early 1980s: "There had not been [in Brazil] a previous experience to draw on, as in Argentina, no earlier movement, no exiles to speak of, and therefore, they started from scratch and the movement was amateurish."[43]

The Brazilian gay movement, however, was not internationally isolated. Green notes that "SOMOS looked to Western Europe and the U.S. for ideas and inspiration."[44] Green himself became a conduit for these ideas. He arrived in São Paulo in 1977 as a graduate student and served as host in Brazil to Winston Leyland, the editor of the San Francisco tabloid journal *Gay Sunshine*, whose visit Green deems "an outside catalyst" for the rise of an organized gay rights movement in Brazil.[45] Among other things, Leyland's visit paved the way for the emergence of *Lampião da Esquina* ("street lamp on the corner," in reference to gay street life), a gay publication that, as seen later, was pivotal in informing the ideological orientations of the Brazilian gay rights movement.[46] Green also helped shaped the movement: "I had lived in the United States and had repressed my sexual desires before Stonewall. The movement had transformed me . . . I believe that a similar transformation was possible in Brazil."[47]

Other key figures of the early period of Brazilian gay activism with international connections included the Argentine poet and anthropologist Néstor Perlongher, a cofounder of the FLH, who was part of a wave of Argentine gay exiles that came to Brazil after 1976, and the writer and avant-garde filmmaker João S. Trevisan, who had spent time in Berkeley, California, where he came in contact with American gay activists. Trevisan's memoirs are especially revealing of the kind of activist energy he was exposed to while living in the United States for an extended period of time. They also reveal the isolated climate he encountered in Brazil upon his return from abroad. "Having lived with militant American gays, foreign feminists, and exiled Brazilian revolutionaries, I felt doubly alone when I returned 'home.' I could not exchange ideas with my old comrades, I was shocked by the lack of punctuality and the irresponsibility of drivers, and I was irritated by the consumer mentality of the enlarged gay ghetto which I found in Brazil at the end of the seventies."[48]

SOMOS reflected the model of gay liberalization pioneered in Latin America by the FLH: Marxist in ideological orientation but also committed to fighting the social hierarchy of heterosexual society, and the many myths and prejudices about homosexuality promoted by the state, the Catholic Church, and the medical establishment. Edward MacRae, an anthropologist involved in the formation of the group, notes that "*Somos*, from the beginning, placed itself against any hierarchical type of structure. It emphasized instead a utopian equality among its members, who even tried to negate the differences between the situation of the male homosexuals and that of the lesbians."[49] He adds that SOMOS sought with little success to popularize the use of the word *bicha* (queen) to refer to all homosexuals, an attempt at "emptying the word from its pejorative connotation" and enforcing "a form of treatment among equals."[50] But many men who identified as homosexual rejected the term given its association with *bicha louca* (screaming queen), while lesbians resented having their identity repressed, forcing them to leave and form their own organization, the Lesbian Feminist Action Group. Its creation responded to "sexism prevalent among gay men" and "the homophobia found among feminist activists."[51]

Gay Politics under Military Rule

Despite their slow start, Brazilian gay organizations grew in size and diversity during the late 1970s and 1980s. Their growth was aided by the *abertura* (opening) policy begun in 1973–1974 by President Ernesto Geisel to return Brazil to civilian rule. The policy came in the wake of the defeat of virtually all opposition to the military regime, including the guerrilla resistance movement that rose in opposition to the 1964 military coup. Political scientist Maria Helena Moreira Alves notes that "the year 1973 was a turning point in the history of the Brazilian opposition. Guerrilla groups disappeared and other groups in opposition recognized that armed actions were allowing the state to justify a violent policy of repression against the population as a whole."[52] As it played itself out in the years after 1974, *abertura* entailed a process of political liberalization from above paired with mobilization and pressure from below by "large sections of Brazilian civil society" including "middle-class actors, church-based groups, opposition politicians, and working-class unions."[53] A gradual opening, or "decompression," ensued that returned the country to democracy by 1985, less than two years after the transition in Argentina.

Among the key beneficiaries of the new political climate was the gay community. By the early 1980s, Brazil was home to Latin America's most important gay newspaper, the aforementioned *Lampião*, edited in Rio de Janeiro. Although focused mostly on gay culture and the sexual liberation movement, *Lampião*'s thirty-eight issues tackled a wide range of subjects, including discrimination based on gender and race, machismo, and environmentalism.[54] More importantly, by the early 1980s, Brazil was well on its way toward emerging as the most vibrant site of gay rights activism in Latin America. This development was marked in 1987, when the GGB, founded by Mott, became the first gay organization in Latin America to be granted legal status by the government. GGB made much of this. Given that in Brazilian colloquial language "legal" means "good" or "cool," after

GGB was legalized, "The official slogan of the gay movement became *É legal ser homosexual* (it is legal to be homosexual)."[55]

The thriving gay community that developed in Brazil during the late 1970s and early 1980s, which stands in striking contrast to the traumatic environment prevalent within the gay community in neighboring Argentina around the same time, mirrors the fact that the state-sponsored political violence in Brazil, although significant, was much less of a factor than it was in Argentina. While the Argentine truth commission, organized in the wake of the collapse of the military dictatorship in the mid-1980s, recognizes some ten thousand people who were killed or disappeared between 1976 and 1983 (human rights organizations put the figure at thirty thousand), the Brazilian truth commission, which was organized only in 2011 and issued its final report in 2014, puts the number of people killed or disappeared by the military between 1965 and 1985 at 434.[56] These numbers provide quite the contrast, considering that Argentina's population is about a fifth that of Brazil and that the period of military rule in Brazil was considerably longer than in Argentina. Ironically, the Brazilian truth commission, unlike the Argentine truth commission, recognizes the LGBT community, alongside unionists, indigenous peoples, and university students and professors, as among the groups targeted by the military.

Less apparent is the paradoxical attitude of the Brazilian military toward homosexuality. For much of the time of military rule, the attempt to uphold public morals led to the occasional ban of gay carnival balls and the censorship of plays and films about homosexuality.[57] The military police were also in the habit of rounding up gays, lesbians, transsexuals, and prostitutes in São Paulo and Rio de Janeiro as part of moralist crusades intended to clean up downtown areas. As reported by MacRae, "The methods were the same as always—lighting strikes at meeting sites, illegal imprisonment for the investigation of criminal or political antecedents, even in the case of people whose documents were in order, and the use of an extreme brutality, especially with prostitutes and transvestites."[58] The military also sought to close *Lampião* on charges that the paper had violated "morality and good customs."[59] In an act of solidarity, the publication was defended by the Brazilian Press Association and by well-known cultural and artistic figures, and the military dropped the case. This harassment of the gay community was legal under the 1968 Institutional Act No. 5, the most infamous of all the institutional acts enacted by the military to rule the country. Act No. 5 overruled the constitution and suspended habeas corpus and judicial review.

But the Brazilian military was also known for its tolerance of homosexuality, a sentiment widely shared by longtime observers of the Brazilian gay community. According to Jorge Schwartz, an author and former professor at the

University of São Paulo active with SOMOS in the 1970s: "The military generals were tolerant of gay-transvestite behavior, viewing it as part of Brazilian culture." He points to the thriving gay social life that developed in Brazilian cities by the late 1970s, with the emergence of bars, cafes, restaurants, and saunas that catered exclusively to the gay community, gay periodicals, such as *Lampião*, as evidence that "unless you directly challenged the state you were basically left alone."[60] Mott echoes Schwartz by noting that: "The generals were relatively tolerant of pornography and of flamboyant homosexuality."[61]

LAUNCHING A GAY RIGHTS CAMPAIGN, 1982–1995

At the start of democracy, rather than coalescing around a single organization, as in Argentina, gay activists were spread around a triumvirate comprised of the São Paulo–based SOMOS, the Rio de Janeiro–based Grupo Homossexual Triângulo Rosa (Pink Triangle), and the Salvador-based GGB. Another difference from Argentina was the social forces inspiring gay activists during the democratic transition. There was nothing in the domestic arena in Brazil comparable to Argentina's human rights community to inspire gay activists, since human rights abuses were not a big political issue during the Brazilian transition. As seen previously, the level of violence in Brazil, while not insignificant, pales in comparison to the reign of terror that the military imposed in Argentina. This made it easier for the military to secure a broad amnesty law in 1979 that protects the old regime from prosecution. At the time the law was "widely accepted in both civil and political circles as mutual amnesty."[62] And, in any case, it is worth remembering that in the early 1980s human rights in Latin America were strictly associated with political repression and not with homosexual advocacy.

There was, however, a tradition in Brazil of minority groups historically discriminated against that saw themselves as a population deserving of civil rights protection from the state, which served as a template for the gay rights movement. Notable among these groups was the Afro-Brazilian civil rights movement, reorganized in 1978 as the Movimento Negro Unificado (MNU).[63] Since at least the 1930s, the Afro-Brazilian movement has been battling the notion that there is no racial discrimination in Brazil, a sentiment articulated in Gilberto Freyre's *The Masters and the Slaves*. More than any other, this 1933 book encouraged the myth of Brazil as a "racial democracy," a country whose miscegenation-rich experience with slavery unified Europeans, indigenous peoples, and Africans, leading to the creation a superior race in Brazil that was spared the ugly history of discrimination found in societies like the United States.

Gays and Afro-Brazilian activists began collaborating, at least as far back as 1979, when SOMOS members participated in a protest march organized by the MNU in observation of the National Day of Black Consciousness. This act of solidarity was an effort to consolidate ties between both groups. Such gestures were not always welcomed, however. According to Green, while many feminists and members of the black consciousness movement were receptive to an alliance proposed by gay and lesbian activists, "These movements by no means universally embraced the recently formed gay and lesbian groups."[64] Bringing gays and Afro-Brazilians together was the conviction that they "shared the same marginal status in Brazilian society."[65] This point was reaffirmed by the fact that a disproportionate number of gay killings in Brazil happen to be Afro-Brazilians. Yet another thing that Afro-Brazilians and gays had in common was a strong suspicion of the Left. Attempting to keep the working class as a single, monolith group, the Brazilian left has historically been reluctant to recognize racism in Brazilian society, preferring instead to put the blame on capitalism.

Like the Afro-Brazilian movement and the Brazilian feminist movement, gay activists in Brazil entered their political activism through an affiliation with the Workers' Party. The PT's emphasis on internal democracy and social mobilization over participation in institutional settings made it especially appealing to most, if not all, of the progressive Brazilian social movements around the time of the democratic transition.[66] Green reports that around the time of the formation of the party, in 1978–1980, "a small number of gays and lesbians began to approach the ranks of the PT, seeing it as an umbrella opposition political party which might seriously support their demands."[67] It is not, however, as if the gay movement had many suitors. Neither one of the two parties allowed by the military regime, the military-backed National Renewal Alliance Party and the center-right Brazilian Democratic Movement Party, had any interest in the gay vote.

Of the four left-wing parties that emerged during the transition (the PT, the Communist Party, the Democratic Labor Party, and the Socialist Party), only the PT saw fit to welcome gays and lesbians into its ranks. Such a lukewarm response mirrored the general hostility of the orthodox Left toward homosexuality, especially the Socialist and Communist parties. This behavior appears to have been carried into the new democracy and made the PT's welcoming of gay issues all the more significant.[68] Writing around the time of the transition, MacRae noted:

> The orthodox left had yet to begin to assimilate the postures of the Brazilian youth, especially those stemming from the sexual liberty made possible by the

advent of the birth control pill and other factors. Sexual relations outside of marriage, together with homosexuality and drug use, were severely repressed within orthodox Left organizations. Indeed, militants who engaged in such activities faced expulsion from their organizations.[69]

To its credit, the PT's embrace of the gay community was no mere formality, and this factor explains the loyalty that many gay activists feel toward the party to this day. From its very inception, PT leaders aimed at making the party the most inclusive and diverse of all Brazilian parties. Explicit support for gay rights was stated in the PT's first platform: "We will not accept that homosexuality be treated as a disease or a matter for the police, and we will defend respect for homosexuals, calling them to the greater mission of constructing a new society."[70] During the 1982 elections, which featured Lula's first attempt to run for the governorship of São Paulo, the PT was also the only party to support a constitutional ban on discrimination based on sexual orientation.

The PT also stood out for its opposition to the classification of homosexuality as an illness by the World Health Organization (paragraph 302.0). While other contenders wavered on the issue, the PT was resolute. "Paragraph 302.0 is a violation of human rights. The discrimination contained in this paragraph is a shameful conceit, as the sexuality of the individual is a universal right," declared a PT representative in a forum on gay rights hosted by *A Folha de São Paulo* in 1982.[71] During the electoral campaign, the PT also fielded eight gay candidates, including an incumbent, João Batista Breda, who declared his homosexuality on national television, unleashing "an unprecedented national discussion of gay life in the media and the arts."[72]

By 1981, gay and lesbian groups were marching in PT demonstrations, alongside trade unionists, feminists, and human rights activists. Within a few years, the vast majority of gay activists were fully ensconced within the PT, especially in the PT's home base of São Paulo state. By the early 1990s, the party was host to the annual gathering of gay and lesbian activists, and it sponsored the creation of an LGBT congressional caucus. The caucus was formed for the purpose of "increasing the visibility of gays and lesbians within the PT" and "pressuring PT parliamentarians across the country to push for pro-GLT legislation."[73] This participation by gay activists within PT structures was clearly at odds with SOMOS's intentions during the early 1980s of building "an autonomous gay and lesbian movement," but it demonstrated "overwhelming support for the Workers' Party as the only electoral alternative in Brazil."[74]

Working alongside and within the PT afforded gay activists unprecedented access to the legislature. Between 1985 and 1988, the years leading to the drafting of a new constitution, and under the presidency of José Sarney (1985–1990), Brazil's first civilian president in decades, PT leaders and gay activists undertook efforts to make homosexuals a constitutionally protected class, such as Afro-Brazilians, indigenous peoples, women, and the elderly. That initiative failed to garner much support beyond the PT, as suggested by the partisan nature of the vote. Only 23.2 percent of members of Congress supported the measure. To their credit, all sixteen representatives from the PT endorsed the measure, alongside members from the Communist and Socialist parties. Support from the parties from the right and the center-right was virtually nonexistent.

Despite its failure, the attempt to incorporate a ban on antigay discrimination in the constitution left an important legacy for the development of gay rights in Brazil. It led to the enactment of antigay discrimination legislation across numerous Brazilian states, cities, and towns. PT leaders, gay leaders, and human rights groups were also successful in declaring healthcare a constitutionally protected right; articles 196–198 declare that "health is a right of all and a duty of the State and shall be guaranteed by means of social and economic policies aimed at reducing the risk of illness and other hazards and at the universal and equal access to actions and services for its promotion, protection, and recovery."[75] This constitutional guarantee, as seen later, had important consequences for the development of HIV/AIDS policy.

The new constitution also allowed for the rise of "participatory budgeting," or policies intended to give grassroots groups and groups historically discriminated against, such as the poor, the elderly, Afro-Brazilians, and the LGBT community, a say in the budget-setting process.[76] Participatory budgeting was especially prominent in the cities and towns that first came under the control of the PT, including Porto Alegre, Belem, Recife, Aracaju, and, most importantly, São Paulo, the nation's most populous city and its economic engine. In each of these localities, participatory budgeting, rhetorically called "the PT way of governing," left an important legacy for the gay community.[77] Among the gay initiatives facilitated by this policy are the Homosexual Reference Center in Campinas and São Paulo's Coordination of Sexual Diversity. Both promote greater societal acceptance and understanding of sexual diversity together with practical services, such as a hotline for victims of homophobic violence.

Access to state funding made possible by the participatory budgeting process also served to offset the crisis in gay rights organizing that came alongside the end of the euphoric period of democratic transition. Indeed, the posttransition years were trying for the gay rights movement. By the late 1980s, of the twenty gay groups that formed during the early 1980s, only a handful were still in existence. This precipitous decline was not surprising. On the one hand, most gay organizations were small and poorly funded and could barely afford a national presence. Mott notes that this was especially the case of gay groups in the Northeast, home to the GGB. In that region, membership is racially mixed and poor, and thus usually unable to contribute to the maintenance of gay organizations; indeed, only very few could even afford a place to meet.[78] On the other hand were the pressures and stresses of the posttransition years. Green notes that "the relative collapse of the gay movement between 1983 and 1987" was exacerbated by "the recession, AIDS, and the exhaustion of the first generation of gay activists."[79]

Despite the visibility and resources that came with the PT affiliation, the affiliation was not free of negative side effects. An obvious problem was the outsized importance that gay activists put on the legislature to press for gay civil rights legislation, which likely came at the expense of engaging the culture at large in support of gay rights and pursuing other venues for advancing gay rights, such as the courts and public opinion. Between 1988 and 1995, gay activists devoted much of their energy to passing an impressive string of gay rights bills in the national legislature.[80] Among the most notable was a 1995 bill to legalize same-sex civil unions (Project of Law 1151/1995). Authored by Congresswoman and future São Paulo Mayor Marta Suplicy, the bill was the first of its kind for a Latin American nation. Revised versions of the bill were resubmitted in 2001 (Project Law 5252/2001), fashioned after France's Law of Civil Solidary Pacts, which would have made civil unions available to both gay and straight couples; and again in 2009 (Project Law 4914/2009). Other proposed legislation of this period included an amendment to the Brazilian Constitution banning discrimination on the basis of sexual orientation; and bills to allow sex-reassignment operations for transsexuals under the national healthcare system, to establish June 28 as National Gay Pride Day, to outlaw discrimination (including sexual orientation) in the hiring and promotion of public sector employees, and to make it illegal to reject blood donations from homosexuals.

None of the proposed bills made it into law; most of them did not even get a vote in Congress. A hostile social environment certainly contributed to this fate. When explaining the defeat of the 1988 constitutional amendment, the late João Antonio Mascarenhas of Triângulo Rosa, who alongside Mott is credited with devising the "interest group" approach to gay politics in Brazil's new democracy,[81] noted that gay activists were unable to overcome "opposition to the rights of sexual minorities in the federal legislature" posed by "conservatism, machismo, homophobia, and religion."[82] Similar arguments can be made about the travails of the civil unions bill. No accommodation on the part of gay activists appeared sufficient to placate conservative legislators—from excluding adoption under the original Suplicy bill of 1995, to allowing heterosexuals to avail themselves of civil unions in the 2001 revision, to guarantees that civil unions were not the equivalent to marriage in the 2009 bill.

But less apparent is that support from the PT for gay rights has been tepid, the result of internal squabbles within the PT leadership about how hard to push for the rights of the gay community. Although the party's platform allowed gay issues to be aired within the party, getting support for gay issues outside the party was a different matter altogether. For many PT activists and leaders, especially during the party's early years, gay rights were a distraction from the party's agenda to transform Brazil. This was especially the case for those groups with the greatest influence within the party, which also happened to be the party's founding movements: the militant São Paulo auto- and metalworkers' movement, the "organized Left" (Marxists, Maoists, etc.), and the progressive Catholic Left. The leaders of last group have traditionally been openly contemptuous of the gay movement, believing that homosexuality is at odds with their religious beliefs. A notable example is Hélio Pereira Bicudo, a founding member of the PT who ran as Lula's vice-gubernatorial candidate during the PT's first campaign in 1982 in São Paulo and later served as vice mayor in the Suplicy mayoralty (2001–2004). Bicudo strongly opposed gay rights because of his deeply held religious views and repeatedly undercut efforts by the party to be more forceful on issues of homosexuality both within São Paulo politics and on the national stage.

Unsurprisingly, charges of homophobia within the PT by gay activists are not unheard of; neither are countercharges by heterosexual PT leaders that gay leaders are unrealistic about how far the party can be expected to push a gay rights agenda. The "family feud" between gay activists and PT leaders burst into open view during the 1989 presidential campaign, which featured a complicated drama regarding the nomination of Fernando Gabeira as Lula's vice-presidential nominee. A founder and leader of the Partido Verde, PV (Green Party), Gabeira was known for his counterculture positions, such as support for the environment, legalization of marijuana, and gay rights, which many in the PT leadership felt would expand the PT's base (and along the way co-opt the PV, a potential competitor to the PT).

There was a lot to be concerned about in Gabeira's past, however, including his participation in guerrilla activity during the military dictatorship. This participation included coordinating the kidnapping in 1969 of American Ambassador Charles Burke Elbrick. But it was Gabeira's unabashed and very visible progay stance that most troubled PT leaders, especially those with an orthodox left-wing bent. Gabeira's staunch support for the gay community, which fueled persistent allegations that he was a closeted homosexual, doomed his candidacy. As reported by Green: "A behind the scene campaign relying on a generalized perception that Gabeira was 'a citizen under suspicion' contributed to his failure to secure the nomination."[83]

By the mid-1990s, with Lula's viability as a presidential candidate on the rise, the PT undertook a political makeover to make the party look more "like its catchall or electoral-professional competitors."[84] This transformation all but rendered the gay movement an inconvenient ally for the party. A turning point came during the 1994 presidential campaign, which pitted Lula against Fernando Henrique Cardoso, the former finance minister who had successfully tamed Brazil's stratospheric inflation rate right before launching his presidential bid. In a desperate and failed attempt to defeat Cardoso, the PT began to shore up support among the Christian Base Communities, a progressive Catholic movement. As part of this effort, the PT dropped its support for abortion and LGBT advocacy was dramatically scaled down when Lula recanted his support for same-sex civil unions. Fronting the "rediscussion" of the PT's 1994 Plan for Governing, which included the programmatic shift in the party's long-standing support for abortion and gay rights, were party leaders Irma Passoni, who was closely tied to the Catholic wing of the party, and Benedita da Silva, Brazil's first Afro-Brazilian senator.[85]

Some gay activists were dismayed at seeing the PT abandon some of its core principles, but others were more sanguine, believing that Lula's rise to the presidency more than compensated for any short-term compromises. This very pragmatic sentiment began to consolidate even as the PT (at least at the national level) was trying to keep gay activists at bay. According to Green, "While its tepid support for gay and lesbian rights discouraged some activists who had looked at the Workers' Party as an electoral alternative, the significant strengthening of the movement nationwide in 1995 propelled activists into closer relationships with this sector of the Brazilian left which continued to be the only political force willing to offer legislative alliance to the movement."[86] In the end, however, the PT's programmatic shift was for naught, as Cardoso won a resounding victory, ensuing from his success as finance minister.

Ironically, the picture for gay organizations began to improve by the mid-1990s with the full onset of the HIV/AIDS crisis, which generated an extraordinarily successful alliance between public officials and gay activists to fight the epidemic under the Cardoso administration (1995–2003).[87] The HIV virus was first detected in Brazil in 1982 and was initially confined to gay enclaves in urban centers. These early trends led to a slow response to the epidemic by Brazilian public authorities, which was typical of most Latin American nations. During its early years, HIV/AIDS in Brazil was associated with a very small fragment of Brazilian society, especially "well-to do individuals who enjoyed the luxury of dividing their time between Rio de Janeiro and São Paulo and foreign centres such as New York and Paris."[88]

By the early 1990s, however, HIV/AIDS began expanding to the general population, especially women. Indeed, by then, the HIV infection rate was rising dramatically in Brazil, at the fastest rate of any country outside of Africa. Approximately one million Brazilians were infected with the HIV virus in 1993, roughly the same number as the United States, even though the population in the United States at the time was almost a third larger than Brazil's (150 million for Brazil vs. 255 million for the United States).[89] Fears that the epidemic's sick and dead would overwhelm the healthcare system were widespread and well founded. In São Paulo state alone, the number of deaths from AIDS quadrupled in four years, rising from 1,067 in 1987 to 4,134 in 1991.[90] By 1994, the situation had grown so dire that the World Bank famously warned Brazilian public officials to brace for nothing short of catastrophe.

Responses to the epidemic first emerged at the state and local levels, especially in São Paulo, home to some of Brazil's most important gay organizations, human rights groups, and, more importantly, a very vibrant public health movement. In 1983, São Paulo's Secretariat of Health, at the instigation of gay leaders, local politicians, and health professionals, created the Grupo de Apoio à Prevenção à AIDS (AIDS Prevention Support Group), GAPA. Its purpose was to find ways to slow down the rate of infection and to provide healthcare to those battling HIV/AIDS. GAPA transformed AIDS national policy and the gay movement itself by becoming the prototype for the Programa Nacional DST/AIDS (PNDA)—a program cited by international health organizations as "one of the developing world's largest, and arguably most successful, AIDS treatment programs."[91] Popularly referred to as "the Brazilian Model," the PNDA is anchored in federal law 9.313 (passed in November 1996), which guarantees free and universal access to antiretroviral therapy through the national healthcare system to anyone infected with the HIV virus.

The PNDA was controversial from the start, since it ran contrary to the advice of many international organizations, including that of the World Bank, that developing countries should emphasize affordable prevention over costly treatment. By choosing to treat everyone who was infected, Brazil ran afoul of powerful international pharmaceutical companies. In order to meet its pledge of universal care for all HIV/AIDS victims, the government threatened to violate any international patent agreement and produce all HIV treatment locally. Brazil was uniquely prepared to carry through with this threat because of the size and sophistication of its pharmaceutical industry. In retaliation, US officials filed a complaint with the World Trade Organization in which they argued that Brazil's intentions were in violation of international patent laws and that Brazil's stance would discourage the drug industry in the United States from bringing new drugs into the market. In the end, the United States dropped the complaint, facing a wave of indignation from other nations, international AIDS activists, and the United Nations.

Brazil's AIDS policy also attracted controversy because it rejected what is popularly known as the "ABC approach" for fighting AIDS: abstinence, being faithful, and controlled use of condoms. This conservative paradigm has dominated American international AIDS policy since the early 2000s. Aside from depending upon extensive consultation between state agencies, the scientific community, and a variety of NGOs, Brazil's AIDS policy also relies on the liberal distribution of condoms (especially at large public events, such as Carnival in Rio and São Paulo's gay pride parade), and enlisting sex workers to promote the use of condoms as a means of helping curb HIV infection. These measures made Brazil ineligible for American funding, which stipulates that all recipient countries must embrace the view that prostitution is degrading and dehumanizing and thus is not suited for involvement in official government business.

But it is hard to argue with success. Above all, the PNDA is credited with "reversing the Africanization of AIDS in Brazil."[92] By the mid-2000s, the AIDS caseload in Brazil stood at about eight hundred thousand, half of what the World Bank had predicted in 1994.[93] Much of this success is credited to President Cardoso, who greatly expanded the role of the federal government in the fight against HIV/AIDS. But sustained and smart activism also played a critical role. By pressing the government into action, gay and human rights activists capitalized on the provision in the 1988 Brazilian constitution that guarantees universal healthcare to make the case that HIV/AIDS treatment was a human rights issue. According to Brazilian lawyer Miriam Ventura, Brazil's AIDS policy was "the successful result of a model of action adopted by organized civil society. This mobilization utilized the language of human rights and the strategic application of national laws and succeeded in placing on the political agenda questions that affect the life of people living with HIV/AIDS, and in so doing altered public and state policies regarding health care."[94]

To some extent, the partnership between and the state and the gay movement triggered by the HIV/AIDS crisis in Brazil was a natural one, given the long history of the Brazilian state of co-opting social movements and interest groups. Fry notes that "it seems as though all social movements in Brazil end up funded by the state, even those that claim to be against the state."[95] He adds that "the government correctly perceived that it needed the gay NGOs in its battle to inform the public about HIV." There was considerable agency, however, on the part of gay activists in crafting their alliance with the state. They saw the state's willingness to engage the gay community on the issue of AIDS as an opportunity both to address a threat that posed a risk to the existence of the gay community and to prevent the collapse of the gay rights movement. Anthropologist João Biehl notes that "with AIDS increasingly viewed as a development problem and with international funds available, AIDS activists left behind antagonism to the state and together with health technicians, epidemiologists, medical and social scientists, economists, and psychologists constituted a new epistemic community within the state."[96]

As might be expected, the PNDA's impact extended beyond health concerns. To no small degree, the program reshaped the Brazilian gay movement in a way that illustrates how state policies can transform social movements and their activism. By 2007, the state's engagement in HIV/AIDS had resulted in the "NGO-ization" of the gay movement, with the emergence of some seven hundred NGOs involved in HIV/AIDS.[97] State support for AIDS organizations included support for their work beyond AIDS advocacy, such as affirming homosexual identities. In 1995, the Seventeenth International Lesbian and Gay Association (ILGA) annual meeting was held in Rio de Janeiro with financial support from the government's AIDS policy program, the first time that the ILGA had organized its annual gathering in a South American country. As part of the ILGA conference, Brazil held its first pride parade in Rio de Janeiro. Held on the fashionable and very prominent Atlantic Avenue, the parade left little doubt about the diversity, vibrancy, and growing political influence of Brazil's LGBT community. "The movement had come of age," reports Green in his effusive review of the ILGA's Rio gathering.[98] In keeping with the local custom, the parade mixed gay activism with a carnival-style atmosphere.

HIV/AIDS funding also accelerated the centralization of the Brazilian gay rights movement with the emergence in 1995 of the Associação Brasileira de Gays, Lésbicas, Bissexuais, Travestis e Transexuais (ABGLT), a national network of some three hundred LGBT groups that claims the title of Latin America's largest gay rights confederation. It was organized by Toni Reis, an activist from the state of Paraná in southern Brazil who had spent time in Italy and England during the late 1980s and early 1990s, where he became active with gay rights groups and "saw how far behind we were in Brazil."[99] Under Reis's leadership, the new organization challenged the hegemony of older gay groups, such as GGB, and rapidly became the "official" voice of the Brazilian LGBT community. Fueling the rise of the ABGLT was the need for national organizations capable of channeling the considerable financial resources being made available by federal government funds directed to gay NGOs involved in HIV/AIDS.

Almost from its inception, the ABGLT's collaborative relationship with the state extended beyond the state agencies responsible for HIV/AIDS policy—mainly the Ministry of Health—to other ministries, such as those of education, human rights, culture, and tourism. Under the Cardoso presidency, ABGLT leaders were consulted on the drafting of the Programa Nacional de Direitos Humanos (PNDH), which was implemented in two phases, in 1996 and 2002.[100] Among other things, the program sought to compensate for the failure of the 1988 constitution to ban antigay discrimination and to repair Brazil's troubled image ensuing from rampant human rights abuses, especially toward the LGBT community. The Cardoso administration also incorporated ABGLT leaders into the Conselho Nacional Contra Discriminação. This governmental commission was created in 2001 to study the stipulations of the United Nations World Conference against Racism, Racial Discrimination, Xenophobia and Related Intolerance, held in Durban, South Africa, that same year.

But there were disadvantages for gay activists working closely with the state and in using public funds to finance their activities, such as not being able to critically engage the government on issues of concern to the gay community beyond HIV/AIDS. Although the PNDH's final report recognized gays, lesbians, and transvestites among Brazil's most vulnerable minorities, the Cardozo government took no steps to battle homophobia and antigay violence. Cardozo had endorsed same-sex civil unions during his 1998 reelection campaign, but he did nothing to advance them during his second term in office. Gay activists, the ABGLT in particular, however, were hesitant to criticize Cardozo for the shortcomings of his gay rights policies. They were even more reluctant to mobilize the gay community against Cardozo, giving rise to criticisms that gay activists were privileging the health concerns of the gay community over their civil rights.[101]

Reis is unapologetic about his organization's collaboration with the state, even at the expense of pushing for a more civil rights-oriented agenda. To his mind: "emergency issues needed urgent solutions."[102] He notes that since the beginning of the AIDS epidemic, which in raw numbers affected Brazil more than any other country in Latin America, gays have been among the hardest hit. He adds that despite the progress that had been made in recent decades, the situation remains serious. Since the beginning of the third millennium the number of AIDS cases reported annually has remained high, exceeding four thousand; and among the young gay population, ages fifteen to twenty-four, the number of cases between 1998 and 2010 increased by 10.1 percent, compared with a decrease of 20.1 percent among the heterosexual population in the same age group.

THE LULA ERA, 2003–2010

Concerns that the ABGLT under Lula had become "an appendix of the PT," rather than an independent force within civil society, grew in intensity under the Lula administration (2003–2010), which started on a high note with Lula tasking the Human Rights Secretariat with devising a policy program to address the needs of the LGBT community. PT allies of the gay movement also reorganized their presence in Congress in anticipation of facilitating Lula's gay rights agenda with the formation in 2003 of the Parliamentary Front for the Freedom of Sexual Expression, created to defend the interests and rights of sexual minorities and to propose legislation of concern to the LGBT community. By 2005, the Front had a membership of eighty-five legislators (76 federal deputies and nine senators of a total of 513 deputies and eighty-one senators); 56 percent of the members came from the PT, with members of leftist parties accounting for 81 percent of all the members of the Front.[103]

Ironically, the Lula era would become the source of much frustration for gay activists. During Lula's two terms in office, Brazil did not enact any major federal gay civil rights legislation. The closest that the Lula administration came to achieving a legislative win on gay rights was an antidiscrimination bill that included sexual orientation as a category, which was approved by Chamber of Deputies in 2006 and then stalled in the Senate. What kept Brazil from making greater progress on gay rights under the Lula administration is a subject of much debate among gay activists. Reis puts the blame squarely on Congress: "The Brazilian gay movement operates within a uniquely unfavorable legislative context," pointing not only to the clout of the Evangelical bloc but also to the need to form coalitions with numerous parties, "many of them socially conservative, to get virtually any legislation enacted."[104] For Mott and other gay activists unaffiliated with the PT, however, the answers lie directly at Lula's feet, especially his failure to invest some of his considerable political capital on one of his oldest and most loyal constituencies, and to use the power of the Brazilian presidency to set the legislative agenda to advance gay rights.

Lula, according to Mott, "spoke the language of gay rights without being willing to commit the needed resources to see gay rights fully succeed."[105] To back up his view, Mott notes not only the administration's failure to enact a law banning antigay discrimination but also that Brasil sem Homofobia, the administration's high-profile initiative to combat antigay violence (designed by several agencies of the federal government and the ABGLT and coordinated by the Special Secretariat of Human Rights), was poorly funded and thinly staffed. Mott also blames Lula's allies within the gay community, especially the ABGLT, for their "uncritical" embrace of "PT-ism" and for "downscaling the ambition of gay rights activism." He notes that "the ABGLT was always close to Lula, although the government funding in health, culture, etc., have decreased comparatively since the Cardoso years. This support for the PT, even without significant achievements, is rooted in a mistaken strategy of preserving the dialog with those sectors of the state closest to the gay movement, especially the Ministry of Health, which finances many programs for the LGBT community."[106]

Both perspectives are valid, but they overlook what most scholars point to as the main reason why Lula over the course of the years dramatically altered his relationship with many of the progressive movements that brought him to power: electoral motivation.[107] Signs of this motivation were more than self-evident well before Lula entered office in 2003. During the 1998 presidential election, which marked a second defeat for Lula at the hands of Cardoso, Lula all but threw the gay community under the bus by telling a Catholic radio station in Rio de Janeiro that he was "against abortion and against gay marriage."[108] In the next election cycle (2002), from which Lula would emerge triumphant, Lula further upset many in the gay community with the selection of José Alencar to be his vice-presidential running mate. Alencar, a textile magnate and leader of the Liberal Party, a pro-business party with ties to conservative groups and a member of the Universal Church of the Kingdom of God, was meant to signal to voters that a PT victory would not entail a cultural and economic revolution. Hoping to avoid giving ammunition to the opposition, Lula skipped São Paulo's 2002 gay pride parade, although other notable PT politicians, including São Paulo's Mayor, Marta Suplicy, were in attendance.

Ironically, electoral concerns would grow most intense while Lula was in office, especially as the 2006 presidential contest was approaching. The 2006 contest found Lula obsessed with avoiding a runoff election (Brazilian electoral law requires presidential candidates to clear a 50 percent majority vote for an outright win). Lula had an unfortunate history with runoffs (he had twice lost the presidency in the final stretch of the race), so avoiding a runoff in 2006 became an objective for the so-called Lula machine.[109] Complicating the picture for Lula in 2006 was a series of political scandals involving members of Lula's inner circle. The most notorious was the *mensalão* scandal, an alleged cash-for-votes scheme involving PT leaders, which forced Lula to distance himself from his own party and its history of progressive politics. Lula the personal brand rather than the PT was front and center during the 2006 presidential race.[110]

In 2006, the main order of business was to assiduously court the fast-growing Pentecostal/Evangelical vote, much of it Afro-Brazilian, which eluded Lula in 2002. To the dismay of the liberal factions within the PT, including the gay movement, Lula held numerous private meetings with influential Evangelical pastors, hoping to secure their support. In one highly publicized visit to the temple of the Assembly of God in the outskirts of Rio, Brazil's biggest Evangelical church, Lula made an impassioned plea for the Evangelical vote. "For many years of my life, people said if I was elected, I would close the doors of evangelical churches. I say today that the Evangelical church does not have any doubts about President Lula, and President Lula has no doubts about the Evangelical church."[111] Lula also began to bring Evangelicals into his cabinet, including Marina Silva, a born-again Afro-Brazilian from the Amazonian state of Acre, who was appointed Brazil's environmental minister in 2003. More suggestively, Lula began to strike political alliances with politicians from parties, like the Republican Party, with considerable sway over Evangelicals. One such politician courted by Lula was Marcelo Bezerra Crivella, a Rio de Janeiro senator best known for his opposition to a federal law to criminalize homophobia. Crivella is a bishop of the Universal Church of the Kingdom of God and a nephew of the church's founder, Edir Macedo.

Predictably, Lula's progressively blatant dialing back of his support for gay rights triggered a serious rift within the gay community. At the 2003 Third National Plenary Meeting of Lesbians, Gays, Travesties, Transsexual and Bisexuals of the PT, the issue of affiliation with the PT took center stage. According to a summary of the meeting, many gay activists stressed the need for the gay movement to reconsider its ties with the PT, seeing "a close alliance between social movement organizations and political parties as a threat to the organizations' and the movement's autonomy."[112] These same leaders were also critical of the expanding bureaucratization of gay issues with the creation of state agencies to deal with the question of sexual diversity. They regarded these agencies as "blurring the line separating the state and civil society" and as compromising the ability of the gay community "to pressure, criticize and monitor the state." But many others saw no problem with their affiliation with the PT, believing that "party affiliation flows from the similarity between their view of society and the political change espoused by the PT." Furthermore, these activists pointed out that despite numerous problems posed by affiliation with the PT, "having the party in power nonetheless opens up more opportunities for change than would be the case with another party."

Trying to mend fences with the gay community, and with electoral concerns behind him, Lula reengaged with gay rights. An initial move was convening the first National Conference of Gays, Bisexuals, Transvestites and Transsexuals, in June 2008, in Brasilia. This was a high-profile occasion, with Lula and much of his cabinet, including Justice Minister Tarso Genro and Human Rights Secretary Paulo Vannuchi, in attendance. Its purpose was to promote "the citizenship and human rights of the LGBT community." To that end, the conference called for some fifty-one policies, including civil unions for gay couples, legalization of gay adoptions, sexual diversity educational programs for the military and the police, lifting restrictions on homosexuals wishing to donate blood, and adding discussion of homosexual families in educational textbooks—basically every piece of gay legislation the PT had been trying to get through the Congress for the past fifteen years.

In remarks that drew the ire of profamily groups and delighted an audience of some seven hundred people, Lula declared homophobia "the most perverse disease impregnated in the human head" and pledged to do "all that is possible to criminalize homophobia and to approve same-sex civil unions."[113] In a follow-up television interview, Lula reiterated his support for same-sex civil unions by noting: "Gay couples exist and we must give them recognition. There are men living with men, women living with women, and many times they live extraordinarily well. They live together, they work together, and I am favorable." At the request of gay activists, the Lula administration also agreed to create the National LGBT Council, a body that incorporates representatives from fifteen government ministries and leading gay organizations to propose policy on how to combat antigay discrimination. Much of this was for naught, however, with Lula already a lame-duck president and the Congress and the political class already looking forward to the 2010 presidential contest. Thus, Lula ended what is widely regarded as the most successful presidency in modern Brazilian history (at least as suggested by a personal approval rate of 80 percent) with a disappointing gay rights legacy.

Oddly enough, the Lula administration had more success promoting gay rights abroad than at home. Pressured by gay activists, Lula pushed hard to see the implementation of the World Trade Organization's 2001 Doha Declaration. This international agreement, inspired by Brazil's national AIDS policy, allows nations to circumvent patent laws on drugs deemed vital for the survival of people living with HIV. In 2004, the Brazilian delegation to the United Nations proposed a resolution, "Human Rights and Sexual Orientation," that called for the protection of human rights irrespective of people's sexual orientation. This resolution became the blueprint for the 2008 Organization of American States Human Rights, Sexual Orientation and Gender Identity Resolution and for an analogous resolution adopted by the United Nations Human Rights Council in 2011.

SAVED BY THE COURTS

Under the PT administration of Dilma Rousseff (Lula's former chief of staff, and Brazil's first ever female president), significant gay rights progress has come to the country, such as same-sex civil unions in 2011 and same-sex marriage in 2013. Yet, unlike in Argentina, where another female president (Cristina Fernández de Kirchner) put her reputation on the line and used every political resource available to her to see legislation on same-sex marriage enacted by the national legislature, this was not case in Brazil. Rousseff is on record as opposing same-sex marriage, a point she underscored during her historic 2010 presidential run and reiterated during her 2014 re-election campaign. "I am in favor of gay civil unions, since I think marriage is a religious issue. I, as an individual, would never tell a religion what it can and cannot do; we must respect," Rousseff said in an interview for the TV show *Roda Viva* of TV Cultural of São Paulo. The subject of same-sex marriage became an issue during the 2010 Brazilian presidential campaign after its legalization in Argentina that same year.

Instead of the executive branch or the legislature, it was the judiciary that ushered in civil rights for same-sex couples in Brazil with a string of historic rulings that have dramatically reshaped the landscape of gay rights in the country. In 2010, the Superior Court of Justice, the country's top appellate court, ruled unanimously that gay couples had the right to adopt. That ruling was followed by another unanimous decision by the Federal

Supreme Court (the country's highest court) in May 2011 (ten votes in favor and none against—one justice, José Antonio Dias Toffoli, abstained from voting, having already spoken in favor of same-sex unions as attorney general) forcing the state to put homosexual and heterosexual relationships on the same legal footing.[114] With this ruling, the Court deemed homosexual couples deserving of all the rights accorded to a homosexual couple. In justifying this ruling, Justice Carlos Ayres Britto, the author of the ruling, noted that "the freedom to pursue one's sexuality is part of an individual's freedom of expression."[115]

In May 2013, the National Council of Justice, a body that oversees the judicial system, effectively ordered the federalization of same-sex marriage in Brazil. They did this by compelling all notary publics to issue marriage certificates to same-sex couples requesting one. The ruling was needed to deal with the growing patchwork of marriage laws across Brazil. By 2013, some ten states had legalized same-sex marriage, without judicial approval, starting in Alagoas in January 2012 and São Paulo, the nation's most populous state, in December 2012. In forcing all notary publics to issue marriage certificates to same-sex couples, Chief Justice Joaquim Barbosa, who also heads the National Council of Justice, noted on the council's website that "our society is going through many changes and the National Council of Justice should not be indifferent to them." The statement added that "the Supreme Court affirmed that the expression of homosexuality and heterosexual affection cannot serve as the basis for discriminatory treatment, which has no support in the Constitution."

Considerable impatience with the intransigence of the Congress on gay issues was a key factor behind the courts' gay rights rulings in Brazil, itself a reflection of how protective of sexual minorities Latin American courts have become in recent years. Then-Chief Justice Cezar Peluso noted that the court's 2011 decision was prompted by "the legal lacuna" created by Congress.[116] Justice Gilmar Mendes added that "same-sex couples found themselves in a legal limbo, so the Court had an obligation to respond to protect gay couples. This legal limbo contributes to discrimination, even to the violent practices that we have seen in the news."[117] "Brazil is moving beyond patriarchy," said Justice Ricardo Lewandowski, adding that "nontraditional relationships are emerging among us, beside the traditional patriarchal family."[118]

Interestingly, this was not the first time that the justices had chastised the political class for its inaction on gay rights. As far back as 1998, the justices had been urging the legislators to take action with fairly strong language. Then-Chief Justice Celso Mello commented in an interview with *O Estado do São Paulo*: "It is of no use commemorating the fiftieth anniversary of the Universal Declaration of Human Rights if unjust practices which deny homosexuals their basic human rights continue to exist. The Executive, legislative, and judicial bodies need to take note of these cruelties and acknowledge our need to confront the conditions of grave adversaries in which members of this extremely vulnerable groups are forced to exist."[119]

Shifting Course

The court's rulings, however, were not a mere sign of judicial indignation. These rulings were also a vindication of the longstanding argument by gay activists that the failure of Brazilian law to recognize same-sex unions amounted to a violation of human dignity and equality. The rulings also mirror shifting trends in Brazilian gay rights activism, especially the emergence of a new wave of gay rights activism prompted by the perception that the emphasis on the legislature employed by gay activists in the past had run its course and that the executive branch will only go so far in pushing for gay rights.

This last point is underscored not only by Lula's tenure in office, but also by Rousseff's first term, which amounted to a long string of disappointments for the gay community. In 2011, under pressure from Evangelical legislators, Rousseff canceled an educational campaign to fight homophobia and gay bulling in schools (the so-called kit homophobia)—designed by gay activists and several state agencies. In 2012, Rousseff failed to convince Congress to pass an antidiscrimination bill. In 2013, she banned an HIV prevention video that recommended safe sex for young people, which Evangelical leaders argued promoted promiscuity.

At the forefront of the new wave of gay activism in Brazil is the Grupo de Advogados pela Diversidade Sexual e de Gênero (Group of Lawyers for Sexual and Gender Diversity), or GADvS, founded in São Paulo in 2010 and legalized in 2012. Unlike other gay organizations, GADvS is not connected to any political party, and its core mission is not to lobby the legislature but rather to develop legal strategies for advancing gay rights. According to its president-director, Paulo Iotti, GADvS's emergence responds to a gap in the Brazilian gay rights movement created by what he calls the "hegemonic groups," an indirect slight against groups such as the GGB and ABGLT and their focus on congressional politics. "Despite the great number of gay NGOs active in Brazil, none of them have legal advocacy for LGBT human rights as its main focus. Resorting to the courts was our last recourse, our last stand to advance equality for the gay community in Brazil."[120]

It is also the case, as Iotti points out, that by 2010 the political and judicial climate had changed dramatically from what it had been during the 1990s.[121] While by 2010 Congress had grown more conservative, the judiciary had become more liberal, as suggested by the composition of the Federal Supreme Court, and this encouraged activists to shift their attention from Congress to the courts. It is almost inconceivable, Iotti argues, that the conservative Federal Supreme Courts of the 1990s could have issued the court's 2011 ruling. For instance, in the mid-1990s, the court famously rejected the petition by a transsexual (male to female) to have a name and sex change. Especially notable is the ideological transformation that the Federal Supreme Court underwent after Lula's election in 2003, including the appointment of a new crop of liberal justices, especially Joaquim Barbosa, the first Afro-Brazilian Chief Justice.

Unlike an earlier generation of gay activists who endeavored to enshrine in the Brazilian Constitution an actual ban on homosexual discrimination, for the GADvS the text of the 1988 constitution provides ample room for ending antigay discrimination in Brazil. Article 1, for instance, cites "a human dignity principle," while article 3 states that "the fundamental objectives of the Federal Republic are to promote the welfare of everyone, without prejudices or origin, race, sex, color, age and any other form of discrimination." And then there is article 226, which states that "the family, the basis of the state, has special protection by the state." That is the article that has been most central to gay activists' claims in recent years for advancing gay rights. In contrast to the previous constitution (that of 1967), the 1988 constitution does not define a family as "constituted by marriage." Therefore, gay activists contend, the constitution protects all families. That argument took center stage in the Federal Supreme Court's landmark 2011 decision that ruled that homosexual families were deserving of the same rights as heterosexual families.

The plaintiff in the case was Rio de Janeiro Governor Sérgio Cabral, a centrist politician who believed that gay state workers and their families deserved equal treatment under the law. He was joined in this effort by Rio de Janeiro Attorney General Roberto Gurgel, who was of the view that the Brazilian constitution does not prohibit a same-sex civil union. Brazilian law allows selected public officers, including governors, to file cases directly with the Federal Supreme Court. At the heart of the case was not same-sex marriage, which has never been a demand of any gay rights organization in Brazil, but rather, it was the constitution's notion of family. As noted by Iotti, who was part of the legal team that argued the case before the Federal Supreme Court, "The court was not asked to decide on the constitutionality of same-sex marriage but rather to define the notion family within the framework of the 1988 constitution."[122] Framing the legal issue around the idea of family, Iotti argues, was wise given how polarized the Brazilian public remains on the issue of same-sex marriage, to say nothing of the stanch opposition to same-sex marriage by the Catholic establishment and the Evangelical movement.

To buttress their case that homosexual couples were deserving of constitutional protection, the plaintiffs worked closely with Maria Berenice Dias. The first female judge in the court of appeals of the state of Rio Grande do Sul, Dias is an expert on Brazilian family law. *A Folha de São Paulo* has hailed her as "a gay rights pioneer."[123] In particular, Dias is known for her advocacy of "homo-affection," a theory that challenges the view that homosexual couples only seek sexual gratification and that proposes, instead, that they aspire to loving and stable relationships, just as heterosexual couples do.[124] Moreover, the plaintiffs contended that the current provisions in the law for same-sex couples essentially forced them to enter into "business arrangements," which was a violation of their dignity, a constitutionally protected right. These arguments, which were echoed in the many amicus briefs filed by gay rights organizations in support of the suit, were broadly supported by the court's decision. The ruling stated that "denying same-sex unions recognition was a violation of the 1988 constitution which guarantees dignity and equality to all Brazilian citizens."

Fittingly, gay activists greeted the 2011 ruling as a milestone for Brazilian families (not just the gay community) since it meant that gay couples (which according to the 2010 census numbered some sixty thousand) would be treated as a "family entity," entitled to all the benefits befitting that status, such as the ability of one partner to give the other health benefits, inheritance, and a pension, as well as the ability to adopt children. Reis, speaking on behalf of the ABGLT, noted that the ruling was "historic" since "prior to the decision, same-sex unions could only be formalized by means of a business contract, as if the couple were partners in a firm."[125] GGB's Cerqueira observed that "This is a historic moment for all Brazilians. This judgment will change everything for us in society—and for the better. Gays, lesbians and transsexuals will be more accepted by having our rights honored."[126]

Sensing that the courts are willing to support gay rights claims of constitutional protection for sexual minorities in the absence of specific protections for sexual minorities in the constitution, gay activists are now eyeing the courts as they seek to enact laws already blocked by Congress. Another lawsuit making its way to the Federal Supreme Court aims to recognize "homotransphobia" as a constitutional crime akin to racism. This law would ask the Federal Supreme Court to criminalize gay discrimination.

According to Iotti, the precedent for this ruling is a 2003 ruling by the court declaring anti-Semitism a form of racism.[127] In that case, the court deemed anti-Semitism to be an ideology that "ran contrary to the constitution by seeking to dehumanize and treat a group of people as inferior."

While the courts have become the gay community's great savior in Brazil, it is unclear whether legislating gay rights from the bench will bring the country around to support gay rights. According to Iotti, despite the positive impact of recent judicial rulings, "victories in court have not increased societal acceptance of homosexuality and LGBT identities in general."[128] In fact, the evidence so far suggests that judicial victories, although vindicating gay activists, are helping to fuel rather than to quell the culture war over gay rights in Brazil. The attempt by conservative politicians to try to circumvent the Federal Supreme Court's rulings is a case in point. Thus, finding ways to increase societal acceptance of homosexuality remains the great challenge for gay rights in Brazil.

"Getting some laws in the books," Iotti notes, will certainly help in increasing societal acceptance of homosexuality, given the societal discussions that making laws usually entails. But he also stresses the need for Brazilian activists to be more proactive in reaching out directly to society, with the aim of influencing hearts and minds. Reaching out to society, Iotti concedes, "is something that Brazilian activists as a collective have not been very effective at." Bruno Bimbi, one of the architects of Argentina's same-sex marriage campaign, now living in Brazil, where he advises gay activists outside of the "historic" LGBT movement, such as Iotti and openly gay congressman Jean Wyllys, echoes Iotti's lament.

When contrasting gay activists' strategies in Argentina and Brazil, Bimbi questions the blinding faith that Brazilian activists have placed on enacting laws to criminalize homophobia as a means for dealing with widespread antigay discrimination and antigay violence. "The difference between the models promoted by the Brazilian LGBT movement to advance gay equality and the model adopted by Argentina is enormous: instead of using the Penal Code to punish the homophobes, we in Argentina opted for convincing the homophobes that they were wrong and we questioned the hegemonic collective conscience that made the homophobes feel comfortable in their thinking." He adds that rather than insisting on getting their rights, Brazilian activists have opted instead for punishing those who would deny gay people their rights. "This is rarely a winning strategy: it builds resentment rather than support."[129]

CHAPTER 6
Insights from the Revolution

L atin America's gay rights revolution underscores the need to unpack the domestic context in order to understand how and why these rights have erupted in such a dramatic fashion throughout the region in recent decades. Popular narratives of Latin America's gay rights advances as a byproduct or offshoot of the globalization of American homosexual culture, the socialization of Latin American countries into international human rights norms, and the diffusion among states of gay rights policies such as antidiscrimination laws and same-sex civil unions and marriage, although compelling, are insufficient and even misleading. Instead, this study has called for decentering gay politics in Latin America. The intention has not been to deny the importance of international influence in the spread of gay rights across Latin America, but instead to demonstrate how the domestic context has worked to mediate the speed and scope with which international gay rights ideas have penetrated the region.

The focus of the analysis has been on those domestic factors that in recent decades have made Latin America an especially receptive environment for the development of gay rights. Cultural, legal, and political factors—such as modernization, constitutional and judicial reforms, and the advent of socially liberal governments in several countries—have certainly made a big difference. Among other things, these factors have lessened the role of religion in public life, made ordinary Latin Americans more accepting of homosexuality, emboldened the courts to expand the rights of sexual minorities, and lowered the risks for politicians willing to support gay rights. But the most decisive factor has been the activism of gay rights organizations, a social movement long neglected even by scholars of Latin American social movements.

In particular, the analysis has highlighted the role of Latin American gay rights activists in crafting gay rights campaigns that although influenced by international trends are firmly grounded in the local environment. Argentina, where the campaign for gay rights, especially marriage equality, was provocatively framed as a human rights crusade, premised on the view that the freedom of sexuality is a basic human right, provides the most compelling example. Argentine gay activists appropriated the international language of human rights and folded themselves into Argentina's own large and influential network of human rights organizations as a way to lend legitimacy to their struggle, to disarm their opponents, and to gain acceptance into the political community.

Gay activists in Argentina also adopted much of the playbook of the local human rights movement, like retaining independence from the political system, aggressive litigation, political pressure tactics (such as the famous *escraches*), and media campaigns intended to influence hearts and minds. Along the way, Argentine gay activists married ideas to action by exploiting a myriad of political opportunity structures to advance their gay rights policy objectives—such as the military trials of the posttransition era, the reformation of the Argentine constitution in 1994, and the social justice movement spawned by the economic implosion of 2001, and made critical allies within the state, the economy, and most sectors of civil society.

To be sure, there is much that is unique about Argentina that limits how much the case can serve as a model to other countries in Latin America and to the rest of the developing world. Above all, it is hard to understand the successful framing of the Argentine campaign for gay rights as a human rights crusade without accounting for the flourishing human rights culture that accompanied the democratic transition. Argentina is, after all, as close to a "human rights state" as one is likely to find anywhere. This was a direct byproduct of the massive scale of the human rights abuses committed by the military dictatorship between the years of 1976 and 1983, which far exceeded the human rights abuses of sister dictatorships in South America.[1] Such a dark legacy made connecting human rights to antigay discrimination in Argentina less of an abstraction than anywhere else in Latin America. Indeed, the political excesses of the old regime in Argentina gave the domestic struggle for gay rights a cultural and political resonance and a moral rooting that was unique in all of Latin America, perhaps the world.

Gay activists in Argentina also operated within the very unusual political environment that is Buenos Aires, a sprawling city that is home to roughly a third of all Argentines. While it is an over-statement to say that "as Buenos Aires goes so goes Argentina" (this point is underscored by the failure of Buenos Aires' civil unions ordinance to go nationwide after 2002), the city dominates national politics like no other case in Latin America. The relevance of this, as explained by James N. Green, is that the convenience of having "one city, one state, and one nation all packed into one geographic location" allowed a small, closely knit group of male intellectuals to coordinate activities, to lobby the political class, to influence public opinion, and to shape national policy in ways that would not had been possible anywhere else in Latin America.[2]

But the uniqueness of Argentina is in many regards the point. It underscores the importance of modeling the campaign for gay rights in a manner that evokes and/or capitalizes upon the domestic context rather reproducing any particular international path or strategy. This point is also broadly supported by the Brazilian experience, especially the recent successes by gay activists in having the courts declare that homosexual families deserve the same legal protections as heterosexual families, which opened the way for the legalization of same-sex civil unions and same-sex marriage. These victories hinged upon the development of homegrown arguments about the nature of homosexual relationships that resonated deeply with elements of the Brazilian Constitution stressing dignity and equality for all.

In this conclusion, I focus on three insights. I deliberately use the word "insights" rather than the more conventional "lessons" because of the still-evolving nature of gay rights politics in Latin America. I first discuss the importance of "decentering" gay politics by putting the domestic context front and center in trying to understand the global spread of gay rights. I then touch on the primacy of "strategy" over "resources" in dictating domestic gay rights policy outcomes, a point that challenges prevailing assumptions about what makes for a successful social movement. In this section I incorporate evidence from the US experience, where gay rights at the federal level appear to have had a harder time getting off the ground than in Latin America. Lastly, I argue that the rise of gay rights in Latin America, a major milestone for democracy in the region, is not without its dark side, especially increased violence against the LGBT population. This contradiction ensues from the fact that in many Latin American countries, even those where gay rights have made the most significant inroads, the culture and public opinion trail the law with respect to gay rights and homosexuality more generally.

LATIN AMERICA AND THE GLOBAL SPREAD OF GAY RIGHTS

The Latin American experience has much to say about the recent global spread of gay rights.[3] First and foremost is the overwhelming importance of the domestic context and national histories in determining whether gay rights arise in the first place and whether these rights prove sustainable in the long term. This assertion goes a long way toward explaining why, for all the talk of a global spread of gay rights and rising acceptance of homosexuality the world over, the geographic scope of this spread is a lot less impressive than is often presumed. As noted by *The Atlantic*'s Uri Friedman, "Gay rights aren't advancing globally as much as they are expanding in certain parts of the world while regressing or languishing in others."[4] Friedman's point is underscored by the fact that the number of countries that still criminalize homosexuality has not decreased much in recent years: eighty-five in 2007 and seventy-six in 2013.[5] Understandably, decriminalizing homosexual behavior, rather than promoting same-sex marriage or civil unions, is the top priority for gay rights activists at major international human rights organizations.

It is telling that the kind of dramatic advances in gay rights that have taken place in Latin America are on the whole missing from other parts of the developing world. Indeed, at the same time that gay rights have been advancing throughout Latin America, including same-sex marriage, they have been receding in other parts of the developing world.[6] In 2013, the year that Brazil and Uruguay introduced same-sex marriage, Uganda passed a bill that calls for life imprisonment for some homosexual acts and a seven-year jail term for anyone who conducts a gay marriage ceremony. This law was actually an improvement over the original 2009 bill, the so-called "kill the gays bill," which called for the death penalty for gay Ugandans and sentences of up to seven years for family and friends who failed to report them to the authorities.

Also in 2013, Russia enacted a law banning the promotion of "sodomy, lesbianism, bisexuality and transgenderism." The law is so broad that, in principle, it outlaws pride parades, public displays of affection by same-sex couples, and symbols of the LGBT community such as the rainbow flag. Even an admission of homosexuality, unless made for the purpose of casting homosexuality in a negative light, could be a violation of the law. In the wake of these legal setbacks in Uganda and Russia came a shocking rash of attacks on gays and lesbians. India's Supreme Court reinstated a colonial-era prohibition on homosexual sex that, according to one estimate, "doubled the number of gay people in the world who can be imprisoned for their sexuality."[7] Brunei increased the penalty for homosexuality to death by stoning, as part of an effort to impose Islamic sharia law. Iran conducted a series of public hangings of gay males intended to reassert it laws that deem homosexuality a crime punishable by death. Sharia judges in Iraq and Nigeria began sentencing people to death for engaging in homosexual conduct. In Egypt, eight gay men were convicted and sentenced to three years in prison for "inciting debauchery" after the authorities detected their faces in an Internet video of an alleged gay wedding on a cruise down the Nile.

How uneven, perhaps schizophrenic, the global picture for gay rights has become is highlighted in "The Global Divide on Homosexuality." This Pew study demonstrates that while gay rights have flourished in the Americas and Western Europe, they are basically frozen in the rest of the world.[8] The survey, based on the question "Should Society Accept Homosexuality?" is led by Spain, where an impressive 88 percent of people surveyed answered in the affirmative, followed by Germany (87 percent), Canada and the Czech Republic (tied at 80 percent). Among Latin American nations, Argentina led with 74 percent of the population expressing acceptance of homosexuality, in the same bracket as most Western European countries; followed by Chile (68 percent), Mexico (61), and Brazil (60), the same as for the United States. On the opposite end of the spectrum we find the likes of Russia, where only 16 percent of the population expresses approval of homosexuality, Turkey (9 percent), Egypt (3 percent), and Nigeria (1 percent).

According to Pew, underlying the global divide on homosexuality are local differences with regards to affluence and religiosity. Gay rights have grown and expanded most rapidly in countries with the highest incomes and the highest standards of living, especially access to education, a development that is often accompanied by a rising tide of secularism, as seen in Western Europe, the United States, and Latin America. Gay rights have failed to get off the ground or even receded in places where poverty remains endemic, such as much of Africa, or where religion remains an important aspect of people's lives. This latter feature is confined, albeit not exclusively, to the poorest regions of the world, like Africa and the Middle East. Across these regions, there has been a robust revival of Islam that is boosting attempts by some governments to make state laws conform to Islamic law (sharia), which makes homosexuality a mortal sin.

A decidedly less observed variable is the political regime, a point underscored by the fate of democracy in many parts of the developing world.[9] Gay rights are faring best in those countries where political freedoms, the rule of law, and civil society have taken hold, as in the nations of Latin America. By contrast, gay rights are languishing where authoritarianism is on the rise and civil society is under attack, as in Russia, most of Africa, and much of the Middle East. As seen in this study, among the many factors that made democracy a boon for gay rights in Latin America are the political opportunity structures that it provides to gay activists and their allies to promote their policy objectives. Democratic governance has afforded handholds such as access to the courts, the party system, and the legislature—as well as a social environment that allows gay people to live their lives more openly and honestly. The last point is often underappreciated in understanding societal acceptance of homosexuality.

The survey data show that knowing someone gay is one of the best indicators for supporting gay rights. A 2009 Gallup study confirmed that "many views toward gay and lesbian issues are related—in some instances, strongly so—to personal experience with individuals who are gay or lesbian." The study raises two plausible explanations. One is that exposure to gays and lesbians leads to greater acceptance of them, regardless of one's ideological leanings. The other is that people who are more accepting of gays and lesbians are more likely to put themselves in situations where they are exposed to gays and lesbians. Regardless of the direction of causality, the data strongly support the proposition "that knowing someone who is gay or lesbian fosters more accepting attitudes on many of the issues surrounding gay and lesbian relations today."[10]

Another point about the global spread of democracy suggested by the Latin American experience is that international influence is not the one-way street that it is generally perceived to be. While we are inclined to think that external influence flowing from the developed North through globalization and policy diffusion is working to make developing nations more welcoming of gay rights, the opposite is often the case. As seen already, in some parts of Latin America, like Brazil, Central America, and the Caribbean, foreign intervention is generating a host of homophobic policies. The situation is more extreme in other parts of the developing world where the domestic environment for gay rights is not as favorable as in Latin America. In much of Africa and the Middle East, a full-scale antigay backlash is underway. This backlash has been credited to the very success of the gay rights movement in the developed West. Graeme Reid of Human Rights Watch accurately notes that "globalization has had paradoxical effects for the LGBT rights movement—on the one hand it has facilitated the movement—on the other hand it has provoked a backlash."[11]

Support for such assertions is provided by the rationalization given for enacting antigay legislation. When enacting nefarious antigay laws, countries such as Uganda and Russia cite not only a concern for stopping "Western influence," but also an actual threat to the nation, a threat articulated in ways intended to generate outright panic. Ugandan parliamentarians contended that their antigay bill was needed because "foreigners are coming into Uganda and spending millions of dollars to recruit children into homosexuality."[12] The Kremlin and the Russian Orthodox Church instigated passage of the law in "an effort to promote Russian values as opposed to Western liberalism," which is seen as "corrupting Russian youth."[13] This theme was echoed in Putin's 2013 state-of-the-union address, which cast Russia "as a defender of conservative values against the genderless and infertile Western tolerance that equates good and evil."[14]

Interestingly, pressure by the international community has done little to force Africans and Russians to back down on their antigay stances. This stands much in contrast to the positive impact of campaigns to shame Latin American nations for their treatment of homosexuals during the 1980s and 1990s. Many Western nations, including the Netherlands and Sweden, have suspended their foreign aid to Uganda. The World Bank has put on hold a US$90 million healthcare loan to Uganda as part of a new policy "meant to eliminate institutionalized discrimination," including antigay discrimination, which the Bank has deemed an "urgent task."[15] But this pressure, as reported by the *New York Times*, has bred "resentment towards the West" and has emboldened the Ugandans and kept the antigay bill alive "by increasing its popularity."[16]

Ironically, the rise of homophobic policies across the developing world intended to curb external influence is itself a fruit of external influence. It has been reported that behind the gay rights backlash in countries like Uganda and Nigeria are American Evangelical missionaries who for several years have been fanning the flames of homophobia in Africa.[17] These missionaries are accused of running a "neocolonial" enterprise that imports antigay strategies and discourse already discarded in most Western societies. According to one report, "Perhaps the biggest actors in Uganda's gay rights drama are American evangelicals who travel there every year by the thousands to spread their Gospel from the far pastures of Charismatic Christianity."[18] Principal among these groups is the International House of Prayer, a Kansas City–based megachurch that since 1999 has "poured millions of dollars into Uganda—much of it filtered into local churches and missions with explicitly anti-gay agendas."

The critical relevance of the domestic context to the rise and persistence of gay rights should be of paramount importance in how nations where gay rights are most advanced, as in Latin America, respond to the gay rights backlash currently underway in most of Africa, parts of Asia, the Middle East, and Russia. Thus far, as suggested previously, the tendency has been to name, shame, and punish. But, as seen previously, this approach is not yielding much in the way of positive results. In fact, the approach may be backfiring. A more fruitful approach might be to boost democracy, the rule of law, and civil society.[19] After all, these are the very things that turned Latin America, once one of the darkest environments for gay people in the developing world, into one of its brightest.

The Latin American experience with gay rights also has much to say about what makes for a successful gay rights movement. In particular, the contrasting experiences of Argentina and Brazil suggest the counterintuitive and provocative point that bigger is not always better when it comes to gay rights activism. In Argentina, a small, low-key, and politically independent movement has been more successful in bringing about societal change about homosexuality than a large, highly visible, and politically connected movement in Brazil. In large part this is because being smaller allowed for greater discipline, more nimbleness, and even more determination. Indeed, the Argentines appear to have turned their relative smallness and weakness into a virtue. At the end of day, Argentine gay rights activists proved more successful in advancing their demands than their Brazilian counterparts not because they were stronger and more resourceful (they decidedly were not) but because they were forced to be bolder and smarter. While Brazilian activists aimed to change the law, Argentine activists targeted transforming society and the culture at large.

More importantly, this study suggests the primacy of "strategy" in shaping gay rights struggles, especially how the campaign for gay rights is crafted. This emphasis on strategy is hardly new to the study of social movements, but more often than not the issue gets lost in the analysis. For one thing, activism itself is barely reflected in the dominant analytical narratives about social change. There is a general propensity among social scientists to either diminish or dismiss the agency of activists in advancing social change, and the case of gay rights is no exception. The political development literature sees rights as evolving organically and sequentially, with the consolidation of "political" rights, such as the right to vote and the right of association, serving as a precursor for the advent of "social rights," including gay civil rights.[20] Modernization scholars view the advent of laws and regulations intended to end discrimination against women, racial and ethnic minorities, and indigenous peoples as flowing from the rise of so-called postmaterial values within the electorate of mature democratic publics. Missing from this perspective is any hint of citizen or activist agency.[21] Scholars of transnationalism, as seen already, generally view the spread of gay rights as a byproduct of globalization, international socialization, and policy diffusion.

On the other hand, among theorists of social movements the issue of strategy is often overshadowed by the nearly hegemonic paradigm known as "resource mobilization," which stresses the importance of organizational assets, like large memberships, financial resources, ties to civil society networks, and access to the political system to the success of social movements.[22] As argued by social movements theorists, these are the things that define social movement strength and that allow social movements to exploit "political opportunity structures," those junctures provided by the political environment that allow social movements to bolster collective action.[23] It is questionable, however, whether the resource mobilization paradigm has the same explanatory currency in the context of advancing gay rights. After all, gay rights organizations in Latin America (and anywhere else for that matter), do not resemble most other social movements, such as organized labor. Given the biases inherent in the resource mobilization paradigm, it is hardly surprising that the eruption of gay rights around the world was never anticipated, much less predicted, by existing social movement theories.

Instead of focusing on organizational resources, the Latin American experience suggests that we might be better off looking at the kinds of claims that gay activists make, the arenas they choose in which to make those claims, and the tailoring of those claims for the local context. At the root of the success of Argentina's gay rights campaign lies not only the clever use of human rights arguments to anchor the campaign, but also a willingness to take the fight for gay rights beyond the political arena and straight into society and the culture at large. In the end, it appears that it is in society and the culture at large, rather than in the legislature or the courts, where gay rights victories are actually won.

The United States through Latin American Lenses

These assertions find much resonance in the American experience, which serves as an interesting counterpoint to the Latin American experience. It is interesting to note that, as in Latin America, the most impressive gay rights victories in the United States have not come in those states where the gay movement is most visible and, arguably, strongest, California and New York readily come to mind, but rather in Massachusetts, where a tight cluster of gay and lesbians centered around "small and staid" Boston laid down the legal groundwork that eventually led Massachusetts to become the first American state to legalize same-sex marriages.[24] "New York was sexier. San Francisco was *really* sexy. But Boston was smarter," argues historian Michael Bronski.[25]

On the other hand, despite having birthed the contemporary gay rights movement with the 1969 Stonewall riots, and by all measures having developed the largest, most resourceful, and most sophisticated network of gay rights organizations in the world, legislating gay rights at the federal level appears to have been a steeper hill in the United States than in Latin America. Not only did several Latin American nations beat the United States in legalizing same-sex marriage and civil unions at the federal level (including Argentina and Brazil, but also Chile, Bolivia, Ecuador, and Colombia), the Latin Americans have also bested the United States in enacting anti-gay discrimination laws. The Employment Non-Discrimination Act, better known as ENDA—a law intended to prevent antigay discrimination in the workplace—has languished in the US Congress since it was first introduced in 1974.[26] This means that only in those American states that have explicit laws banning discrimination on the basis of sexual orientation (about a third of them), are gay Americans protected from discrimination.

Also noteworthy is the backlash against gay rights in the United States, which has no parallel anywhere in Latin America. The backlash began in earnest in 1993, triggered by fears that the Hawaiian Supreme Court would legalize same-sex marriage and force other states into recognizing those marriages under the US Constitution's Full Faith and Credit Clause. In reaction to this prospect, in 1996, a panicked US Congress, with veto-proof majorities in both the Senate and the House of Representatives, passed the Defense of Marriage Act (DOMA). That infamous law prevented the federal government from recognizing same-sex marriages conducted in states where those marriages were legal. It inspired some thirty state laws and constitutional amendments banning same-sex marriage and in some cases same-sex civil unions and domestic partnerships. DOMA was invalidated in June 2013 by the US Supreme Court, which at the same time struck down California's Proposition 8, a popular referendum that in 2008 overturned California's same-sex marriage law.[27] DOMA, the Court ruled, "stigmatizes" and "humiliates" gay people, prompting dozens of federal and state courts across to conclude that bans on same-sex marriage were unconstitutional.[28] These rulings served as a prelude for the landmark June 2015 ruling by the Supreme Court in *Obergefell v. Hodges* that declared same-sex marriage a constitutionally protected right.

Even as they celebrate being able to marry, same-sex couples in the United States are bracing themselves for a new wave of discriminatory laws. These laws are emerging directly because of the expansion of same-sex marriage, especially so-called religious freedom laws that allow individuals and or corporations to deny services to gays and lesbians, like a wedding cake, if a "sincerely held religious belief" prevents them from doing so. New laws that just went into effect in Utah and North Carolina will allow any notary public to claim a religious exemption to issue a marriage certificate to a same-sex couple. A similar law, the Marriage and Religious Freedom

Act, introduced in the US House of Representatives, will do the same at the federal level. Several Republican senators have promised to introduce an amendment to the US Constitution that would allow individual states to reinstate same-sex marriage bans.

Some of the same variables examined in this study to understand the gay rights experience in Latin America can help make sense of why several Latin American nations have outperformed the United States on gay rights. For starters, despite having lower levels of social and economic development, Latin America offers a more advantageous religious environment. The primary reason for this is that Catholics overwhelmingly dominate in Latin America, quite in contrast to the United States, where Protestants are the dominant group. According to Pew: "On average, Catholics are less morally opposed to abortion, homosexuality, artificial means of birth control, sex outside of marriage, divorce and drinking alcohol than are Protestants."[29] It is further noted that "the differences between Catholics and Protestants on most of these issues hold true even when accounting for levels of religious observance."

It is also the case that the Latin American constitutions provide a more expansive notion of social rights than the American Constitution. Most Latin American constitutions have been either rewritten or replaced with brand-new ones in the last three decades with an eye toward eviscerating social discrimination and enhancing human rights protections. This is a direct consequence of Latin America having spent the better part of the 1970s and 1980s under the yoke of authoritarianism. New constitutional protections have made it easier for the high courts in places like Brazil and Mexico to rule decisively in favor of same-sex marriage, and simpler for gays and lesbians to access the courts demanding civil rights protections. By contrast, the American Constitution remains by and large remarkably faithful to its eighteenth-century foundations.

Another difference in the legal environment between Latin America and the United States is how the courts view international jurisprudence. The high courts in Latin America have in recent years indulged in "transnational legalism" to advance gay rights. Curiously, much of the foreign inspiration for the Latin American justices when mandating gay rights, same-sex marriage in particular, has come from American jurisprudence. The ruling by Mexico's Supreme Court that opened the way for the federalization of same-sex marriage among Mexican states is a clear example of this phenomenon. The unanimous 2012 ruling that declared denying the right to marry to three gay couples from the state of Oaxaca cited *Loving v. Virginia*, the landmark case that struck down anti-miscegenation laws in the United States. The US Supreme Court, by contrast, has, traditionally, been loath to cite legal precedents from other countries or international courts. Justice Ruth Bader Ginsburg recently lamented this when noting that the global influence of the American high court was diminishing because it had not regularly used foreign law in reaching its decisions. "You will not be listened to if you don't listen to others," she admonished law students at Ohio State University.[30]

A less apparent factor in shaping gay politics in the United States and Latin America, and the one with the most direct connection to this study, is the crafting of the campaign for gay rights. More so than in any other country, the campaign for gay rights in the United States has been waged as a "minority rights" struggle in search of civil rights, with activists trying to justify gay rights under the equal protection clause of the Fourteenth Amendment to the US Constitution. This followed the example set by the American civil rights movement. As noted by historian George Chauncey, the civil rights movement "pioneered the concept of minority rights and made it easier for gays to begin to depict themselves as a minority who deserved the same civil rights that other Americans and other minorities did."[31]

But selling gay rights as minority rights in the United States has proven to be a real challenge; a harder challenge, in fact, than the attempt by gay activists in Latin America to justify gay rights as human rights. It is only since DOMA's demise, in 2013, that American courts began to rule in favor of same-sex marriage as a violation of the Fourteenth Amendment. Significant portions of the American public, especially conservative African Americans, resent the notion that the Fourteenth Amendment, which deals explicitly with the issue of slavery, applies to homosexuals.

For all the power of the argument that equal protection under the law applies to the homosexual population, it is telling that support for same-sex marriage did not begin to take hold within American society until after gay activists shifted discourse strategies. Over time, the rhetoric about same-sex marriage went from emphasizing equal rights to stressing instead that gay people's desire for marriage is rooted in love, commitment, and responsibility, much in the same way in which straight people justify their desire for marriage.[32] Pressing this new campaign was Freedom to Marry, an organization created in 2003 by Evan Wolfe, widely regarded as the father of the American marriage equality movement, with the mission of changing perceptions of how Americans felt about gay marriage. In researching the issue of gay marriage, Freedom to Marry found that Americans' opposition to gay marriage was rooted in "antigay stereotypes," such as "gay people wanted marriage for selfish reasons while they themselves wanted to express love and commitment." Once the argument shifted from equal rights to love and commitment, attitudes toward gay marriage began to shift as well.

It is questionable, of course, whether the human rights framing approach that proved so influential in Latin American in the struggle for gay rights could have been pursued successfully in the United States. Human rights do not resonate with the American public in the same way they do in Latin America, given the wanton disregard for basic civil and political liberties that Latin Americans endured for much of the twentieth century. Moreover, despite the American leadership demonstrated during the drafting of the 1948 Universal Declaration of Human Rights, American courts generally do not recognize the legitimacy of international human rights laws. Not surprisingly, attempts by American social movements to use human rights arguments to advance their goals have on the whole been unsuccessful. The most notable attempt was by African Americans, who in the wake of World War II and the horrors of the Holocaust attempted unsuccessfully to use the emerging human rights framework to eradicate race-based segregation and discrimination in the United States. As the work of historians suggests, the tarnishing of human rights (by conservatives during the Cold War) as a Communist-inspired threat to the American way of life all but doomed African American leaders' embrace of human rights as a means for advancing black equality.[33]

POST-GAY RIGHTS LATIN AMERICA

Finally, it is interesting to ponder what the advent of gay rights means for Latin America. If, as is often noted, the character and quality of any country's democracy should be measured by how it treats its weakest and most vulnerable citizens, then the advent of gay rights in Latin American countries signals the dawn of a new era for democracy, citizenship, and human rights in the region. The rise of gay rights in Latin America should also help bury the region's stereotype as a social backwater, a trope that has been outdated for quite some time. For younger Latin Americans, notes sociologist Hector Carrillo in the New York Times, machismo "has become a dirty word."[34]

To be sure, "retro-machismo" still permeates many corners of Latin America, especially those corners where gay rights have been slowest to develop.[35] During the last presidential campaign in Venezuela, President Nicolás Maduro referred to his political opponent, Henrique Capriles (a forty-year-old single man) as "a little princess," while adding that "unlike my opponent I do have a wife and I like women." Capriles responded to Maduro's homophobic attacks by declaring himself "a womanizer," noting

"I am telling the whole country, right here and now, that women are my weakness."[36] During his electoral campaign, Paraguay's right-wing President, Horacio Cartes, rallied against gay marriage by characterizing it as "something that monkeys swinging from a tree do." He added that "he would shoot himself 'in the balls'" if he discovered that his twenty-eight-year-old son had married another man.[37] Bolivian President Evo Morales famously contended that "eating chicken could cause men to become bald and homosexual because too many fowl are injected with hormones."

But even in those countries where gay rights have made significant advances, homophobia remains pervasive. A case in point is the 2014 Brazilian presidential campaign, which came in the wake of the federalization of same-sex marriage by the Federal Supreme Court. Arguably, the most memorable moment of the campaign was a cringe-inducing episode about gay rights from the candidates' penultimate debate. During the section of the debate in which candidates were allowed to directly question each other, Socialism and Freedom Party candidate Luciana Genro asked Levy Fidelix, of the center-right Labor Renewal Party, why conservative politicians who say they support families refuse to accept the families of same-sex couples. Fidelix responded with a homophobic rant that was heard around the nation. In very crude language, he argued that homosexual sex is not conducive to procreation and added that because of a propensity toward pedophilia, gays "should be kept far away from society and given psychological help," before describing as "shameful and ugly" the sight of same-sex couples walking on Avenida Paulista, São Paulo's main street and the site of Brazil's largest gay pride parade. Fidelix's comments drew laughter from the audience, and none of the six other candidates at the podium, including incumbent Dilma Rousseff of the Workers' Party, felt compelled to repudiate them.[38]

More significant is the troublesome persistence of antigay violence. This has created a situation in which some of the most progressive legislation in the world regarding gay rights coexists with widespread antigay violence. Of course, this phenomenon of gay rights going hand in hand with antigay violence is not unique to Latin America. The American gay rights revolution has also been marred by violence against LGBT people. And even today, despite the milestones achieved at both the state and federal levels, gays in American society remain a vulnerable minority. According to a 2010 study by the Southern Poverty Law Center (SPLC), "Gays and lesbians face more violent hate crime than any other American minority and . . . the attacks are generally far more savage than other crimes."[39] Based on an analysis of fourteen years of hate crime data culled from Federal Bureau of Investigation, the SPLC study found that "gays and lesbians are more than twice as likely to be attacked in a violent hate crime as Jews or blacks; more than four times as likely as Muslims; and 14 times as likely as Latinos." The study concluded that "LGBT people are far more likely than any other minority group in the United States to be victimized by violent hate crime."

But what is striking about Latin America is the magnitude of antigay violence, at least as suggested by the available evidence, which is not very comprehensive. Few governments in the region collect statistics on violence against sexual minorities, since hardly any of them record "hate crimes," and international organizations tend to subsume the issue within the larger subject of "sexual violence."[40] Academics, for their part, are more prone to focus on violence in general in Latin America, including state-sanctioned armies, drug traffickers, gangs, and guerrillas.[41] Both perspectives are, of course, legitimate and make the very important point of highlighting violence in contemporary Latin America as both a public health concern and an egregious violation of human rights. But neither one provides an accurate picture of the unique problem of antigay violence or of the factors underpinning this pathology, nor what connection antigay violence might have with the recent spread of gay rights.

Undoubtedly, the most discussed case of antigay violence in Latin America is Brazil, where, as seen already, gay activists have claimed for years of the existence of a "homocaust" that takes hundreds of lives annually. The contrast with the United States is striking. According to the National Coalition of Anti-Violence Programs, in 2012 anti-LGBT and HIV-related homicides in the United States stood at twenty-five, a decrease of 16 percent from 2011.[42] As in other parts of Latin America, the roots of violence against LGBT people in Brazil are varied and complex, including homophobia, poverty, race, and social marginalization, a point underscored by a recent report from Global Rights drawing on data from the Brazilian government.[43] The majority of victims of gay violence in Brazil are sex workers and transsexuals. Out of the 338 LGBT murders recorded for 2012, 138 were transsexuals. The rural/urban divide is very important as well. Violence against LGBT people is more likely to take place in rural areas; it is also more likely to go unreported. Class is yet another relevant factor. Affluent gays, especially males, occupy a rarified environment of relative privilege in Latin America's most cosmopolitan cities, such as Buenos Aires, Rio de Janeiro, and Mexico City, not unlike that encountered in the developed West.

It is also the case that the advent of gay rights in Latin America has emboldened opposition to homosexuality in some quarters and that this, in turn, has made for a more dangerous climate for LGBT people. The growing opposition to gay rights by Evangelicals in Brazil has contributed a great deal to a climate that encourages violence against LGBT people. This can be appreciated in the virulent antigay activism of Evangelical preachers, who are leading the fight against gay rights by using their megachurches as the main venues in which to spread their venom against gay people. Religious leaders in Brazil are also active within the structures of the state. As seen previously, under the improbable leadership of Federal Deputy Marco Feliciano, an Evangelical pastor, the Committee on Human Rights and Minorities, a body created by the Brazilian Congress to defend LGBT rights, has become a tool with which to undermine these very rights.

Gay activists in Mexico point to a spike in violence against LGBT people between the years of 2004 and 2008, around the time the Catholic Church began to rally against the legalization of same-sex marriage in the Federal District in 2008.[44] Cardinal Norberto Rivera deemed gay rights "one of Mexico's most serious problems, comparable to violence, poverty and unemployment." The Archdiocese of Mexico published an article calling the Mexico City Council "a secular Taliban." In what activists described as an endorsement of violence against gays, Armando Martínez, head of Mexico's Catholic Lawyers College, argued that gay marriage would unleash a backlash against gays that the city assembly would be unable to contain. "The promoters of this law are promoters of homophobia. Why? Because Mexican culture is not ready for these things and they can release a level of homophobia that no one will be able to stop."[45]

Gay activists across Latin America are keenly aware about what is ahead: to bring societal attitudes about homosexuality in line with where the law is. This is a challenge in its own right; one likely to be as steep, if not steeper, than getting gay rights enacted into law in the first place. Perhaps because gay rights have come so swiftly in Latin America, the extent to which these rights actually challenge a social order that since colonial times has seen homosexuality through the darkest of prisms, can often go unacknowledged. But bringing society around is an obligatory challenge, one that has already been met for the most part in places like Argentina. If there is such a thing as a truism in gay politics is that gay rights victories in the legislature and the courts will prove sustainable only if accepted by the majority in society.

NOTES

INTRODUCTION

1. The term "gay rights" is understood in this study to stand for policies and legislation intended to eradicate discrimination on the basis of sexual orientation. The word "gay" is employed in this study as shorthand for gays and lesbians; when needed, however, I use the terms "gay males" and "lesbians." When speaking about a broader set of sexual identities I use the more inclusive "LGBT" (lesbian, gay, bisexual, and transgender) term.

2. "Gay Rights in Latin America: Out of the Closet," *The Economist*, March 8, 2007, http://www.economist.com/node/8819803 (accessed August 10, 2015).

3. "Why Is Latin America So Progressive on Gay Rights?" *New York Times*, January 29, 2014, http://www.nytimes.com/roomfordebate/2014/01/29/why-is-latin-america-so-progressive-on-gay-rights (accessed August 10, 2015).

4. "Rainbow Tide Rising: How Latin America Became a Gay Haven," *Alternet*, February 13, 2014, http://www.alternet.org/world/how-latin-america-became-haven-gay-rights (accessed August 10, 2015).

5. "Rainbow Coalition: A Gay Rights Revolution Is Sweeping across the Americas," *Foreign Policy*, January 24, 2013, http://foreignpolicy.com/2013/01/24/rainbow-coalition/ (accessed August 10, 2015).

6. On the GFI see Javier Corrales, Mari Crook, and Mario Pecheny, "Argentina: World Champion in LGBT Rights: How Did This Happen?" Paper presented at the annual meeting of the American Political Science Association, Seattle, WA, September 1–4, 2011.

7. Omar G. Encarnación, "Gay Rights and Human Rights," *Current History*, January 2013.

8. In 2013, the frequency of gay killings in Latin America was deemed serious enough for the Inter-American Commission on Human Rights to start a database to track down these killings. See "An Overview of Violence Against LGBTI Persons in the Americas: A Registry Documenting Acts of Violence between January 1, 2013 and March 31, 2014," http://www.oas.org/en/iachr/media_center/PReleases/2014/153A.asp (accessed August 28, 2015).

9. "Legal in Unlikely Places: Now Mature in the West, Gay Power Is Growing in Unlikely Places, Even in the Land of Machismo," *Newsweek International*, September 17, 2007.

10. See, especially, Martin B. Duberman, *Stonewall* (New York: Dutton, 1993).

11. Dennis Altman, "Rupture or Continuity? The Internationalization of Gay Identities," *Social Text* 14 (3) (1996), 77–94.

12. On international socialization, see Thomas Risse and Kathryn Sikkink, "The Socialization of International Human Rights Norms into Domestic Practices: Introduction," in *The Power of Human Rights*, ed. Thomas Risse, Stephen C. Ropp, and Kathryn Sikkink (New York: Cambridge University Press, 1999). An application of these theories to Latin America is Elisabeth Jay Friedman, "Constructing the Same Rights with the Same Names: The Impact of Spanish Norm Diffusion on Marriage Equality in Argentina," *Latin American Politics and Society* 54 (4) 2012, 29–59.

13. See Ryan R. Thoreson, *Transnational LGBT Activism: Working for Sexual Rights Worldwide* (Minneapolis: University of Minnesota Press, 2014).

14. See Adriana Piatti-Crocker, "Diffusion of Same-Sex Policies in Latin America," in *Same-Sex Marriage in the Americas*, ed. Jason Pierceson, Adriana Piatti-Crocker, and Shawn Schulenberg (New York: Lexington Books, 2010). On policy diffusion see Zachary Elkins and Beth Simons, "On Waves, Clusters, and Diffusion: A Conceptual Framework," *Annals of the American Academy* 598 (March 2005), 33–51; and Everett M. Rogers, *Diffusion of Innovations* (New York: Free Press, 2003).

15. José Guillermo de los Reyes Heredia, "Gay Rights and Movements," in *Iberia and the Americas: Culture, Politics and History*, ed. J. Michael Francis (Santa Barbara: ABC-CLIO, 2006), 516.

16. See Maria Berenice Dias, *União Homossexual: O Preconceito & a Justiça*, 2nd ed. (Porto Alegre: Editora Livraria do Advogado, 2001).

17. See "The Export of Hate: Global Advocacy of American Anti-LGBT Extremists Exposed," Human Rights Campaign Fund, September 15, 2014, http://www.hrc.org/campaigns/exporters-of-hate (accessed August 11, 2015).

18. Alex Seitz-Waltz, "Evangelicals Are Winning the Marriage Fight—in Africa and Russia," *National Journal*, January 25, 2014, http://www.nationaljournal.com/gay-washington/evangelicals-are-winning-the-gay-marriage-fight-in-africa-and-russia-20140123 (accessed May 1, 2015).

19. Risse and Sikkink, "Socialization," 5.

20. This growing literature includes Pierceson, Piatti-Crocker, and Schulenberg, *Same-Sex Marriage*; Shawn Schulenberg, "The Construction and Enactment of Same-Sex Marriage in Argentina," *Journal of Human Rights* 11 (1) 2012, 106–125; and Jordi Diez, *The Politics of Same-Sex Marriage in Latin America: Argentina, Mexico and Chile* (New York: Cambridge University Press, 2015).

21. Quoted passages from this section draw from Robert D. Benford and David A. Snow, "Framing Processes and Social Movements: An Overview and Assessment," *Annual Review of Sociology* 26 (2000): 614.

22. Ibid., 615–616.

23. Hank Johnston and John A. Nokes, "Frames of Protest: A Road Map to a Perspective," in *Frames of Protest: Social Movements and the Framing Perspective*, ed. Hank Johnston and John A. Nokes (Lanham, MD: Rowman and Littlefield, 2003), 11.

24. Ibid.

25. See, especially, John D. McCarthy and Mayer N. Zald, "Resource Mobilization and Social Movements: A Partial Theory," *American Journal of Sociology* 8 (6) (May 1977), 1212–1241.

26. Sidney Tarrow, *Power in Movement: Social Movements and Contentious Politics* (New York: Cambridge University Press, 1998).

CHAPTER 1

1. Charles Kaiser, *The Gay Metropolis, 1940–1996* (New York: Houghton Mifflin, 1997), 197.

2. See Elizabeth A. Armstrong and Suzanna M. Crage, "Movements and Memory: The Making of the Stonewall Myth," *American Sociological Review* 71 (5) (2006): 724–751. This analysis is notable for highlighting the series of gay riots that took place in Los Angeles and San Francisco during the 1950s, today forgotten save for the most detailed histories of the US gay rights movement.

3. For a fuller account of these events see David Carter, *Stonewall: The Riots That Sparked the Gay Rights Revolution* (New York: St. Martin's Press, 2004).

4. Martin B. Duberman, *Stonewall* (New York: Dutton, 1993), preface.

5. See, for instance, James Miller, *Democracy in the Streets: From Port Huron to the Siege of Chicago* (New York: Simon and Schuster, 1987); and Todd Gitlin, *The Sixties: Years of Hope, Days of Rage* (New York: Bantam, 1987).

6. On the rise and fall of homophile movement, see Barry D. Adam, *The Rise of a Gay and Lesbian Movement* (Boston: Tawyne, 1987), 64–75.

7. John D'Emilio, "Cycles of Change, Questions of Strategy: The Gay and Lesbian Movement after Fifty Years," in *The Politics of Gay Rights*, ed. Craig A. Rimmerman, Kenneth D. Wald, and Clyde Wilcox (Chicago: University of Chicago Press, 2000), 33.

8. Adam, *Rise of Movement*, 64.

9. Ibid., 75.

10. Neal Broverman, "The History of the Gay Rights in 348 Pages," *The Advocate*, July 3, 2012, http://www.advocate.com/arts-entertainment/books/2012/07/03/victory-author-linda-hirshman-discusses-meaning-stonewall (accessed January 5, 2014).

11. Michael Bronski, *Culture Clash: The Making of Gay Sensibility* (Boston: South End Press, 1984), 202.

12. This typology of gay rights draws upon the literature on "negative" and "positive" rights typically associated with the evolution of human rights, as summarized by Jack Donnelly in *Universal Human Rights in Theory and Practice* (Ithaca, NY: Cornell University Press, 2003), 30. According to Donnelly, "negative" rights only require "forbearance on the part of others," whereas "positive" rights require others to provide "goods, services, or opportunities." He adds that "the right to protection against torture is defined as the archetypical negative right, since it requires of the state nothing more than to refrain from incursions on personal liberty and bodily integrity. But protecting people against torture always requires positive endeavors by the state."

13. See, especially, Donn Teal, *The Gay Militants* (New York: Stein and Day, 1971).

14. Terence Kissack, "Freaking Fag Revolutionaries: New York's Gay Liberation Front, 1969–1971," *Radical History Review* 62 (1995): 105.

15. Craig A. Rimmerman, *From Identity to Politics: The Lesbian and Gay Movements in the United States* (Philadelphia: Temple University Press, 2001), 24.

16. Ibid; and Steven Epstein, "Gay and Lesbian Movements in the United States: Dilemmas of Identity, Diversity, and Political Strategy," in *The Global Emergence of Gay and Lesbian Politics*, ed. Barry Adam, Jan Willem Duyvendak, and Andre Krouwel (Philadelphia: Temple University Press, 1999), 41.

17. See Fred Fejes, *Gay Rights and Moral Panic: The Origins of America's Debate on Homosexuality* (New York: Palgrave Macmillan, 2008).

18. See, especially, Chris Bull and John Ghallager, *Perfect Enemies: The Religious Right, the Gay Movement and the Politics of the 1990s* (New York: Crown Publishers, 1996).

19. Liberation-type organizations, however, have never disappeared from the landscape of gay organizations. The 1990s, for instance, witnessed a revival of sexual liberation organizations such as Queer Nation and the Lesbian Avengers. On these movements see Epstein, "Gay and Lesbian Movements," 60–62.

20. See Craig A. Rimmerman, "Beyond Political Mainstreaming: Reflections on Lesbian and Gay Organizations and the Grassroots," in Rimmerman, Wald, and Wilcox, *Politics of Gay Rights*; and Rimmerman, *From Identity to Politics*, 18–44.

21. See, especially, Urvashi Vaid, *Virtual Equality: The Mainstreaming of Gay and Lesbian Liberation* (New York: Anchor Books, 1995).

22. See, especially, Andrew Sullivan, *Virtually Normal: An Argument about Homosexuality* (New York: Vintage, 1996); Evan Wolfson, *Why Marriage Matters: America, Equality and Gay People's Right to Marry* (New York: Simon and Schuster, 2005); Jonathan Rauch, *Gay Marriage: Why It Is Good for Gays, Good for Straights and Good for America* (New York: Henry Holt, 2006), and Kathleen E. Hull, *Gay Marriage: The Cultural Politics of Law and Love* (New York: Cambridge University Press, 2006).

23. See David A. Richards, *Identity and the Case for Gay Rights* (Chicago: University of Chicago Press, 1999), and Craig A. Rimmerman and Clyde Wilcox, eds., *The Politics of Same-Sex Marriage* (Chicago: University of Chicago Press, 2007).

24. Josh Zeitz, "The Making of the Marriage Equality Revolution," *Politico*, April 28, 2015, http://www.politico.com/magazine/story/2015/04/gay-marriage-revolution-e van-wolfson-117412.html#.VUFjZIu4lzg (accessed April 28, 2015).

25. See, especially, Peter A. Jackson, "Capitalism and Global Queering: National Markets, Parallels among Sexual Cultures, and Multiple Queer Modernities," *Gay and Lesbian Quarterly* 15 (3) (2009): 357–395. "Queer theory" is a staple of gay and lesbian studies. It reconceptualizes the word "queer," once a slur for homosexuals, to question gender norms and to introduce new dialogues about sexual identities and the politics such identities. For a primer on queer theory, see Annamarie Jagose, *Queer Theory: An Introduction* (New York: New York University Press, 1996).

26. Ken Plummer, "Speaking Its Name: Inventing a Gay and Lesbian Studies," in *Modern Homosexualities: Fragments of Lesbian and Gay Experience*, ed. Ken Plummer (London: Routledge 1992), 17.

27. Dennis Altman, "Rupture or Continuity? The Internationalization of Gay Identities," *Social Text* 14 (3) (1996): 33.

28. Arnaldo Cruz Malavé and Martin F. Manalansan IV, "Introduction: Dissident Sexualities/Alternative Globalisms," in *Queer Globalizations: Citizenship and the Afterlife of Colonialism*, ed. Arnaldo Cruz Malavé and Martin F. Manalansan IV (New York: New York University Press, 2002), 1.

29. Jackson, "Capitalism and Global Queering," 358.

30. Martin F. Manalansan IV, "In the Shadows of Stonewall: Examining Gay Transnational Politics and the Diasporic Dilemma," *Gay and Lesbian Quarterly* 2 (1995): 424.

31. Ibid., 427.

32. Christopher Pullen, ed., *LGBT Transnational Identity and the Media* (New York: Palgrave, 2012).

33. Reid Wilson, "Will, Grace, and a Decade of Change on Gay Rights," *National Journal*, June 26, 2013, http://www.nationaljournal.com/columns/on-the-trail/will-grace-and-a-decade-of-change-on-gay-rights-20130626 (accessed May 1, 2015).

34. William L. Leap and Tom Boellstorff, eds., *Speaking in Queer Tongues: Globalization and Gay Language* (Urbana: University of Illinois Press, 2004).

35. Dennis Altman, *Global Sex* (Chicago: University of Chicago Press, 2002), 70–71.

36. See Marc Carl Rom, "Gays and AIDS: Democratizing Disease?" in Rimmerman, Wald, and Wilcox, *Politics of Gay Rights*, 217–248.

37. See ibid.

38. Jonathan Rauch, "Not Whether but How: Gay Marriage and the Revival of Burkean Conservatism," *South Texas Law Review*, Winter 2009.

39. See Matthew W. Roberts, "Emergence of Gay Identity and Gay Social Movements in Developing Countries: The AIDS Crisis as Catalyst," *Alternatives* 20 (1995): 243–264.

40. Altman, "Rupture or Continuity?" 85.

41. Epstein, "Gay and Lesbian Movements," 55.

42. See Josh Gamson, "Silence, Death, and the Invisible: AIDS Activism and Social Movement Newness," *Social Problems* 36 (4) (October 1989): 351–367.

43. Jason DeParle, "Rude, Rash and Effective: ACT-UP Shifts AIDS Policy," *New York Times*, January 3, 1990, http://www.nytimes.com/1990/01/03/nyregion/rude-rash-effective-act-up-shifts-aids-policy.html (accessed August 11, 2015).

44. Thomas Risse and Kathryn Sikkink, "The Socialization of International Human Rights Norms into Domestic Practices," in *The Power of Human Rights*, ed. Thomas Risse, Stephen C. Ropp, and Kathryn Sikkink (New York: Cambridge University Press, 1999), 11.

45. Omar G. Encarnación, "Gay Rights and Human Rights," *Current History*, January 2013.

46. Risse and Sikkink, "Socialization," 11.

47. Ibid., 13.

48. Margaret E. Keck and Kathryn Sikkink, "Transnational Advocacy Networks in International and Regional Politics," *International Social Science Journal* 51 (1999): 89.

49. Ibid., 89–90.

50. Peter Nardi, "The Globalization of the Gay and Lesbian Socio-political Movement: Some Observations about Europe with a Focus on Italy," *Sociological Perspectives* 41 (3) (1998): 573.

51. According to the ILGA's website, as of 2012, membership in the organization included some 750 gay groups from around the world.

52. Encarnación, "Gay Rights."

53. *Breaking the Silence: Human Rights Violations Based on Sexual Orientation* (London: Amnesty International 1995).

54. "Hall of Shame' Shows Reach of Homophobia," Human Rights Watch, May 17, 2006, http://www/hrw.org/english/docs/2006/05/07/global13393.htm (accessed March 16, 2015).

55. Dave Bohon, "Conservatives Respond to Obama's Foreign Aid for 'Gay' Rights Policy," *New American*, December 8, 2011, http://thenewamerican.com/culture/faith-and-morals/10109-conservatives-respond-to-obamas-foreign-aid-for-gay-rights-policy (accessed February 25, 2012).

56. Dan Robinson, "Obama Elevates Gay Rights as a Foreign Policy Priority," *Voice of America*, December 6, 2011, http://www.voanews.com/english/news/usa/Obama-Elevates-Gay-Rights-as-a-Foreign-Policy-Priority-135136743.html (accessed February 7, 2012).

57. Ibid.

58. See Everett M. Rogers, *Diffusion of Innovations* (New York: Free Press, 2003), 5.

59. Andrew Sullivan, "Here Comes the Groom: The Case for Gay Marriage," *New Republic*, August 28, 1989.
60. *The Economist*, January 6, 1996, 84.
61. Richard G. Parker, "Changing Brazilian Constructions of Homosexuality," in Murray, *Latin American Male Homosexualities*, 249.
62. This is a dominant theme in the literature on Latin American male homosexuality. See, for instance, Stephen Murray, ed., *Latin American Male Homosexualities*, and Matthew C. Gutmann, ed., *Changing Masculinities in Latin America* (Durham, NC: Duke University Press, 2003).
63. See Gutmann, *Changing Men and Masculinities*.
64. Charles Klein, "The Ghetto Is Over, Darling: Emerging Gay Communities and Gender and Sexual Politics in Contemporary Brazil," *Culture, Health and Sexuality* 1 (3) (1999): 240.
65. See Benigno Trigo, ed., *Foucault and Latin America: Appropriations and Deployments in Discursive Analysis* (New York: Routledge, 2002).
66. See Lynda Johnson, *Queering Tourism: Paradoxical Performances of Gay Pride Parades* (New York: Routledge, 2005).
67. Javier Corrales, "Latin American Gays: The Post-left Lefties," March 29, 2010, http://www.americasquarterly.org/gay-rights-Latin-America (accessed September 11, 2013).
68. The most comprehensive account of AIDS in Latin America is Shawn Smallman, *The AIDS Pandemic in Latin America* (Chapel Hill: University of North Carolina Press, 2007).
69. Tim Fracas, *AIDS in Latin America* (New York: Palgrave, 2005), 6.
70. Shawn Smallman, "A Case for Guarded Optimism: HIV/AIDS in Latin America," *NACLA Report on the Americas*, July–August 2008, 15.
71. James Brooke, "AIDS in Latin America—a Special Report: In Deception and Denial, an Epidemic Looms," *New York Times*, January 25, 1993.
72. See M. Alfredo González, "Latinos ACT UP: Transnational AIDS Activism in the 1990s," *NACLA Report on the Americas*, July–August 2008.
73. Ibid.
74. *HIV/AIDS in Latin American Countries: The Challenges Ahead* (Washington, DC: World Bank, 2003).
75. This program is discussed in some detail in chapter 5.
76. Pan American Health Organization, "Campaigns against Homophobia in Argentina, Brazil, Colombia and Mexico," Washington, DC, 2008, http://www.paho.org/English/AD/FCH/AI/Homofobia.pdf (accessed April 2, 2012).
77. Ibid.
78. Katherine E. Bliss, "XVII International AIDS Conference in Mexico City: Implications for Latin America and the Caribbean," *Hemisphere Focus* 16 (3) (September 15, 2008).
79. Kathryn Sikkink, "The Emergence, Evolution, and Effectiveness of the Latin American Human Rights Network," in *Constructing Democracy: Human Rights, Citizenship, and Society in Latin America*, ed. Elizabeth Jelin and Eric Hershberg (Boulder, CO: Westview Press, 1996), 70–71.
80. Website of the International Gay and Lesbian Human Rights Commission, http://www.iglhrc.org/cgi-bin/iowa/content/about/ourhistory/index.html (accessed February 24, 2013).
81. See Juan Pablo Ordóñez, *No Human Being Is Disposable: Social Cleansing, Human Rights, and Sexual Orientation in Colombia* (San Francisco: International Gay and Lesbian Human Rights Commission, 1994).

82. Amy Lind, "Gay Rights in Latin America," *NACLA Report on the Americas*, May 1995.

83. Ibid.

84. Clyde H. Farnsworth, "Argentine Homosexual Gets Refugee Status in Canada," *New York Times*, January 14, 1992, http://www.nytimes.com/1992/01/14/world/ argentine-homosexual-gets-refugee-status-in-canada.html (accessed September 22, 2013).

85. Luiz Mott, *Epidemic of Hate: Violations of the Human Rights of Gay Men, Lesbians, and Transvestites in Brazil* (San Francisco: International Gay and Lesbian Human Rights Commission, 1996).

86. Amnesty International, "Violaciones de los Derechos Humanos de los Homosexuales," Madrid, Spain, January 1994, http://www.amnesty.org/es/ library/asset/POL30/001/1994/es/9a5f5d5a-ec2c-11dd-8d9d-a7825928c0bf/ pol300011994es.pdf (accessed January 1, 2014).

87. Amnesty International, May 31, 2001, http://www.amnesty.org/en/library/info/ AMR13/015/2001/en (accessed December 31, 2013).

88. Mario Vargas Llosa, "La caza del gay," *El País*, April 8, 2012, http://elpais.com/ elpais/2012/04/04/opinion/1333540547_113226.html (accessed August 8, 2015).

89. US State Department of State Fact Sheet, "Promoting Human Rights of LGBT People," December 6, 2011, http://iipdigital.usembassy.gov/st/english/texttran s/2011/12/20111206162231su0.6575587.html#axzz2Ta8iUVLC (accessed May 17, 2010).

90. The Latin American delegation included Jaime Parada of the Movement for Homosexual Integration and Liberation in Chile; Laura Bronzino, president of the Misiones LGBT Association in Argentina; Henry Peralta, general director of the LGBT Equality Foundation in Bolivia; Marcela Sánchez, executive director of Colombia Diversa; Brazilian congressman Jean de Matos; Francisco Madrigal of the Center for the Investigation and Promotion of Human Rights in Central America in Costa Rica; Efraín Soria, president of the Equity Foundation in Ecuador; José Lopéz, vice president of Comunidad Cultural de Tijuana LGBTI in Mexico; and Panamanian activist Augustín Rodríguez.

91. Rafael De la Dehesa, *Queering the Public Sphere in Mexico and Brazil* (Durham, NC: Duke University Press, 2010), 4.

92. For a translated version of the speech see http://www.gayliberation.net/ opinion/2005/1220zapatero.html.

93. Elisabeth Jay Friedman, "Constructing 'The Same Rights with the Same Names': The Impact of Spanish Norm Diffusion on Marriage Equality in Argentina," *Latin American Politics and Society* 54 (4) (Winter 2012): 29.

94. See Bonnie Field, "A 'Second Transition' in Spain? Policy, Institutions and Interparty Politics under Zapatero, 2004–08," *South European Society and Politics* 14 (4) (December 2009): 379–387.

95. Author's interview, Buenos Aires, July 20, 2012.

96. Omar G. Encarnación, "Latin America's Gay Rights Revolution," *Journal of Democracy* 22 (2011): 105.

97. Michael Levers, "Mexican Supreme Court Finds Gay Marriage Ban," *Washington Blade*, February 19, 2013.

98. See David F. Greenberg, *The Construction of Homosexuality* (Chicago: University of Chicago Press, 1988).

99. See especially John D'Emilio, "Capitalism and Gay Identity," in *The Lesbian and Gay Studies Reader*, ed. Henry Abelove, Michèle Aina Barale, and David M. Halperin (New York: Routledge, 1993), 467–478.

100. The literature on homosexuality and urbanization is quite voluminous by now. See, especially, George Chauncey, *Gay New York: Urban Culture and the Making of the Gay Male World, 1890–1940* (New York: Basic Books, 1994), Susan Stryker and Jim Van Buskirk, *Gay by the Bay: The History of Queer Culture in the San Francisco Bay Area* (San Francisco: Chronicle Books, 1996); Kaiser, *The Gay Metropolis, 1916–1996*; John Donald Gustav-Wrathall, *Take the Young Stranger by the Hand: Same Sex Relations and the YMCA* (Chicago: University of Chicago Press, 1998); Marc Stein, *City of Brotherly and Sisterly Loves: Lesbian and Gay Philadelphia* (Chicago: University of Chicago Press, 2004); and Matt Houlbrook, *Queer London: Perils and Pleasures in the Sexual Metropolis, 1918–1957* (Chicago: University of Chicago Press, 2005).

101. Osvaldo Bazán, *Historia de la Homosexualidad en la Argentina: De la Conquista de America al Siglo XXI* (Buenos Aires: Marea, 2004).

102. Daniel Bao, "Invertidos Sexuales, Tortilleras, and Maricas Machos: The Construction of Homosexuality in Buenos Aires, Argentina, 1900–1950," *Journal of Homosexuality* 24 (3–4) (1993): 208.

103. James N. Green, *Beyond Carnival: Male Homosexuality in Twentieth-Century Brazil* (Chicago: University of Chicago Press, 1999), 7.

104. Ibid., 11.

105. Ibid., 7.

106. Hector Anabitarte, email communication, July 12, 2012.

107. Author's interview, Buenos Aires, June 1, 2012.

108. Adam, *Rise of Movement*, 89 and 142.

109. Ibid., 143.

110. Stephan Likosky, ed., *Coming Out: An Anthology of Gay and Lesbian Writings* (New York: Pantheon, 1992), 246.

111. James N. Green, "(Homo)sexuality, Human Rights, and Revolution in Latin America," in *Human Rights and Revolutions*, ed. Jeffrey N. Wasserstrom, Greg Grandin, Lynn Hunt, and Marilyn B. Young (Lanham, MD: Rowman and Littlefield, 2002), 140.

112. Frente de Liberación Homosexual, "Sex and Revolution," trans. Sam Larson, in Likosky, *Coming Out*.

113. Author's interview, Buenos Aires, June 1, 2012.

114. De la Dehesa, *Queering the Public Sphere*, 5.

115. Human Rights Campaign Foundation, "Exposed: The World Congress of Families," August 2014, http://hrc-assets.s3-website-us-east-1.amazonaws.com//files/assets/resources/ExposedTheWorldCongressOfFamilies.pdf (accessed August 29, 2014).

116. Ibid.

117. Philip Pullella, "Pope Says Gay Marriage a Threat to Creation," Reuters, January 11, 2010.

118. Omar G. Encarnación, "Pope Francis' Latin Lessons," Foreign Affairs.com, May 14, 2014, http://www.foreignaffairs.com/articles/141424/omar-g-encarnacion/pope-francis-latin-lessons (accessed August 28, 2014).

119. This section on the spread of the ex-gay movement draws upon the reporting from Jandira Querioz, Fernando D'Elio, and David Maas, *The Ex-Gay Movement in Latin America: Therapy and Ministry in the Exodus Network* (Somerville, MA: Political Research Associates, 2013), http://www.politicalresearch.org/wp-content/uploads/downloads/2013/04/Ex-Gay-Movement-in-Latin-America.pdf (accessed December 30, 2013).

120. See André Corten and Ruth Marshall Fratani, eds., *Between Babel and Pentecost: Transnational Pentecostalism in Africa and Latin America* (Bloomington: University of Indiana Press, 2001) and Sturla J. Stalsett, ed., *Spirits of Globalization: The Growth of Pentecostalism and Experiential Spiritualities in a Global Age* (London: SCM Press, 2007).

121. "The Ex-Gay Movement on the Rise in Latin America," *The Edge*, February 21, 2012, http://www.edgeboston.com/index.php?ch=news&sc=international&sc3=&id=130139 (accessed May 17, 2013).

122. Jandira Querioz, "Christian Evangelical Right Sets up American Foothold in Brazil," January 26, 2013, http://oblogdeeoblogda.me/2013/01/26/christian-evangelical-right-sets-up-american-style-foothold-in-brazil/ (accessed January 12, 2014).

123. "U.S. Evangelicals Cheer on Latin Americas Culture Wars," *Reuters*, August 10, 2014, http://news.yahoo.com/u-evangelicals-cheer-latin-american-culture-wars-161634218.html (accessed August 8, 2015).

124. Reed Johnson, "Honduras Measure to Ban Same-Sex Measure Mobilizes Rights Groups," *Los Angeles Times*, January 19, 2005, http://articles.latimes.com/2005/jan/19/world/fg-gaymarriage19 (accessed February 24, 2014).

125. Wendy Wright, "Backlash Begins against Obama's LGBT Agenda," Catholic Family and Human Rights Institute, January 19, 2012, http://www.c-fam.org/fridayfax/volume-15/backlash-begins-against-obama's-lgbt-agenda.html (accessed February 7, 2012).

126. Cheryl Chumley, "Dominican Republic Outraged over Obama's Pick of Gay Ambassador," *Washington Times*, July 12, 2013, http://www.washingtontimes.com/news/2013/jul/12/dominican-republic-outraged-over-obamas-pick-gay-a/ (accessed December 23, 2013).

CHAPTER 2

1. Ronald Inglehart and Wayne E. Baker, "Modernization, Cultural Change, and the Persistence of Traditional Values," *American Sociological Review* 65 (1) (February 2000): 19.

2. Reported in Howard Wiarda and Harvey F. Kline, eds., *Latin American Politics and Development* (Boulder, CO: Westview Press, 2014), 11.

3. See "Brazil Bolsa Familia Program," World Bank, http://www.mfdr.org/sourcebook/6-1Brazil-BolsaFamilia.pdf (accessed April 23, 2015).

4. Ronald Inglehart and Christian Welzel, *Modernization, Cultural Change, and Democracy* (New York: Cambridge University Press, 2005).

5. Ronald Inglehart, *The Silent Revolution: Changing Values and Political Styles among Western Publics* (Princeton, NJ: Princeton University Press, 1977).

6. "Evangelicalism and Gay Rights in Latin America," Latin American Public Opinion Project, Vanderbilt University, 2012, http://www.vanderbilt.edu/lapop/ (accessed September 22, 2013).

7. This finding is in sync with survey data from the United States. A 2013 poll by Quinnipiac University Polling Institute found that "Catholic voters are leading American voters toward support for same-sex marriage." According to the survey 54 percent of Catholics favor gay marriage and 38 oppose it, versus 47 percent supporting and 43 opposing for the general public.

8. Ronald Inglehart, "Cultural Change, Religion, Subjective Well-Being and Democracy in Latin America," in *Religious Pluralism, Democracy and the Catholic Church in Latin America*, ed. Frances Hagopian (Notre Dame, IN: Notre Dame University Press, 2009), 67–95.

9. "The Global Catholic Population," Pew Research Center, February 13, 2013, http://www.pewforum.org/2013/02/13/the-global-catholic-population/ (accessed February 24, 2015).

10. Omar G. Encarnación, "The Catholic Crisis in Latin America: Even an Argentine Pope Can't Save the Church," Foreign Affairs.com, March 19, 2013, http://www.foreignaffairs.com/articles/139066/omar-encarnacion/the-catholic-crisis-in-latin-america (accessed August 28, 2014).

11. Frances Hagopian, "Latin American Catholicism in an Age of Religious and Political Pluralism: A Framework for Analysis," Working Paper No. 332, Helen Kellogg Institute for International Studies, December 2006, 3.

12. These figures come from the polling service Latinobarometro and are cited by Catholic News Service, http://www.catholicnews.com/data/stories/cns/0503707.htm (accessed February 26, 2012).

13. Liliam Kwon, "Pentecostal Impact Growing in Latin America," *Christian Post*, November 9, 2006, http://www.christianpost.com/article/20061109/pentecostal-impact-growing-in-latin-america/index.html (accessed August 5, 2010).

14. Countries where the percentage of Evangelicals exceeds 10 percent of the population include Argentina, Brazil, Guatemala, El Salvador, Nicaragua, and Chile. These countries are led by Guatemala, where, according to LAPOP, a stunning 34.2 percent of the population regards itself as "Evangelical-Charismatic."

15. See "Religion in Latin America," Pew Research Center, http://www.pewforum.org/2014/11/13/religion-in-latin-america/ (accessed February 25, 2015).

16. See David Martin, *Tongues of Fire: The Explosion of Protestantism in Latin America* (New York: Wiley Blackwell, 1993) and David Stoll, *Is Latin America Turning Protestant? The Politics of Evangelical Growth* (Berkeley: University of California Press, 1991).

17. Diego Cevallos, "Catholic Church Losing Followers in Droves," *Inter Press Service*, October 21, 2004, http://ipsnews.net/print.asp?idnews=25966 (accessed July 18, 2010).

18. "World In Brief: Argentina: Catholic Bishops Apologize for Civil War Crimes," *Los Angeles Times*, April 28, 1996, http://articles.latimes.com/1996-04-28/news/mn-63749_1_dirty-war (accessed February 23, 2012).

19. Encarnación, "Catholic Crisis."

20. Jason Berry, "How Fr. Maciel Built His Empire," *National Catholic Reporter*, April 12, 2010, http://ncronline.org/news/accountability/how-fr-maciel-built-his-empire (accessed August 6, 2010).

21. "The Reverend Marcial Maciel," *Telegraph*, February 2, 2010, http://www.telegraph.co.uk/news/uknews/1577304/The-Reverend-Marcial-Maciel.html (accessed August 6, 2010).

22. Rachel Donadio, "Pope Reins in Catholic Order Tied to Abuse," *New York Times*, May 1, 2010, http://www.nytimes.com/2010/05/02/world/europe/02legion.html?_r = 1 (accessed August 6, 2010).

23. This section draws from José Manuel Vidal, "Maciel plagió el libro de cabecera de los legionarios," *El Mundo* (Madrid), December 12, 2009, http://www.elmundo.es/elmundo/2009/12/12/internacional/1260637560.html (accessed August 6, 2010); Tracy Wilkinson, "Vatican Orders Overhaul of Group after Investigation of Sexual Abuse," *Los Angeles Times*, May 1, 2010, http://articles.latimes.com/2010/may/01/world/la-fg-vatican-abuse-20100501 (accessed August 6, 2010); and

Alma M. Muñoz, "Reclaman derechos hereditarios tres hijos mas de Maciel," *La Jornada* (Mexico), August 11, 2009.

24. Hagopian, "Latin American Catholicism."

25. "Bergoglio dice que la boda gay es "la pretensión destructiva del plan de Dios," *La Nación*, July 8, 2009, http://www.lanacion.com.ar/1282778-bergoglio-dice-que-la-boda-gay-es-la-pretension-destructiva-del-plan-de-dios (accessed August 17, 2015).

26. Mariano Obarrio, "La Presidenta lleva a China a opositoras del matrimonio gay," LaNación.com, July 10, 2010, http://www.lanacion.com.ar/nota.asp?nota_id = 1283380 (accessed July 28, 2010).

27. Dan Fastenberg, "International Gay Marriage," *Time*, July 22, 2010, http://content.time.com/time/world/article/0,8599,2005678,00.html (accessed September 22, 2013).

28. Matthew Cullinan Hoffman, "Cardinal Has Proof That Mexican Judges Were Bribed for Gay Marriage Vote," LifeSiteNews.com, August 18, 2010, http://www.lifesitenews.com/news/archive/ldn/2010/aug/10081801 (accessed September 23, 2013).

29. Tracy Wilkinson, "Mexico City's Gay Marriage Law Still Igniting Debate," *Los Angeles Times*, August 18, 2010, articles.latimes.com/2010/aug/18/world/la-fg-mexico-gays-20100818 (accessed September 22, 2013).

30. Hoffman, "Cardinal Has Proof."

31. Bertha Teresa Ramírez, "El Cardenal se Retracta o sera Demandado: Ebrard," *La Jornada* (Mexico City), August 17, 2010, http://www.jornada.unam.mx/2010/08/17/index.php?section=politica&article=003n3pol (accessed February 23, 2012).

32. "Uruguay Mulls Allowing Adoptions by Homosexuals Despite Catholic Opposition," *Catholic News Agency*, August 31, 2009, http://www.catholicnewsagency.com/archive/2009/08/31/ (accessed July 28, 2010).

33. "Uruguay to Legalize Gay Adoptions," *RET News World*, September 10, 2009, http://www.rte.ie/news/2009/0910/uruguay.html (accessed February 25, 2012).

34. Joseph Contreras, "Legal in Unlikely Places: Now Mature in the West, Gay Power is Growing in Unlikely Places, Even in the Land of Machismo," *Newsweek International*, September 17, 2007.

35. For a broader view of the rise of these reforms see Jodi Finkel, *Judicial Reform as Political Insurance: Argentina, Peru, and Mexico in the 1990s* (South Bend, IN: Notre Dame University Press, 2008) and Javier Corrales, "Constitutional Rewrites in Latin America, 1987–2009," in *Constructing Democratic Governance in Latin America*, ed. Jorge I. Domínguez and Michael Shifter, 4th ed. (Baltimore: Johns Hopkins University Press, 2013), 2–13.

36. See Rachel Sieder, *Multiculturalism in Latin America: Indigenous Rights, Diversity and Democracy in Latin America* (New York: Palgrave 2002), Deborah Yashar, *Contesting Citizenship in Latin America* (New York: Cambridge University Press, 2005), and Joseph Tulchin and Meg Ruthenberg, eds., *Citizenship in Latin America* (Boulder, CO: Lynne Rienner, 2006).

37. Jason Pierceson, "Variations in the Judicialization of Politics of Same-Sex Marriage Policy in Latin America," in *Same-Sex Marriage in the Americas*, ed. Jason Pierceson, Adriana Piatti-Crocker, and Shawn Schulenberg (New York: Lexington Books, 2010), 57.

38. Pierceson, "Variations in the Judicialization," 57.

39. Jodi Finkel, "Judicial Reform as Insurance Policy: Mexico in the 1990s," *Latin American Society and Politics* 46 (1) (2005): 91.

40. Ibid.

41. Víctor Manuel Collí Ek, "Improving Human Rights in Mexico: Constitutional Reforms, International Standards, and New Requirements for Judges," *Human Rights Brief* 20 (1) (2012), http://www.wcl.american.edu/hrbrief/20/1ek.pdf (accessed December 14, 2013).

42. On federalism and democratization in Latin America see Merilee Grindle, *Audacious Reforms: Institutional Invention and Democracy in Latin America* (Baltimore: Johns Hopkins University Press, 2000), Kent Eaton, *Beyond the Capital: The Design of Subnational Institutions in South America* (Stanford, CA: Stanford University Press, 2004), and Edward Gibson, ed., *Federalism and Democracy in Latin America* (Baltimore: Johns Hopkins University Press, 2004).

43. See Barry Ames, *The Deadlock of Democracy in Brazil* (Ann Arbor: University of Michigan Press, 2001) and Alfred Stepan, "Brazil's De-centralized Federalism: Bringing Government Closer to the People?" *Daedalus* 129 (2) (Spring 2000): 145–170.

44. See Rebecca Neaera Abers, *Inventing Local Democracy: Grassroots Politics in Brazil* (Boulder, CO: Lynne Rienner, 2000).

45. Alberto Alesina, Alberto Carrasquilla, and Juan José Echevarría, "Decentralization in Colombia," working paper, Fedesarrollo, August 2000, http://www.fedesarrollo.org.co/wp-content/uploads/2011/08/WP-No.-15-Decentralization-in-Colombia-inglés.pdf (accessed January 3, 2013).

46. Ruth Morris, "Offbeat Leftist's New Take on Bogota," *Los Angeles Times*, November 2003.

47. Jodi Finkel, "Judicial Reform in Argentina: How Electoral Incentives Shape Institutional Change," *Latin American Research Review* 39 (3) (2004): 58.

48. Finkel, "Judicial Reform as Insurance Policy," 90.

49. Linn Hammergren, "Do Councils Further Judicial Reform? Lessons from Latin America," working paper, Carnegie Endowment for International Peace, June 21, 2002, http://carnegieendowment.org/2002/06/21/do-judicial-councils-further-judicial-reform-lessons-from-latin-america/3bey (accessed January 2, 2014).

50. Pierceson, "Variations in the Judicialization," 25.

51. A transcript of the decision can be found at http://www.corteconstitucional.gov.co/relatoria/2007/c-075-07.html (accessed December 15, 2013).

52. This case is discussed in greater detail in chapter 6.

53. See Jorge G. Castañeda, "Latin America's Left Turn," *Foreign Affairs*, May–June 2006; Kurt Weyland, Raúl L. Madrid, and Wendy Hunter, eds., *Leftist Governments in Latin America: Successes and Shortcomings* (New York: Cambridge University Press, 2010); and Steven Levitsky and Kenneth Roberts, eds., *The Resurgence of the Latin American Left* (Baltimore: Johns Hopkins University Press, 2011).

54. "South America's Leftward Sweep," BBC, March 2, 2002, http://news.bbc.co.uk/2/hi/americas/4311957.stm (accessed July 4, 2012).

55. Shawn Schulenberg, "The Lavender Tide? LGBT Rights and the Latin American Left Today," in Pierceson, Piatti-Crocker, and Schulenberg, *Same-Sex Marriage*, 25.

56. Elisabeth Jay Friedman, "Seeking Rights from the Left: Gender and Sexuality in Latin America," in *Women's Movements in the Global Era: The Power of Local Feminism*, ed. Amrita Basu (Boulder, CO: Westview Press, 2010), 285.

57. Ibid.

58. Edward MacRae, "Homosexual Identities in Transitional Brazilian Politics," in *The Making of Social Movements in Latin America: Identity, Strategy, and Democracy*, ed. Arturo Escobar and Sonia Alvarez (Boulder, CO: Westview Press, 1992), 186.

59. James N. Green, *Beyond Carnival: Male Homosexuality in Twentieth-Century Brazil* (Chicago: University of Chicago Press, 1999), 271.

60. James N. Green, "Who Is the Macho Who Wants to Kill Me? Male Homosexuality, Revolutionary Masculinity, and the Brazilian Armed Struggle of the 1960s and 1970s," *Hispanic American Historical Review* 92 (3) (August 2012): 443.

61. Ibid.

62. Mario Vargas Llosa, "La caza del gay," *El País*, April 8, 2012, http://elpais.com/elpais/2012/04/04/opinion/1333540547_113226.html (accessed August 8, 2015).

63. Javier Corrales and Mario Pecheny, "The Comparative Politics of Sexuality in Latin America," in *The Politics of Sexuality in Latin America: A Reader on Lesbian, Gay, Bisexual and Transgender Rights*, ed. Javier Corrales and Mario Pecheny (Pittsburgh: University of Pittsburgh Press, 2010), 24.

64. Ibid.

65. Chris Lewis, "Rainbow Tide Rising: How Latin America Became a Gay Haven," *Alternet*, February 13, 2014.

66. See Michael K. Levers, "Cuban LGBT Leaders Cite Progress, on-going Harassment," *The Washington Blade*, September 17, 2012, http://www.washingtonblade.com/2012/09/17/cuban-lgbt-activists-cite-progress-ongoing-harassment/, accessed August 21, 2015.

67. See Ian Lumsden, *Machos, Maricones and Gays: Cuba and Homosexuality* (Philadelphia: Temple University Press, 2010).

68. Levers, "Cuban LGBT Leaders Cite Progress, on-going Harassment."

69. Allen Young, *Gays under the Cuban Revolution* (San Francisco: Grey Fox Press, 1981), 7–8.

70. "Soy el responsable de la persecusión de los homosexuals que hubo en Cuba: Fidel Castro," *La Jornada*, August 31, 2010.

71. Castro made this remark in May 2012 at a talk at the Americas Society in New York City attended by the author.

72. Kurt Weyland, "The Performance of Leftist Governments in Latin America: Conceptual and Theoretical Issues," in Weyland, Madrid, and Hunter, *Leftist Governments*, 3.

73. Weyland, "Performance of Leftist Governments," 3.

74. See Margaret Keck, *The Workers' Party and Democratization in Brazil* (New Haven: Yale University Press, 1992).

75. Elisabeth Jay Friedman, "Gender, Sexuality and the Latin American Left: Testing the Transformation," *Third World Quarterly* 30 (2) (2009): 429.

76. "Chile Presidential Candidates, Bachelet, Matthei Square Off in Debate Ahead of Elections," Associated Press, December 6, 2013, http://www.canada.com/news/Chile+presidential+candidates+Bachelet+Matthei+square+debate+ahead/9255381/story.html (accessed December 30, 2013).

77. Mala Htun and Timothy J. Power, "Gender, Parties, and Support for Equal Rights in the Brazilian Congress," *Latin American Society and Politics* 48 (4) (December 2006): 83–104.

78. "The Mystery behind Mujica's Mask," *Economist*, October 22, 2009, http://www.economist.com/node/14700728 (accessed September 23, 2013).

79. It is interesting that the various edited volumes about the "return" of the Left in Latin America published since the mid-2000s by and large neglect to highlight gay rights as a policy issue.

80. See Friedman, "Gender, Sexuality."

81. See Herbert Kitschelt, *The Transformation of European Social Democracy* (New York: Cambridge University Press, 1994).

82. See Omar G. Encarnación, "Spain's New Left Turn: Party Driven or Society Instigated?," *Southern European Society and Politics* 14 (4) (2009): 399–415.

83. Fastenberg, "International Gay Marriage."

84. Wilkinson, "Gay Marriage Law."

85. Hoffman, "Cardinal Has Proof."

86. See Stephan Haggard and Robert R. Kaufman, *The Political Economy of Democratic Transitions* (Princeton, NJ: Princeton University Press, 1995).

87. Diego Sempol, "The Creation of Civil Partnerships in Uruguay," in Pierceson, Piatti-Crocker, and Schulenberg, *Same-Sex Marriage*, 93.

88. See Susan Eckstein, ed., *Power and Popular Protest: Latin American Social Movements* (Berkeley: University of California Press, 1989).

89. See Wiarda and Kline, *Latin American Politics*.

CHAPTER 3

1. Argentina's first female president, Isabel Martínez de Perón (1974–1976), inherited the job after the death of her husband, Juan Domingo Perón, who had chosen her as his vice president.

2. Javier Corrales, Mari Crook, and Mario Pecheny, "Argentina: World Champion in LGBT Rights: How Did This Happen?," paper presented at the annual meeting of the American Political Science Association, Seattle, WA, September 1–4, 2011.

3. This point is, of course, arguable. In its defense, see Matthew C. Gutmann, ed., *Changing Men and Masculinities in Latin America* (Durham, NC: Duke University Press, 2003).

4. Uki Goni, "Last Tango for Machismo as Gay Tourists Flock to Argentina," *Observer*, June 24, 2004.

5. David William Foster, *Buenos Aires: Perspectives on the City and Cultural Production* (Gainesville: University of Florida Press, 1993), 87.

6. This is a broad theme of some of the better-known histories of homosexuality in Argentina, especially Osvaldo Bazán, *Historia de la Homosexualidad en la Argentina: De la Conquista de America al Siglo XXI* (Buenos Aires: Marea, 2004).

7. "Argentina: Shrouded in Silence," trans. Sam Larson, in *Coming Out: An Anthology of Gay and Lesbian Writings*, ed. Stephan Likosky (New York: Pantheon, 1992), 71.

8. Stephen Brown, "'Con discriminación y represión no hay democracia': The Lesbian and Gay Movement in Argentina," *Latin American Perspectives* 29 (2) (March 2002): 130.

9. Amy Lind, "Out of the Closet and into la Calle," *NACLA Report on the Americas*, May 5, 1997.

10. See Amy Becker, "Determinants of Support for Same-Sex Marriage: Generational Cohorts, Social Contract and Shifting Attitudes," *International Journal of Public Opinion Research* 24 (4) (2012): 524–533.

11. United Nations Development Program, Human Development Report, 2014.

12. This section draws from "Religion in Latin America," Pew Research Center, November 13, 2014, http://www.pewforum.org/2014/11/13/religion-in-latin-america/ (accessed February 24, 2014).

13. A 2012 Survey from the Latin American Public Opinion Poll (LAPOP) at Vanderbilt University that tested acceptance of homosexuality based on whether people would mind having a homosexual as a neighbor and if gay people should be allowed to run for public office found that "Evangelicals do not differ greatly from

their mainline counterparts. They do, however, differ more so when compared to other religious groups such as Roman Catholics and Other." The survey theorizes that the difference in level of acceptance of homosexuality is due to the fact that Evangelicals are poorer and less educated than other groups. See "Evangelicalism and Gay Rights in Latin America," AmericasBarometer, Latin American Public Opinion Project, Vanderbilt University, 2013, http://www.vanderbilt.edu/lapop/ (accessed September 20, 2013).

14. See Michael A. Burdick, *For God and the Fatherland: Religion and Politics in Argentina* (Albany: SUNY University Press, 1996).

15. See Jason Pierceson, "Variations in the Judicialization of Politics of Same-Sex Marriage Policy in Latin America," in *Same-Sex Marriage in the Americas*, ed. Jason Pierceson, Adriana Piatti-Crocker, and Shawn Schulenberg (New York: Lexington Books, 2010), 53–72.

16. Brown, *"Con discriminación y represión,"* 122.

17. See the introduction for a review of these terms.

18. Pablo E. Ben, "Male Same-Sex Sexuality and the Argentine State, 1880–1930," in *The Politics of Sexuality in Latin America: A Reader on Lesbian, Gay, Bisexual and Transgender Rights*, ed. Javier Corrales and Mario Pecheny (Pittsburgh: University of Pittsburgh Press, 2010), 34–35.

19. Jorge Salessi, *Médicos, maleantes y maricas: Higiene, criminología y homosexualidad en Argentina 1870–1914* (Buenos Aires: Beatriz Viterbo Editora, 1995).

20. Aldo C. Vacs, "Argentina," in *The Politics of Latin America: The Power Game*, ed. Harry E. Vanden and Gary Prevost (New York: Oxford University Press, 2009), 396.

21. Jorge Salessi, "The Argentine Dissemination of Homosexuality, 1890–1914," *Journal of the History of Sexuality* 4 (3) (January 1994): 348.

22. Charles Bergquist, *Labor in Latin America: Comparative Essays on Chile, Argentina, and Colombia* (Stanford, CA: Stanford University Press, 1986), 81.

23. Mariano Ben Plotkin, *Freud in the Pampas: The Emergence and Development of a Psychoanalytic Culture in Argentina* (Stanford, CA: Stanford University Press, 2001), 16.

24. Ibid.

25. Salessi, "Argentine Dissemination of Homosexuality," 348.

26. Plotkin, *Freud in the Pampas*, 16.

27. Positivist philosophy, as influenced by the work of sociologist Auguste Comte, states that all authentic knowledge is scientific rather than intuitive and that it allows for verification. This philosophy was quite popular among Latin American intellectuals in the late 1800s and influenced policies and state building more generally.

28. Richard Cleminson, "Transnational Discourse on the Mala Vida: Male Homosexuality in Madrid, Buenos Aires and Barcelona," *Journal of Spanish Cultural Studies* 10 (4) (2009): 461.

29. Salessi, "Argentine Dissemination of Homosexuality," 470.

30. Donna J. Guy, *Sex and Danger in Buenos Aires: Prostitution, Family and the Nation in Argentina* (Lincoln: University of Nebraska Press, 1991), 93.

31. Salessi, "Argentine Dissemination of Homosexuality," 470.

32. Ibid., 338.

33. Barry D. Adam, *The Rise of a Gay and Lesbian Movement* (Boston: Twayne, 1987), 29.

34. Ricardo D. Salvatore, "Criminology, Prison Reform, and the Buenos Aires Working Class," *Journal of Interdisciplinary History* 23 (2) (Autumn 1992): 287.

35. Ibid., 288.

36. Felipe Pigna, *Los mitos de la historia Argentina* (Buenos Aires: Planeta, 2006), 285.

37. Ben, "Male Same-Sex Sexuality," 36–37.

38. Ibid., 37.

39. Guy, *Sex and Danger*, 5.

40. In his autobiography, Molina writes that while in Uruguay "I wrote a letter directly to Evita, telling her that I wanted to return to go back to work in Buenos Aires, although I did not know if I would encounter any problems entering the country and returning to the stage. One week later, I learned through official channels that I could return to and work in Argentina. Later, I learned that Evita had petitioned my police file and that upon learning that the file showed no pending crimes she gave orders that the police make every effort to facilitate my return. I was grateful to her all of my life, especially having encountered so many mighty who did nothing else but prosecute me." See Miguel de Molina, *Botín de Guerra: Autobiografía* (Barcelona: Planeta, 1998), 245–46.

41. Guy, *Sex and Danger*, 180–203.

42. Ibid., 182–183.

43. Omar Acha and Pablo Ben, "Amorales, patoleros, chongos y pitucos: La homosexualidad masculina durante el primer Peronismo, 1943–1955," Trabajos y Comunicaciones, Universidad Nacional de la Plata, 2004–2005.

44. Valeria Manzano, "Sexualizing Youth: Campaigns and Representations of Youth in Early 1960s Buenos Aires," *Journal of the History of Sexuality* 14 (4) (October 2005): 438.

45. Ibid., 441–442.

46. Ibid., 442–443.

47. The economic rationale of the rise of military power in Argentina in the 1960s is also broadly reflected in political science treatments of the subject. See Guillermo O'Donnell, *Modernization and Bureaucratic Authoritarianism: Studies in South American Politics* (Berkeley, CA: Institute of International Studies, 1973) and David Collier, ed., *The New Authoritarianism in Latin America* (Princeton, NJ: Princeton University Press, 1979).

48. Cyrus Stephens Cousins, "General Onganía and the Argentine Military Revolution of the Right: Anti-Communism and Morality, 1966–1970," *Historia Actual Online* 7 (Fall 2008): 67.

49. See Plotkin, *Fred in the Pampas*. This fascinating book explains why Argentina gave birth to one of the world's largest psychoanalytic communities, encompassing the realms of medicine, education, politics, and popular culture, and which has given Argentina, on a per capita basis, more psychotherapists than any other place on the planet.

50. Ibid.

51. Pablo E. Ben, "Peronism, the LGBT Movement, and Authoritarian Rule in Argentina in the 1960s and 1970s," paper presented at the 125th Annual Meeting of the American Historical Association, Boston, January 6–9, 2011.

52. Nuestro Mundo's founding date remains the subject of some controversy. Although 1969 is the widely cited founding year, Osvaldo Bazán believes that the members began meeting in 1967, which would date the creation of the group to two years before Stonewall, but that they did not regard themselves as a group until 1969. Anabitarte also confirmed 1967 as the founding year of Nuestro Mundo in an interview conducted for this study. He notes that the organization was founded in either October or November 1967 in the city of Lomas de Zamora.

53. Interview, June 1, 2012.

54. Email correspondence with Anabitarte, July 12, 2012.

55. Interview, Buenos Aires, June 1, 2012.

56. Email correspondence with Anabitarte, July 12, 2012.

57. Ibid.

58. Flavio Rapisardi, "Escritura y lucha política en la cultura Argentina: Identidades y Hegemonia en el movimiento de diversidades sexuales entre 1970 y 2000," *Revista Iberoamericana* 74 (225) (October–December 2008): 979.

59. For a broader view of the intellectual work of gay and lesbian intellectuals and the struggle for gay recognition see David William Foster, "Argentine Intellectuals and Homoeroticism: Nestor Perlongher and Juan José Sebreli," *Hispania* 84 (3) (September 2001): 441–450.

60. Néstor Perlongher, *Prosa Plebeya: Ensayos 1980–1992* (Buenos Aires: Colihue, 1997), 77; emphasis on "Gay Power Americano" added. See also Néstor Perlongher, "Una historia del FLH Argentino," mimeo, Buenos Aires, 1977.

61. CHA archives, consulted March 25, 2012.

62. Brown, *"Con discriminación y represión,"* 128.

63. This was part of the FLH's ten points of agreement that governed the organization's activities. On this point see James N. Green, "(Homo)sexuality, Human Rights, and Revolution in Latin America," in *Human Rights and Revolutions*, ed. Jeffrey N. Wasserstrom, Greg Grandin, Lynn Hunt, and Marilyn B. Young (Lanham, MD: Rowman and Littlefield, 2002), 146.

64. Perlongher, *Prosa Plebeya*, 81.

65. Frente de Liberación Homosexual, "Sex and Revolution," trans. Sam Larson, in Likosky, *Coming Out*, 189.

66. Interview, June 1, 2012.

67. Rapisardi, "Escritura y lucha político," 982.

68. Interview with Osvaldo Bazán, Buenos Aires, June 1, 2012.

69. Ibid.

70. See James N. Green, "Who Is the Macho Who Wants to Kill Me? Male Homosexuality, Revolutionary Masculinity, and the Brazilian Armed Struggle of the 1960s and 1970s," *Hispanic American Historical Review* 92 (3) (August 2012): 37–69.

71. Brown, *"Con discriminación y represión,"* 121.

72. CHA Archives, Buenos Aires, consulted March 26, 2012.

73. CHA Archives, Buenos Aires, consulted March 26, 2012.

74. Many books chronicle the horrors of Argentina's Dirty War, including Iain Guest, *Behind the Disappearances: Argentina's Dirty War against Human Rights and the United Nations* (Philadelphia: University of Pennsylvania Press, 1990); Marguerite Feitlowitz, *A Lexicon of Terror: Argentina and the Legacies of Torture*, rev. ed. (New York: Oxford University Press 2011); Antonius C. G. M. Robben, *Political Violence and Trauma in Argentina* (Philadelphia: University of Pennsylvania Press, 2001); Paul H. Lewis, *The Dirty War in Argentina* (New York: Praeger, 2001); and Patricia Marchak and William Marchak, *God's Assassins: State Terrorism in Argentina in the 1970s* (Montreal: McGill-Queen's University Press, 1999).

75. Alfred Stepan, *Rethinking Military Politics: Brazil and the Southern Cone* (Princeton, NJ: Princeton University Press, 1988), 69. Stepan's numbers for Brazil have been updated recently by the Brazilian truth commission. He uses the figure of 125 disappeared in Brazil, which is the figure reported in *Brasil: Nunca Mais*, an unofficial accounting, while the commission reported nearly five hundred missing persons.

76. *Nunca Más: Report of the Argentine National Commission on Disappearance of Persons* (New York: Farrar, Straus and Giroux, 1985).

77. Interview César Cigliutti, Buenos Aires, June 7, 2012.

78. Carlos Jáuregui, *La homosexualidad en la Argentina* (Buenos Aires: Ediciones Tarso, 1987), 170.

79. See, for instance, "Violaciones de derechos humanos y civiles en la República Argentina basadas en la orientación sexual de las personas y de las personas viviendo con VIH/SIDA," Gays por los Derechos Civiles, 3rd ed., December 1995, 3–4.

80. Interview with Pablo Ben, February 19, 2015.

81. To my knowledge, the first article to publish the charge of four hundred gay killings under military rule is Brown, "*Con discriminación y represión*," one of the first accounts of the Argentine gay movements published in English.

82. See Santiago Joaquín Insausti, "los cuatrocientos homosexuals desaparecidos: Memorias de la represión estatal a las sexualidades dissidenes en Argentina," in *Deseo y represion: Sexualidad, género y Estado en la historia reciente argentina* (Buenos Aires: Ediciones Imago Mundi, 2015), 1–18.

83. Email communication with Mr. Insausti, August 25, 2014.

84. Insausti, "los cuatrocientos homosexuales desaparecidos," 5.

85. Ibid.

86. Flavio Rapisardi and Alejandro Modarelli, *Fiestas, baños y exilios: Los gays porteños en la última dictadura militar* (Buenos Aires: Editorial Sudamericana, 2001).

87. CHA Archives, consulted March 24, 2012.

88. Brown, "*Con discriminación y represión*," 121.

89. Diego Sempol, "Violence and the Emergence of Gay and Lesbian Activism in Argentina, 1983–1990," in *The Sexual History of the Global South: Sexual Politics in Africa, Asia, and Latin America*, ed. Saskia Weiringa and Horacio Sívori (New York: Zed Books, 2013), 102.

90. Luiz Mott, "The Gay Movement and Homosexuality in Brazil," in *Latin American Male Homosexualities*, ed. Stephen O. Murray (Albuquerque: University of New Mexico Press, 1995), 222.

91. Nicolas Schumway, *The Invention of Argentina* (Berkeley: University of California Press, 1991).

92. Diana Taylor, *Disappearing Acts: Spectacles of Gender and Nationalism in Argentina's Dirty War* (Durham, NC: Duke University Press, 1997), 34–35.

93. Interview, Buenos Aires, June 1, 2012.

94. Interview, New York, February 18, 2015.

95. Interview, Buenos Aires, June 1, 2012.

96. Interview, New York, February 18, 2015.

97. Mabel Bellucci, *Orgullo: Carlos Jáuregui, una Biografía Política* (Buenos Aires: Editorial Planeta, 2010), 206.

98. Rapisardi, "Escritura y lucha polítical," 987.

99. Ibid.

100. Sempol, "Violence and the Emergence," 116.

101. Email communication with César Cigliutti, July 3, 2013.

102. Interview with Mabel Bellucci, Buenos Aires, May 16, 2012.

103. This section borrows from Sempol, "Violence and the Emergence," 102–3.

104. CHA archives, consulted March 27, 2012.

105. Bellucci, *Orgullo*, 206.

106. Ibid.

107. Rapisardi, "Escritura y lucha política," 990.

108. Gary Marx, "Gays in Latin America Begin to Claim Rights," *Chicago Tribune*, January 28, 1992.

109. Brown, *"Con discriminación y represión,"* 124.

110. Interview, Buenos Aires, June 7, 2012.

111. Ibid.

112. Email correspondence with César Cigliutti, July 3, 2013.

113. See Omar G. Encarnación, "Human Rights and Gay Rights," *Current History*, January 2014.

114. CHA archives, consulted March 27, 2012.

115. CHA archives, consulted March 26, 2012.

116. CHA Document, *Discriminalizacion y sexualidad en la Argentina*, December 1987.

117. Sempol, "Violence and the Emergence," 105.

118. See Urvashi Vaid, *Virtual Equality: The Mainstreaming of Gay and Lesbian Liberation* (New York: Anchor Books, 1995).

119. Sempol, "Violence and the Emergence," 106.

120. Brown, *"Con discriminación y represión,"* 128.

121. Bellucci, *Orgullo*, 12.

122. International Gay and Lesbian Human Rights Commission, "Presentación del Libro *Carlos Jáuregui: Una Biografia Política*," Buenos Aires, April 2010, http://iglhrc.org/content/presentación-del-libro-carlos-jáuregui-una-biograf%C3%AD-po l%C3%ADtica (accessed January 7, 2014).

123. Sempol, "Violence and the Emergence," 106.

124. Bellucci, *Orgullo*, 45.

125. Kathryn Sikkink, "From Pariah State to Global Protagonist: Argentina and the Struggle for International Human Rights," *Latin American Politics and Society* 50 (1) (2008): 1–29.

126. Elizabeth Jelin, "The Politics of Memory: The Human Rights Movement and the Construction of Democracy in Argentina," *Latin American Perspectives* 21 (2) (Spring 1994): 38.

127. See Kelly Kollman, "Same-Sex Unions: The Globalization of an Idea," *International Studies Quarterly* 51 (2007): 329–357.

128. Bellucci, *Orgullo*, 45.

129. Ibid.

130. Kerman Calvo, "Pursuing Membership in the Polity: The Spanish Gay and Lesbian Movement in Comparative Perspective," doctoral dissertation, Instituto Juan March, 2005, 125–126.

131. Ibid, 125.

132. Brown, "Con discriminación y represión," 130–131.

133. This section draws primarily from an interview with Mabel Bellucci (Buenos Aires, May 16, 2012), Bellucci's essay "De la homosexualidad femenina al lesbianismo: Las mujeres de la CHA," provided by Ms. Bellucci to this author, and archival work at CHA headquarters in Buenos Aires.

134. Email communication with Elisabeth Jay Friedman, February 18, 2015.

135. Email correspondence, February 18, 2015.

136. Bellucci, *Orgullo*, 199.

CHAPTER 4

1. This account of the legalization of the CHA draws from interviews with former and present CHA officials, including former CHA president Rafael Freda, former CHA copresident Mónica Santino, and current CHA president César Cigliutti, and from

published accounts available in Horacio Verbitski, *Hacer la corte: la construcción de un poder absoluto sin justicia ni control* (Planeta: Buenos Aires, 1993), *New York Times*, November 13, 1991, *The Advocate*, December 17, 1991, and M. Alfredo González, "Latinos ACT-UP: Transitional AIDS Activism in the 1990s," *NACLA Report on the Americas*, July–August 2008.

2. See the introduction for a discussion of the literature on framing.

3. Hank Johnston and John A. Nokes, "Frames of Protest: A Road Map to a Perspective," in *Frames of Protest: Social Movements and the Framing Perspective*, ed. Hank Johnston and John A. Nokes (Lanham, MD: Rowman and Littlefield, 2003), 11.

4. For an overview of Argentina's human rights movement see Alison Brysk, *The Politics of Human Rights in Argentina: Protest, Change and Democratization* (Stanford, CA: Stanford University Press, 1994).

5. On Las Madres and their political impact see Marysa Navarro, "The Personal Is Political: The Madres de la Plaza de Mayo," in *Power and Popular Protest: Latin American Social Movements*, ed. Susan Eckstein (Berkeley: University of California Press, 1989), 241–258, and Diana Taylor, *Disappearing Acts: Spectacles of Gender and Nationalism in Argentina's Dirty War* (Durham, NC: Duke University Press, 1997).

6. Brysk, *Politics of Human Rights*, 7.

7. On the trials of the military junta see Jaime Malumud-Goti, *Game with No End: State Terror and the Politics of Justice* (Norman: University of Oklahoma Press, 1995).

8. Email communication César Cigliutti, July 3, 2013.

9. Ibid.

10. Alejandro Modarelli, "Honor y Gratitud," *Página 12*, August 20, 2010, http://www.pagina12.com.ar/diario/suplementos/soy/1-1552-2010-08-20.html (accessed March 3, 2015).

11. Mario Pecheny, "Sexual Orientation, AIDS, and Human Rights in Argentina: The Paradox of Social Advance amid Health Crisis," in *Struggles for Social Rights in Latin America*, ed. Susan Eva Eckstein and Timothy P. Wickham-Crowley (New York: Routledge, 2003), 262.

12. Interview, Buenos Aires, June 29, 2012.

13. Interview, Buenos Aires, June 7, 2012.

14. Email communication with César Cigliutti, July 3, 2013.

15. CHA archives, consulted March 26, 2012.

16. Email correspondence with César Cigliutti, July 3, 2013.

17. *Truth and Partial Justice in Argentina: An Americas Watch Report* (New York: Americas Watch Report, 1987).

18. "200 Military Officers are Pardoned in Argentina," *New York Times*, October 7, 1989, http://www.nytimes.com/1989/10/08/world/200-milita ry-officers-are-pardoned-in-argentina.html (accessed August 13, 2015.

19. CHA archives, consulted on March 25, 2012.

20. Email communication with Rafael Freda, February 18, 2015.

21. See Ronaldo Munck, "A New Argentina: Democracy, Menem and Labor," *Latin American Perspectives* 24 (6) (1997): 173–178.

22. Email communication with Irene Ocampo, February 18, 2015.

23. James Brooke, "AIDS in Latin America—a Special Report: In Deception and Denial, An Epidemic Looms," *New York Times*, January 25, 1993.

24. Ibid.

25. Pan American Health Organization, "Campaigns against Homophobia in Argentina, Brazil, Colombia and Mexico," Washington, DC, 2008, http://www.paho.org/English/AD/FCH/AI/Homofobia.pdf (accessed April 2, 2012).
26. Ibid.
27. Pecheny, "Sexual Orientation," 262.
28. This section draws from Juan Carlos Tealdi, "Responses to AIDS in Argentina: Law and Politics," in *Legal Responses to AIDS in Comparative Perspective*, ed. Stanislaw Frankowski (The Hague: Kluwer Law International 1998), 385–387.
29. Interview, Buenos Aires, June 7, 2012.
30. Ibid.
31. Modarelli, "Honor y Gratitud."
32. Interview with Pablo Ben, February 20, 2015.
33. Email correspondence with former CHA vice president Rafael Freda, February 25, 2015.
34. Ibid.
35. Mabel Bellucci, *Orgullo: Carlos Jáuregui, una Biografía Política* (Buenos Aires: Editorial Planeta, 2010), 67.
36. Modarelli, "Honor y Gratitud."
37. Bellucci, *Orgullo*.
38. This account of the constitutional reforms of 2004 draws from Jodi Finkel, "Judicial Reform in Argentina: How Electoral Incentives Shape Institutional Change," *Latin American Research Review* 39 (3) (2004): 56–80.
39. This account of the passage of Buenos Aires' 1996 constitution is based on interviews with CHA officials.
40. "El final de los edictos policiales," *Clarín*, March 13, 1998.
41. Interview, Buenos Aires, June 14, 2012.
42. Javier Corrales, "The Politics of Argentina's Meltdown," *World Policy Journal*, Fall 2002, 29.
43. Alexei Barrionuevo, "Macho Argentina Warms to Gay Dollars and Euros," *New York Times*, December 3, 2007, http://www.nytimes.com/2007/11/29/world/americas/29iht-journal.4.8532361.html (accessed September 22, 2013).
44. Interview, Buenos Aires, June 14, 2012.
45. Interview, Buenos Aires, June 14, 2012.
46. Brian Byrnes, "Wary of Past Abuses, Argentine Capital Approves Gay Rights," *Christian Science Monitor*, July 14, 2003.
47. Renata Hiller, "The Civil Union Law in Buenos Aires," in *The Politics of Sexuality in Latin America: A Reader on Lesbian, Gay, Bisexual and Transgender Rights*, ed. Javier Corrales and Mario Pecheny (Pittsburgh: University of Pittsburgh Press, 2010), 213–214.
48. Interview, Buenos Aires, June 14, 2012.
49. Quoted in Shawn Schulenberg, "The Construction and Enactment of Same-Sex Marriage in Argentina," *Journal of Human Rights* 11 (1) (2012): 110.
50. Quoted in Jordi Diez, "Explaining Policy Outcomes: The Adoption of Same-Sex Unions in Buenos Aires and Mexico City," *Comparative Political Studies* 46 (2) (2014): 224.
51. "Ley de Unión Civil: Un gran paso," *Clarín*, December 12, 2002.
52. "Going Pinker on the Plata," *Economist*, December 4, 2008 http://www.economist.com/node/12725407 (accessed April 4, 2012).
53. Barrionuevo, "Macho Argentina."

54. Global Travel Industry News, "Gay Tourism in Argentina Set to Boom," July 22, 2011, http://www.eturbonews.com/17420/destination-news-gay-tourism-argentina-set-boom (accessed April 5, 2012).

55. Silvia Naishta, "Empresarios de EE.UU. que apuestan al mercado gay," *Clarín*, July 23, 2010.

56. Alejandra Sarda, "Resisting Kirchner's Recipe (Sometimes): LGBTTTI Organizing in Argentina," *NACLA Report on the Americas*, March 2007, 32.

57. Luciana Bertoia, "A Decade of Human Rights: No Turning Back," *Buenos Aires Herald*, May 25, 2013.

58. Interview, Buenos Aires, June 14, 2012.

59. Ibid.

60. See "Discrimination in Argentina: Diagnosis and Proposals," United Nations High Commission for Human Rights, 2005, http://inadi.gob.ar/uploads/publicaciones_inadi/varios/National_Plan_against_Discrimination.pdf (accessed January 21, 2014).

61. Steven Levitsky and Victoria Murillo, "Argentina: From Kirchner to Kirchner," *Journal of Democracy* 19 (2) (2008): 17.

62. Ibid.

63. Adriana Piatti-Crocker, "Policy Innovation in Argentina: From Gender Quotas to Same-Sex Marriage," in *Same-Sex Marriage in the Americas*, ed. Jason Pierceson, Adriana Piatti-Crocker, and Shawn Schulenberg (New York: Lexington Books, 2010), 58.

64. Interview, Buenos Aires, July 20, 2012.

65. Bruno Bimbi, *Matrimonio Igualitario* (Buenos Aires: Editorial Planeta, 2011), 19.

66. Interview with Esteban Paulón by *Gay Star News*, October 17, 2012, http://www.gaystarnews.com/article/how-argentina-bringing-fight-gay-marriage-you171012 (accessed March 25, 2015).

67. Elisabeth Jay Friedman, "Constructing 'The Same Rights with the Same Names': The Impact of Spanish Norm Diffusion on Marriage Equality in Argentina," *Latin American Politics and Society* 54 (4) (Winter 2012): 39.

68. Bimbi, *Matrimonio Igualitario*, 67.

69. Marcela Valente, "The Final Battle for Gay Rights," *IPSNews*, August 26, 2005, http://ipsnews.net/news.asp?idnews=30038 (accessed March 20, 2012).

70. Ibid.

71. Interview, Buenos Aires, June 14, 2012.

72. Interview, Buenos Aires, July 20, 2012. For a broader view of the organization's views on same-sex marriage see Federación Argentina LGBT, *Matrimonio Para Todos: La Ley de Igualidad*, May 9, 2010, http://www.lgbt.org.ar/archivos/Libro_Senadores2.pdf (accessed March 24, 2012).

73. Bimbi, *Matrimonio Igualitario*, 10.

74. Thomas Dollar, "Gay Marriage and Argentine Politics," *FiveThirtyEightPolitics*, July 18, 2010, http://fivethirtyeight.com/features/gay-marriage-and-argentine-politics/ (accessed October 24, 2014).

75. "La Iglesia Alertó Sobre el Matrimonio Gay," *La Nación*, April 21, 2010.

76. Uki Goñi, "Defying Church, Argentina Legalizes Gay Marriage," *Time*, July 15, 2010, http://content.time.com/time/world/article/0,8599,2004036,00.html (accessed March 24, 2012).

77. Soledad Gallego Díaz, "Guerra de Dios contra las bodas gay en Argentina," *El País*, July 14, 2014.

78. Dollar, "Gay Marriage."

79. Juan Marco Vaggione, "Sexual Rights and Religion: Same-Sex Marriage and Lawmakers' Catholic Identity in Argentina," *University of Miami Law Review*, Spring 2011, http://www.lexisnexis.com (accessed March 12, 2015).

80. This section draws from Vaggione's "Sexual Rights and Religion."

81. Piatti-Crocker, "Policy Innovation in Argentina," 57.

82. Bimbi, *Matrimonio Igualitario*, 10.

83. Marcela Valente, "Being Gay No Longer a Bar to Marriage," July 15, 2010, www.globalissues.org/news/2010/07/15/6316 (accessed September 13, 2013).

84. Gustavo Ibarra, "Más voces contra el matrimonio gay en el senado," *La Nación*, June 30, 2010.

85. Interview with César Cigliutti, Buenos Aires, June 7, 2012.

86. "El matrimonio gay, sin dictamen," *Clarín*, November 6, 2009, http://edant.clarin.com/diario/2009/11/06/sociedad/s-02034892.htm (accessed August 16, 2015).

87. The concept of *amparo* is discussed in chapter 2.

88. "BA Mayor Not to Appeal Ruling Allowing Gay Marriage," *Buenos Aires Herald*, November 14, 2009.

89. "Argentinian Men Become First Same-Sex Couple Married in Latin America," *Guardian*, December 29, 2009, http://www.theguardian.com/world/2009/dec/29/argentina-first-gay-marriage (accessed September 22, 2013).

90. Bimbi, Matrimonio Igualitario, 76–78.

91. Ricardo Kirchbaum, "Tolerancia y Diversidad," *Clarín*, July 11, 2010.

92. Good examples include Alejandro Modarelli, "Víctimas sin nombre," *Página 12*, March 20, 2009; and Patricio Lennard, "La lucha continua," *Página 12*, June 26, 2009.

93. This claim of Argentina as a genocidal state now involves revisiting the history of the founding of modern Argentina by President Julio Argentina Roca. His successful victories over indigenous peoples in 1878–1879 led to the conquest of the Patagonia, which, in turn, opened Argentina's heartland to massive European immigration. This history is now being recast as a case of genocide. See Rory Caroll, "Argentine Founder Recast as Genocidal Murderer," *Guardian*, January 13, 2011, http://www.theguardian.com/world/2011/jan/13/argentinian-founding-father-genocide-row (accessed May 25, 2015).

94. Interview, Pablo Ben, February 20, 2015.

95. Alejandro Rebossio, "'Entre la Guerra de Dios' contra el matrimonio gay y el apoyo a la unión civil," *El País*, March 30, 2013. This article reports that following the legalization of same-sex marriage the future pope met with leaders from FALGBT to express his opposition to gay marriage and his support for civil unions for same-sex couples.

96. Andres D'Alessandro and Tracy Wilkinson, *Los Angeles Times*, July 16, 2010.

97. Mariano Obarrio, "La Presidenta lleva a China a opositoras del matrimonio gay," *La Nación*, July 10, 2010.

98. Goñi, "Defying Church."

99. Fernando Laborda, "Matrimonio homosexual: Las razones de los Kirchners," *La Nación*, July 13, 2010.

100. "Gay Marriage in Argentina: A Queer Calculation," *Economist*, July 15, 2008.

101. Interview, Buenos Aires, June 14, 2012.

102. Interview, Buenos Aires, July 20, 2012.

103. "Congress Begins to Debate Gay Marriage," *Momento24*, July 10, 2010, http://m24digital.com/en/2009/10/28/congress-begins-to-debate-gay-marriage/ (accessed March 24, 2012).

104. Juan Forero, "Gay Rights Activists Celebrate Argentine Vote for Same-Sex Marriage," *Washington Post*, July 16, 2010.

105. Rocio Llama, "Todos Unidos Votaremos," *Página 12*, May 20, 2010, accessed March 31, 2012, http://www.pagina12.com.ar/diario/sociedad/3-145981-2010-05-20.html.

106. "Argentina Legalizes Same-Sex Marriage," *National Public Radio*, July 15, 2010, http://www.npr.org/templates/story/story.php?storyId=128536587 (accessed July 1, 2013).

107. "El Senado convirtió en ley en matrimonio homosexual," *Clarín*, July 15, 2010, http://www.clarin.com/sociedad/Senado-convirtio-Ley-matrimonio-homosexual_0_298770299.html (accessed August 24, 2015).

108. Marie Trigona, "Argentina Passes Marriage Law," July 15, 2010, http://mujeres-libres.blogsspot.com/2010/10/07/argentina-passes-gay-marriage-law.html (accessed September 22, 2013).

109. Gisele Sousa Dias, "Cristina promulgó la ley de matrimonio homosexual en un clima de festejos," *Clarín*, July 22, 2010.

110. The rest of this paragraph draws from Viviana Mariño, "En un clima de fiestas, la presidenta promulgó el matrimonio igualitario," July 22, 2010, http://tiempo.infonews.com/notas/clima-de-fiesta-presidenta-promulgo-matrimonio-igualitario (accessed June 24, 2013).

CHAPTER 5

1. See J. Michael Francis, ed., *Iberia and the Americas: Culture, Politics and History* (Santa Barbara, CA: ABC-CLIO, 2006), 517.

2. Richard Guy Parker, *Beneath the Equator: Cultures of Desire, Male Homosexuality, and Emerging Gay Communities in Brazil* (New York: Routledge, 1999), 1; and Richard Guy Parker, *Bodies, Pleasures and Passion: Sexual Culture in Contemporary Brazil* (Boston: Beacon Press, 1991), 136.

3. In 1830, just a few years after gaining independence from Portugal, Brazil eliminated all references to sodomy in a new Imperial Penal Code introduced by Emperor Dom Pedro, a position reaffirmed in 1889, after the Brazilian Republic was created, although public morality laws could still get homosexuals arrested for cross-dressing and same-sex public displays of affection. See James N. Green, *Beyond Carnival: Male Homosexuality in Twentieth-Century Brazil* (Chicago: University of Chicago Press, 1999).

4. Luiz Mott, "The Gay Movement and Human Rights in Brazil," in *Latin American Male Homosexualities*, ed. Stephen O. Murray (Albuquerque: University of New Mexico Press, 1995), 221.

5. Charles Klein, "The Ghetto Is Over, Darling: Emerging Gay Communities and Gender and Sexual Politics in Contemporary Brazil," *Culture, Health and Sexuality* 1 (3) (1999): 241.

6. See Margaret Keck, *Democratization and the Workers' Party in Brazil* (New Haven: Yale University Press, 1995), 187–189.

7. This paradox fits within a larger puzzle of the conservatism of Brazilian laws regarding gender and sexuality. See Mala Htun and Timothy J. Power, "Gender, Parties, and Support for Equal Rights in the Brazilian Congress," *Latin American Society and Politics* 48 (4) (December 2006): 83–104.

8. Rafael De la Dehesa, *Queering the Public Sphere in Mexico and Brazil* (Durham, NC: Duke University Press, 2010), 2.

9. W. W. Hudson and W. A. Ricketts, "A Strategy for the Measurement of Homophobia, *Journal of Homosexuality* 5 (4) (1980): 357–372.

10. See, especially, F. L. Whitam and R. M. Mathey, *Male Homosexuality in Four Societies: Brazil, Guatemala, the Philippines and the United States* (New York: Praeger, 1986).

11. Rich Proulx, "Homophobia in Northeastern Brazilian University Students," *Journal of Homosexuality* 34 (1) (1997): 47–56.

12. Ibid., 47.

13. Luiz Mott, "The Gay Movement in the Land of Carnival," paper presented at the conference "Brazil: 500 Years," Dartmouth College, April 14–15, 2000. Transcript provided by the author.

14. The Pew Research Center, "The Global Divide on Homosexuality," June 4, 2013, http://www.pewglobal.org/2013/06/04/the-global-divide-on-homosexuality/ (accessed October 24, 2014).

15. Mitchell A. Seligson and Daniel E. Moreno Morales, "Gay in the Americas," *Americas Quarterly*, Winter 2010, http://www.vanderbilt.edu/lapop/bolivia/2008-gay.pdf (accessed June 12, 2015).

16. See, especially, Kurt Weyland, *Democracy without Equity* (Pittsburgh: University of Pittsburgh Press, 1996).

17. Grupo Gay da Bahia, *Assassinatos de Homossexuais no Brasil*, http://www.ggb.org.br/ (accessed September 23, 2013).

18. "Governo recebe 3.4 denúncias de homofobia por dia," *A Folha de S. Paulo*, May 17, 2012.

19. "HIV Prevention Hampered by Homophobia," http://www.unaids.org/en/Resources/PressCentre/Featurestories/2009/January/20090113MSMLATAM/ (accessed January 21, 2015).

20. Cited by *Luis Nassif Online*, November 11, 2012, http://jornalggn.com.br/blog/luisnassif/o-mais-recente-delirio-de-veja (accessed December 23, 2013).

21. Email correspondence with Luiz Mott, June 21, 2013.

22. According to Mott, the widespread use of the pejorative term "deer" to refer to gay males also fuels violence against the deer population. He reports of zoos across Brazil whose deer have been "stoned and bludgeoned to death" by those transferring their hatred of gays towards the animals.

23. Email correspondence with Peter Fry, June 5, 2013.

24. "Historical View of Pentecostalism in Brazil," Pew Forum on Religion and Public Life, Pew Research Center, October 5, 2006, http://www.pewforum.org/Christian/Evangelical-Protestant-Churches/Historical-Overview-of-Pentecostalism-in-Brazil.aspx (accessed May 21, 2013).

25. Paul Freston, "Neo-Pentecostalism in Brazil: Problems of Definition and the Struggle for Hegemony," *Archives de Sciences Sociales des Religions* 105 (January–March 1999): 141.

26. See Anderson Antunes, "The Richest Pastors in Brazil," *Forbes*, January 17, 2013, http://www.forbes.com/sites/andersonantunes/2013/01/17/the-richest-pastors-in-brazil/ (accessed May 21, 2013).

27. Simon Romero, "Evangelical Leader Rises in Brazil's Culture Wars," *New York Times*, November 25, 2011.

28. Author's translation of the transcript of the interview provided by *Correio 24 Horas*.

29. Mott, "Gay Movement in the Land of Carnival," 13.

30. Quoted in the blog *Clerical Whispers*, May 6, 2010, http://clericalwhispers.blogspot.com/2010/05/society-is-pedophile-archbishop.html (accessed March 15, 2015).

31. Vincent Bevins, "Brazilian Evangelical Churches Re-write the Rules of Politics," *Los Angeles Times*, October 21, 2012, http://articles.latimes.com/2012/oct/21/world/la-fg-brazil-evangelicals-20121022 (accessed May 24, 2013).

32. "Social Conservatives Gaining Force in the Brazilian Congress," *Associated Press*, October 18, 2013.

33. Barry Ames, *The Deadlock of Democracy in Brazil* (Ann Arbor: University of Michigan Press, 2002).

34. Dan Littauer, "Feminism Turns People Gay, Warns Brazil's Human Rights Boss," *Gay Star News*, March 21, 2013, http://www.gaystarnews.com/article/feminism-turns-people-gay-warns-brazil's-human-rights-boss210313 (accessed March 26, 2015).

35. Oscar López, "Behind Brazil's Gay Pride Parades, a Struggle with Homophobic Violence, *Newsweek*, May 11, 2015, www.newsweek.com/brazils-big-gay-fight-33-562 (accessed June 16, 2015).

36. For broader accounts of the rise of the gay movement in Brazil see James N. Green, "The Emergence of the Brazilian Gay Liberation Movement, 1977–1981," *Latin American Perspectives* 21 (1) (Winter 1994): 38–55; Edward MacRae, *A Construção da Igualdade: Identidade Sexual e Política no Brasil da "Abertura"* (Campinas: Editora da Unicamp, 1990).

37. Green, "Emergence," 45.

38. Ibid., 52.

39. Email correspondence with James N. Green, June 28, 2014.

40. James N. Green, "Desire and Militancy: Lesbians, Gays and the Brazilian Workers' Party," in *Different Rainbows*, ed. Peter Drucker (London: Millivers, 2000), 58.

41. Email correspondence with Peter Fry, June 5, 2013.

42. Mott, "The Gay Movement and Human Rights in Brazil," 223.

43. Email correspondence with James N. Green, June 28, 2014.

44. James N. Green, "Desire and Revolution: Socialists and the Brazilian Gay Liberation Movement in the 1970s," in *Human Rights and Transnational Solidarity in Cold War Latin America* (Madison, WI: University of Wisconsin Press, 2013), 265.

45. Ibid., 249.

46. Leyland is better known for his pioneering role in bringing Latin American gay literature to the American public, as editor of several anthologies of Latin American gay literature. For a review of this interesting but problematic enterprise, see Daniel Balderston and José Quiroga, "A Beautiful, Sinister Fairyland: Gay Sunshine Does Latin America," *Social Text* 21 (3) (Fall 2003): 85–108.

47. Green, "Desire and Revolution," 265.

48. Stephan Likosky, ed., *Coming Out: An Anthology of Gay and Lesbian Writings* (New York: Pantheon, 1992), 247.

49. Edward MacRae, "Homosexual Identities in Transitional Brazilian Politics," in *The Making of Social Movements in Latin America: Identity, Strategy, and Democracy*, ed. Arturo Escobar and Sonia A. Alvarez (Boulder, CO: Westview Press, 1992), 186.

50. Ibid., 195.

51. Sonia A. Alvarez, *Engendering Democracy in Brazil: Women's Movements in Transition Politics* (Princeton, NJ: Princeton University Press, 1990), 117.

52. Maria Helena Moreira Alves, "Interclass Alliances in the Opposition to the Military in Brazil: Consequences for the Transition Period," in *Power and Popular Protest: Latin American Social Movements*, ed. Susan Eckstein (Berkeley: University of California Press, 1989), 288.

53. See Alfred P. Montero, *Brazilian Politics* (London: Polity Press, 2005), 20.

54. The entire collection is available at http://www.grupodignidade.org.br/blog/cedoc/jornal-lampiao-da-esquina/ (accessed May 22, 2015).

55. Mott, "The Gay Movement and Human Rights in Brazil," 223.

56. See Brazilian Truth Commission, http://www.cnv.gov.br/ (accessed April 21, 2015), and *Relatório Final da Comissão Nacional da Verdade* [Final Report of the National Truth Commission], vol. 2 (Brasilia: Comissão Nacional da Verdade, 2014). This report details harrowing episodes of torture by the military between 1964 and 1985, including that of President Dilma Rousseff, who was tortured while in prison in Rio de Janeiro in 1969, then only twenty-two years old, for her work as a Marxist activist. Although the commission recommends prosecutions of human rights offenders, no prosecutions are expected. In 2010, the Federal Supreme Court upheld the constitutionality of the 1979 Amnesty Law that prevents anyone from being prosecuted on human rights abuses linked to the period of military rule.

57. See James N. Green and Renan Quinalha, eds., *Homossexualidade e a ditadura brasileira: Opressão, resistencia e a busca da verdade* (São Carlos: Editora da Universidade Federal de São Carlos, 2014).

58. MacRae, "Homosexual Identities," 191.

59. Ibid, 187.

60. Interview, New York City, April 20, 2014.

61. Email correspondence with Luiz Mott, June 21, 2013.

62. Alfred Stepan, *Rethinking Military Politics: Brazil and the Southern Cone* (Princeton, NJ: Princeton University Press), 69.

63. George Hanchard, *Orpheus and Power: The Movimento Negro of Rio de Janeiro and Sao Paulo, Brazil, 1945–1988* (Princeton, NJ: Princeton University Press, 1994).

64. Green, "Desire and Militancy," 59.

65. Ibid.

66. Keck, *Democratization*, 187–189.

67. Green, "Desire and Militancy," 62.

68. James N. Green, "Who Is the Macho Who Wants to Kill Me? Male Homosexuality, Revolutionary Masculinity, and the Brazilian Armed Struggle of the 1960s and 1970s," *Hispanic American Historical Review* 92 (3) (August 2012): 437–469.

69. MacRae, "Homosexual Identities," 186.

70. Partido dos Trabalhadores, *Resoluções de Encontros e Congressos: Resoluções de Encontros e Congressos, 1979–1998* (São Paulo: Ed. Fundação Perseu Abramo / Diretório Nacional do PT, 1998), 111.

71. Luiz Mott, "Partidos Políticos e a homossexualidade," unpublished manuscript made available to the author on June 21, 2013.

72. Green, "Emergence," 50.

73. Juan Pereira Marsiaj, "Social Movements and Political Parties: Gays, Lesbians, and Transvestites and the Struggle for Inclusion in Brazil," in *The Politics of Sexuality in Latin America: A Reader on Lesbian, Gay, Bisexual and Transgender Rights*, ed. Javier Corrales and Mario Pecheny (Pittsburgh: University of Pittsburgh Press, 2010), 201–203.

74. Email communication with James N. Green, June 28, 2014.

75. Amy Nun, *The Politics and History of AIDS Treatment in Brazil* (New York: Springer, 2009), 40.

76. See, especially, Robert Nylen, *Participatory Democracy versus Elitist Democracy* (New York: Palgrave Macmillan, 2003).

77. Juan Pereira Marsiaj, "Political Parties, Culture and Democratization: The Gay, Lesbian, and Transvestite Movement in the Struggle for Inclusion in Brazil," paper presented at the Annual Meeting of the American Political Science Association, September 1–4, 2005, 17.
78. Email communication with Luiz Mott, June 21, 2013.
79. Email communication with James N. Green, June 28, 2014.
80. For a more detailed view of these bills see Luiz Mello, *Novas Famílias: Conjugalidade Homossexual no Brasil Contemporâneo* (Rio de Janeiro: Garamond, 2005).
81. Rafael de la Dehesa, "Global Communities and Hybrid Cultures: Early Gay and Lesbian Activism in Brazil and Mexico," *Latin American Research Review* 42 (1), (February 2007): 34.
82. Pereira Marsiaj, "Political Parties, Culture and Democratization," 9.
83. Green, "Desire and Militancy," 65.
84. Wendy Hunter, *The Transformation of the Workers' Party in Brazil, 1989–2009* (New York: Cambridge University Press, 2010), 2.
85. Green, "Desire and Militancy," 66.
86. Email communication with James N. Green, June 28, 2014.
87. For a broader view of AIDS politics in Brazil, see Herbert Daniel and Richard Parker, *Sexuality, Politics and AIDS in Brazil: Another World?* (London: Falmer Press, 1993); João Biehl, "The Activist State: Global Pharmaceuticals, AIDS and Citizenship in Brazil," *Social Text* 22 (2) (Fall 2004): 105–132; and Tim Fracas, *AIDS in Latin America* (New York: Palgrave, 2005).
88. Daniel and Parker, *Sexuality, Politics and AIDS*, 9.
89. James Brooke, "AIDS in Latin America: A Special Report," *New York Times*, January 25, 1993.
90. Ibid.
91. Amy Steward Nunn, Elize Massard da Fonseca, Francisco I. Bastos, and Sofia Gruskin, *Heath Affairs* 29 (4) (July–August 2009): 1103.
92. Biehl, "The Activist State," 106.
93. Mariana A. Hacker, Angela Kaida, Robert S. Hogg, and Francisco I. Bastos, "The First Ten Years: Achievements and Challenges of the Brazilian Program of Universal Access to HIV/AIDS Comprehensive Management and Care, 1996–2006," http://www.scielo.br/pdf/csp/v23s3/03.pdf (accessed May 26, 2013).
94. Jane Galvoa, "Brazil and Access to HIV/AIDS Drugs: A Question of Human Rights and Public Health," *American Journal of Public Health* 95 (7) (July 2005): 1112.
95. Email communication with Peter Fry, June 5, 2013.
96. Biehl, "The Activist State," 105.
97. Adrianna R. B. Vianna and Sérgio Carrara, "Sexual Politics and Sexual Rights in Brazil: A Case Study," 37, http://www.sxpolitics.org/frontlines/book/pdf/capitulo1_brazil.pdf (accessed July 27, 2015).
98. James N. Green, "More Love and More Desire: The Building of the Brazilian Gay Movement," in Corrales and Pecheny, *The Politics of Sexuality*, 71.
99. Email communication with Toni Reis, February 20, 2015.
100. See Programa Nacional de Direitos Humanos, Brasília, Presidência da República, Secretaria de Comunicação Social, Ministério da Justiça, 1996, http://portal.mj.gov.br/sedh/pndh/pndh1.pdf (accessed September 17, 2013).
101. R. Facchini, *Sopa de letrinhas? movimento homossexual e produção de identidades coletivas nos anos 90* (Rio de Janeiro: Garamond, 2005).
102. Email communication with Toni Reis, February 20, 2015.
103. Pereira Marsiaj, "Social Movements and Political Parties," 201–203.

104. Email communication with Toni Reis, February 20, 2015.

105. Email communication with Luiz Mott, June 21, 2013.

106. Email communication with Luiz Mott, June 22, 2013.

107. See, especially, Hunter, *Transformation of Workers' Party*.

108. Mott, "Partidos Políticos e a homossexualidade."

109. Lula won the first round of voting (held on October 1, 2006) but failed to get the required 50 percent. He prevailed in the runoff (held on October 29, 2006), garnering 60.8 percent of the vote.

110. See Wendy Hunter and Timothy J. Power, "Rewarding Lula: Executive Power, Social Policy and the Brazilian Elections of 2006," *Latin American Politics & Society* 49 (1) (Spring 2007): 23.

111. "Brazil's Evangelical Movement Has Become a Major Social, Political Force," *Worldwide Religious News*, September 27, 2006, http://wwrn.org/articles/22868/?&place=south-america&section=miscellaneous (accessed September 23, 2013).

112. Quoted passages come from Pereira Marsiaj, "Political Parties, Culture and Democratization," 19.

113. A translated transcript of Lula's speech is available in Corrales and Pecheny, *The Politics of Sexuality*, 265–269.

114. A copy of the decision is available at http://redir.stf.jus.br/paginadorpub/paginador.jsp?docTP=AC&docID=628633 (accessed March 27, 2015).

115. "Brazil Supreme Court Awards Gay Couples New Rights," March 6, 2011, http://www.bbc.com/news/world-13304442 (accessed March 27, 2015).

116. Debora Sampier, "Supreme Court Unanimously Recognizes Legality of a Stable Union Involving Homosexuals," May 5, 2011, http://agenciabrasil.ebc.com.br/new-in-english/2011-05-09/news-english---supreme-court-unanimously-recognizes-legality-stable-union-involving-homosexual (accessed September 23, 2013).

117. Ibid.

118. Taylor Barnes, "Brazil Becomes Largest Nation Yet to Legalize Civil Unions," *Christian Science Monitor*, May 6, 2011, http://www.csmonitor.com/World/Americas/2011/0506/Brazil-becomes-largest-nation-yet-to-legalize-civil-unions (accessed September 16, 2013).

119. Mott, "The Gay Movement in the Land of Carnival," 12.

120. Email correspondence with Paulo Iotti, March 27, 2015.

121. This section draws from author's correspondence with Paulo Iotti, June 8, 2015.

122. Ibid.

123. "Maria Bernice Dias foi pioneira em defender direitos gays," *O Folha de São Paulo*, August 1, 2012.

124. See Maria Berenice Dias, *União Homossexual: O Preconceito & a Justiça*, 2nd ed. (Porto Alegre: Editora Livraria do Advogado, 2001), and Paulo Roberto Iotti, *Manual da Homoafetividade: Da Possibilidade Jurídica do Casamento Civil, da União Estável e da Adoção por Casais Homoafetivos*, 2nd ed. (São Paulo: Ed. Método, 2013).

125. Amnesty International, "Brazil's Supreme Court Recognizes Same-Sex Civil Unions," May 6, 2011, http://www.amnesty.org/en/news-and-updates/brazil-supreme-court-legalizes-same-sex-civil-unions-2011-05-06 (accessed September 16, 2013).

126. "Brazil Approves Same-Sex Civil Unions Despite Catholic Protests," *The Associated Press*, May 6, 2011.

127. Email correspondence with Paulo Iotti, March 27, 2015.

128. Email correspondence with Paulo Iotti, May 16, 2015.

129. Bruno Bimbi, "Hannah Arendt y el matrimonio igualitario: La lucha por los derechos LGBT en Argentina," *Nueva Sociedad*, May–June 2014, 122–123.

CHAPTER 6

1. Alfred Stepan, *Rethinking Military Politics: Brazil and the Southern Cone* (Princeton, NJ: Princeton University Press, 1988), 69.
2. Email correspondence, June 26, 2014.
3. This section draws from Omar G. Encarnación, "Gay Rights: Why Democracy Matters," *Journal of Democracy* 25 (3) (July 2014): 90–104.
4. Uri Friedman, "How Sochi Became the Gay Olympics," *Atlantic*, January 2014, http://www.theatlantic.com/international/print/2014/01/how-sochi-became-the-gay-olympics/283398/ (accessed January 30, 2014).
5. Ibid.
6. See *Together, Apart: Organizing around Sexual Orientation and Gender Identity Worldwide* (New York: Human Rights Watch, 2009).
7. Ibid.
8. "The Global Divide on Homosexuality," Pew Research Center, June 4, 2013, http://www.pewglobal.org/files/2013/06/Pew-Global-Attitudes-Homosexuality-Report-FINAL-JUNE-4-2013.pdf (accessed February 7, 2014).
9. Pew Research on Religion and Public Life, "Russians Return to Religion, but Not to Church," February 10, 2014, www.pewforum.org/2014/02/10/russians-return-to-religion-but-not-to-church.
10. Lymari Morales, "Knowing Someone Gay/Lesbian Affects Views of Gay Issues," Gallup.com, May 29, 2009.
11. Graeme Reid, "A Globalized LGBT Fight," *Global Post*, November 2, 2010, http://www.globalpost.com/dispatch/news/culture-lifestyle/111101/opinion-the-globalization-lgbt-rights-fight (accessed March 6, 2013).
12. Reed Karaim, "Gay Rights: Has the Movement's Success Sparked a Backlash?" *CQ Press* 5 (5) (March 1, 2011): iv. When the legislator in question was asked by the US media if he had any evidence to back up this claim, he could not cite any.
13. Mansur Mirovalev, "Russia Moves to Enact Anti-gay Law Nationwide," *Associated Press*, January 21, 2013.
14. "Vladimir Putin Defends Russia's Conservative Values," *Associated Press*, December 12, 2013, *Washington Times*, http://www.washingtontimes.com/news/2013/dec/12/vladimir-putin-defends-russian-conservative-values/?utm_source=RSS_Feed&utm_medium=RSS (accessed December 17, 2013).
15. "The World Bank: Right Cause, Wrong Battle," *Economist*, April 12, 2014.
16. Josh Kron, "Resentment towards the West Bolsters Uganda's New Anti-gay Bill," *New York Times*, February 28, 2012, http://www.nytimes.com/2012/02/29/world/africa/ugandan-lawmakers-push-anti-homosexuality-bill-again.html?pagewanted=all&_r=0 (accessed December 28, 2012).
17. Kapya Kaoma, *Globalizing the Culture Wars: U.S. Conservatives, African Churches and Homosexuals* (Somerville, MA: Political Research Associates, 2012), 3, http://www.publiceye.org/publications/globalizing-the-culture-wars/pdf/africa-full-report.pdf (accessed December 28, 2013).
18. Jeremy Lybarger, "Foiled in the United States, Anti-gay Evangelicals Spread Hate in Africa," *Mother Jones*, July 9, 2013.
19. I expand on this point in Encarnación, "Gay Rights: Why Democracy Matters," 101–103.

20. See T. H. Marshall and Tom Bottomore, *Citizenship and Social Class* (London: Pluto Press, 1987).

21. See Ronald Inglehart, *The Silent Revolution: Changing Values and Political Styles among Western Publics* (Princeton, NJ: Princeton University Press, 1977).

22. See, especially, John D. McCarthy and Mayer N. Zald, "Resource Mobilization and Social Movements: A Partial Theory," *American Journal of Sociology* 82 (6) (May 1977): 1212–1241.

23. Sidney Tarrow, *Power in Movement: Social Movements and Contentious Politics* (New York: Cambridge University Press, 1998).

24. Leon Neyfalk, "How Boston Powered the Gay Rights Movement," *Boston Globe*, June 2, 2013.

25. Ibid.

26. Gregory B. Lewis and Jonathan L. Edelson, "DOMA and ENDA: Congress Votes on Gay Rights," in *The Politics of Gay Rights*, ed. Craig A. Rimmerman, Kenneth D. Wald, and Clyde Wilcox (Chicago: University of Chicago Press, 2000), 194–216.

27. See Kenji Yoshino, *Speak Now: Marriage Equality on Trial: The Story of* Hollingsworth v. Perry (New York: Crown, 2015).

28. See Jo Becker, *Forcing the Spring: Inside the Fight for Marriage Equality* (New York: Penguin, 2014). Numerous reviewers have harshly criticized this book for over-estimating the work of the "celebrity" lawyers involved in the case, David Bois and Theodore Olsen, and for undermining the longer struggle for gay marriage by gay activists and ordinary gays and lesbians. See, for instance, Adam Teicholtz, "Jo Becker's New Book Disparages Gay Marriage Activists' Years of Hard Work," *New Republic*, April 17, 2014, http://www.newrepublic.com/article/117418/jo-beckers-forcing-spring-undersells-gay-advocates (accessed January 15, 2014); and Adam Goodheart, "A Fight over Marriage Equality and over History," *New York Times*, April 30, 2014, http://www.nytimes.com/2014/05/01/books/forcing-the-spring-by-jo-becker.html (accessed January 15, 2015).

29. Pew Research Center, "Religion in Latin America: Widespread Change in a Historically Catholic Region," November 13, 2014, http://www.pewforum.org/2014/11/13/religion-in-latin-america/ (accessed November 14, 2014).

30. Adam Liptak, "Ginsburg Shares Her Views on Influence of Foreign Law on Her Court and Vice Versa," *New York Times*, April 9, 2009.

31. Interview with *PBS Newshour*, September 2, 2013, www.pbs.org/newshour/bb/nation-July-dec13-civilrights_09-02/ (accessed June 5, 2015).

32. See Marc Solomon, *Winning Marriage: The Inside Story of How Same-Sex Couples Took on the Politicians and the Pundits and Won* (New York: ForeEdge, 2014).

33. Carol Anderson, *Eyes off the Prize: The United Nations and the African-American Struggle for Human Rights, 1944–1955* (New York: Cambridge University Press, 2003).

34. Hector Carrillo, "How Latin Culture Got More Gay," *New York Times*, May 17, 2013, http://mobile.nytimes.com/2013/05/17/opinion/how-latin-culture-got-more-gay.html (accessed September 23, 2013).

35. Tim Padgett, "Why Latin America's Homophonic Leaders Should Stop Their Gay Bashing," Time.com, April 26, 2013, http://world.time.com/2013/04/26/why-latin-americas-homophobic-leaders-should-stop-their-gay-bashing/ (accessed September 22, 2013).

36. Juan Jesús Aznarez, "Nicolás Maduro and Homophobia in Latin America," *El País in English*, March 19, 2013, http://elpais.com/elpais/2013/03/19/inenglish/1363711540_386143.html (accessed December 23, 2013).

37. Janey Street Thorton, "President Sorry for Saying That He Would Shoot His Genitals If Son Was Gay," *Gay Star News*, April 23, 2013, http://www.gaystarnews.com/article/president-sorry-saying-hed-shoot-his-genitals-if-son-was-gay230413 (accessed December 23, 2013).

38. In March 2015, Mr. Fidelix was found guilty of defamation and fined one million reais. He is appealing the sentence.

39. "Anti-gay Violence Fuels Hate Violence," Southern Poverty Law Center, Intelligence Report, Winter 2010, http://www.splcenter.org/get-informed/intelligence-report/browse-all-issues/2010/winter/fuel-on-the-fire (accessed September 22, 2013).

40. See, for instance, Juan Manuel Contreras, "Sexual Violence in Latin America and the Caribbean: A Desk Review," Sexual Violence Research Initiative, 2010.

41. Enrique Desmond Arias and Daniel M. Goldstein, eds., *Violent Democracies in Latin America* (Durham, NC: Duke University Press, 2010).

42. National Coalition of Anti-Violence Programs (NCAVP), "Lesbian, Gay, Bisexual, Transgender, Queer and HIV Violence: Hate Violence in 2012," http://www.avp.org/about-avp/coalitions-a-collaborations/82-national-coalition-of-anti-violence-programs (accessed September 14, 2013).

43. See, especially, *Global Rights: Partners for Justice, Racial Violence. A Reading of Homicide Violence in Brazil* (Washington, DC, 2009).

44. "Mexico's LGBT Community Faces Violence Despite Major Gains in Civil Rights," *Latin American News Dispatch*, August 4, 2011, http://latindispatch.com/2011/08/04/mexicos-lgbt-community-faces-violence-despite-major-gains-in-civil-rights/ (accessed September 14, 2013).

45. Ioan Grillo, "Mexico City's Revolutionary First: Gay Marriage," Time.com, December 24, 2009, http://www.time.com/time/world/article/0,8599,1949953,00.html (accessed July 28, 2010).

INDEX

CPSIA information can be obtained
at www.ICGtesting.com
Printed in the USA
BVOW03s1704230817
492833BV00002B/7/P